Law's Fam

ONE WEEK LOAN

Law in Context

Below is a listing of the more recent publications in the Law in Context Series

Editors: William Twining (University College, London) and Christopher McCrudden (Lincoln College, Oxford)

Law's Families

Alison Diduck
Lecturer in Law
Brunel University

Members of the LexisNexis Group worldwide

United Kingdom	LexisNexis UK, a Division of Reed Elsevier (UK) Ltd, Halsbury House, 35 Chancery Lane, LONDON, WC2A 1EL, and 4 Hill Street, EDINBURGH EH2 3JZ
Argentina	LexisNexis Argentina, BUENOS AIRES
Australia	LexisNexis Butterworths, CHATSWOOD, New South Wales
Austria	LexisNexis Verlag ARD Orac GmbH & Co KG, VIENNA
Canada	LexisNexis Butterworths, MARKHAM, Ontario
Chile	LexisNexis Chile Ltda, SANTIAGO DE CHILE
Czech Republic	Nakladatelství Orac sro, PRAGUE
France	Editions du Juris-Classeur SA, PARIS
Germany	LexisNexis Deutschland GmbH, FRANKFURT, MUNSTER
Hong Kong	LexisNexis Butterworths, HONG KONG
Hungary	HVG-Orac, BUDAPEST
India	LexisNexis Butterworths, NEW DELHI
Ireland	Butterworths (Ireland) Ltd, DUBLIN
Italy	Giuffrè Editore, MILAN
Malaysia	Malayan Law Journal Sdn Bhd, KUALA LUMPUR
New Zealand	LexisNexis Butterworths, WELLINGTON
Poland	Wydawnictwo Prawnicze LexisNexis, WARSAW
Singapore	LexisNexis Butterworths, SINGAPORE
South Africa	LexisNexis Butterworths, DURBAN
Switzerland	Stämpfli Verlag AG, BERNE
USA	LexisNexis, DAYTON, Ohio

© Alison Diduck 2003

A CIP Catalogue record for this book is available from the British Library.

ISBN 0 406 96733 4

Typeset by Sparks Computer Solutions Ltd, Oxford – http://www.sparks.co.uk
Printed and bound in Great Britain by Thomson Litho Ltd, East Kilbride, Scotland
Visit LexisNexis UK at www.lexisnexis.co.uk

Preface: an introductory note on methodology

A socio-legal approach

This book is about families as much as it is about family laws. It is about the ways in which individuals experience relationships they define as familial and about the way in which those experiences are shaped by laws. However, it is also about the way those experiences shape law. It adopts the view that the relationship between law and the society that breathes life into it and into which it breathes life is a mutually sustaining and inextricable one, but it aims to explore more than the (important) connection between social context and legal doctrine. It looks to individuals' family practices (Morgan 1996), as much as to normative statements about family, to reflect upon how family life is lived and regulated in contemporary British society. In this respect, it is a socio-legal study of family law. It follows in the tradition of those socio-legal scholars who teach and research the law as a distinct discipline, but as one that is enriched by the study of other disciplines such as history, sociology, social policy, economics, philosophy and politics. In this tradition, law is profoundly social and political and is not completely comprehensible otherwise.

It is this perspective that has informed the socio-legal approach to the study of law (see, for example, Law and Society Association homepage 2001; Thomas 1997; Wheeler and Thomas 2000; Cotterrell 1993)[1] and family

---

1   The president of the Law and Society Association in the United States in 1990 defined socio-legal studies thus:
      'The term "socio-legal studies" is used here to denote the social study of law, legal process, legal systems, normative ordering, law-related behaviors, and what is

law in particular has been enriched over the years by this broad socio-legal perspective. Socio-legal scholars on the family have studied the theoretical (Collier 1995a; Fineman 1995; O'Donovan 1985 and 1993; Regan 1993 and 1999), ideological (Gittins 1993 and 1998; Barrett and MacIntosh 1991) and interdisciplinary (Morgan 1996; Beck and Beck-Gernsheim 1995; Giddens 1992; Gillis 1985 and 1997; Stone 1990; James, Jenks and Prout 1998; Jenks 1996) nature of law and they have examined the role of individual actors as they engage with law and legal institutions (Ingleby 1992; Sarat and Felstiner 1995; Eekelaar, Maclean and Beinart 2000; Eekelaar 1991; Smart 1984; Davis et al 1994; Smart and Neale 1999; Smart, Neale and Wade 2001; Day Sclater 1999a) as much as they have analysed legal doctrine (Dewar 1992; Hogget, Pearl and Bates 1996 and 2002; Diduck and Kaganas 1999). My work over the years has been inspired by many of these authors and this book certainly owes a debt to them. The socio-legal approach that I adopt here is to review and build upon their enlightening and wide-ranging body of work that has established family law as 'one of the more successful areas for the socio-legal enterprise' (Jolly 1997 p 342)[2].

Part of the reason for the 'success' of the socio-legal approach to family law may be the rapid pace of change in family laws and the encourage-ment of the Law Commission and the Lord Chancellor's Department in promoting and funding research about this change (Jolly 1997). Part of the reason may also be the nature of the relationships under examina-tion. That is to say, if family law is about regulating the relationships of intimates, relationships based not upon the arm's length transactions of the 'rational', liberal legal subject, but upon the 'irrationality' of feelings, morals, or even instinct, it seems, more than other areas of law, to concede the legitimacy of considerations traditionally believed to be extra-legal[3].

<hr/>

endemically legal in society. However broad the scope, it is meant to embrace the study of law as a social phenomena, not the use of social science in or by law. ... [T]he term socio-legal studies ... is inherently interdisciplinary and can integrate and extend the classical characterizations that derive from the older disciplines (eg of sociology of law, anthropology of law, psychology and law, legal history, public law, judicial process, criminology, law and economics)' (Levine 1990 p 8 fn 1).

2   For a comprehensive review of socio-legal work on families to 1997, see Jolly (1997). See also Eekelaar and Maclean (1994), particularly 'Introduction'.

3   O'Donovan suggests that this is an instrumentalist view of law, and in combination with the idea that laws about families are unenforceable – 'we cannot tell people how to behave in their own homes' – that law is a negative force which destroys that which it sets out to help and that law may be too 'pure' to be sullied by the messiness of domestic

This perception has meant that legal scholarship on families can legitimately include insights from disciplines other than law, which can help to illuminate not only legal doctrine and legal policy and the social, moral and affective aspects of our selves and our relationships, but also an apparent political imperative to assert 'the family's' place in the normative social order – one that is in many ways unregulatable, but that always requires regulation.

Thus, in the spirit of a broad understanding of socio-legal studies, including probably irreconcilable debates between it, the sociology of law (see Thomas 1997; Wheeler and Thomas 2000) and critical legal studies[4], I want to look at the regulation of intimate relationships, including relationships between those who, legally, may not be 'family'. This book will thus examine regulation of people's intimate, familial behaviour by 'law-government', as Cotterrell (1993) called it, and it will investigate the normative constitution and bases of familial identities and the often ideological role they play in 'private' or informal regulation, which derives from less official arenas such as the expectations of individual or group moralities. It will draw upon the empirical as well as the theoretical research conducted by socio-legal scholars in the past. It will look at the lawyers' law that comes from cases and legislation as well as the rhetoric of that law and its ideological effects. It will examine some research that may not be considered to be law at all, but rather to be sociology, psychology or history. It will do all this to explore not only law's place in intimate relationships, but also the place and the meaning of justice in those relationships.

life, reflects a liberal political philosophy and a belief in the public/private divide inherent in that philosophy (O'Donovan 1986 p 185). I disagree. It is family law's legitimacy of the 'irrational' that creates the potential for seeing law as a fundamental part of social, affective, emotional, moral and political existence and relationships – in other words, as other than instrumentalist.

4   At the annual meeting of the Socio-Legal Studies Association at the University of Aberystwyth in 2002 the plenary session was to be a debate between Roger Cotterrell, presumably representing the 'sociology of law' camp, and Paddy Hillyard, perhaps representing the 'critical theory' camp, entitled 'Current Issues and Directions in Socio-Legal Research and Theory'. (Their presentations are now published in Cotterrell 2002 and Hillyard 2002) While there were some areas of disagreement, the 'debate' was less oppositional than might have been the case in previous years. It seems that differences in the theory and approach to socio-legal studies may indeed be lessening.

A feminist approach

The second approach this book will take is an explicitly feminist one[5]. Feminism is concerned with women's lives and women's lives traditionally have centred around their families. Family law has thus proved to be fertile ground for the work of feminist legal scholars. In many ways, the history of changes in family law over the years mirrors the history of law's engagement with women as legal subjects; from the Married Women's Property Acts of the nineteenth and early twentieth centuries to recent legislation on maternity leave, law has been a powerful mediator not only in regulating the balance of power between legal subjects, but also in shaping the form those subjects take. Feminist scholars have unpicked the political and legal nature of family relationships and subjected them to a critical analysis, the legacy of which is that the study of families and of family law has been enriched by considerations of gender and sex at the levels of practice, policy and theory.

Feminism means different things to different people. To many legal scholars it means disorder, critique or disruption of law's claims to objectivity and neutrality and also of liberalism's foundational assumptions of individual autonomy and formal equality (Lacey 1998). It is overtly constructionist methodologically, assuming that nothing is natural or given (Lacey 1998) and thus that the structure of the social/legal realm is shaped by conditions over which actors have control. Feminist theory was born of social/political activism and feminist legal theory retains much of those activist roots in this constructivist claim and also in its claim that the 'ways in which sex/gender has shaped the legal realm are presumptively politically and ethically problematic' (Lacey 1998 p 3). It thus aims to subject law(s) to the challenge law sets for itself, that of achieving individual and social justice, even while it may simultaneously challenge taken-for-granted conceptions of what justice means. A feminist approach always asks 'the woman question' and in this way renders women visible in law, attributes value to the concerns of women and ensures that those who traditionally have been excluded from theoretical and pragmatic legal considerations are recognised. Feminism says sometimes that law is gendered, other times that law is but one gendering strategy, but always pays attention to gender as one axis of social and legal analysis and organisation[6]. It thus highlights

---

5   For a discussion of the relationship between feminist theory and socio-legal studies, see O'Donovan 1997.

6   For an excellent review of the feminist legal project, see Conaghan (2000).

not only law's context, but demands a further interrogation of that context itself and of the subject who inhabits it. It asks, for example, how we determine what it means to be a working-class woman, a gay man or a black child (Richardson and Sandland 2000).

Feminism in family law acknowledges that people lead gendered lives in families (Fineman 1995) and in this recognition it has theorised the separate spheres dichotomy at the heart of the liberal polity as the root of women's political and legal subordination (O'Donovan 1985; Olsen 1983; Rose 1987; Ribbens McCarthy and Edwards 2002); it has embraced historical materialist analyses of the relationship between production and reproduction (Barrett and MacIntosh 1991; Boyd 1991 and 1994), and it has opened the way for a new moral and political philosophy to reshape the meaning of justice inside and outside the family context (Young 1990; Gilligan 1982; Sevenhuijsen 1998; Smart 1999). Finally, a feminist approach to family law is particularly concerned with subject identities and positions, and feminist legal theory examines the role that law plays in constituting those positions as we come to law as mothers, fathers, carers, workers or children. Crucially, in this as well as in its more general theoretical enterprise, it is inclusive and maintains an awareness at all times of the importance of all axes of domination, including sex/gender, class, race, generation and sexuality.

It is thus in the feminist and socio-legal spirit of the *politics* of families and family law that I make the enquiries and observations to which I now turn.

Alison Diduck
June 2003

Acknowledgments

This book has benefited enormously from exchanges with many people either in casual conversation or in more formal conference settings. Discussions I have had with Adrian James, Gillian Douglas, Derek Morgan, Alan Norrie, Christine Piper, Michael King, Robert Fine and Felicity Kaganas, in particular, made me think carefully about what I wanted to say. Helen Reece, Michael King, David Seymour, Robert Fine and Jane Jordan read drafts of various chapters and provided insights and valuable assistance that made them better chapters. Of course, I take complete responsibility where I have not adequately addressed their concerns. My friend and colleague Amanda Kunicki assisted with, among other things, putting the words onto the computer, often late into the night and fortified only by pizza. I am grateful to all these people. It may be clichéd, but it is true that this book could not have been written without them.

My thanks also go to Dartmouth Ashgate, Shelly Day Sclater and Christine Piper for permission to base Chapter 6 on work previously published by them in *Undercurrents of Divorce*, 1999, and to Abimbola Olowofoyeku, head of the Brunel Law Department, for finding funds for administrative assistance in completing this book. I am also grateful to Adrian James and Linda Mulcahy who originally encouraged me to write it, and to Christopher McCrudden, William Twining and the editorial staff at LexisNexis UK who allowed it to see the light of day.

My deepest appreciation goes to Christine Piper and Felicity Kaganas, my dear friends in the Brunel Law Department. One always hopes to have congenial and intellectually stimulating colleagues, but in them I have been lucky enough to have found not only two outstanding scholars with whom to work, but two cherished friends. Their moral and practical support throughout was only matched by the thoughtful and perceptive comments they offered after reading the first draft of each chapter, whenever it was nervously presented to them.

This book is about family living in all its manifestations, and writing it has been a profoundly familial experience not only for me, but also for David Seymour and our son Max. Their understanding, love and support was, and is, a continuing source of encouragement for me. I dedicate this book to Max, to his grandparents Peter and Vi Diduck and to the memory of his great-grandmothers Anne Becker and Tekla Diduch. My experience of family with each of them inspires me on a daily basis.

Contents

Table of statutes

Table of cases

Chapter 1

Individual intimacies

'Neither a "back to basics" fundamentalism, trying to turn back the clock, nor an "anything goes" liberalism which denies the fact that how families behave affects us all, is credible any more' (Home Office 1998).

'The family' has almost iconic status in popular and 'official' discourses, even though there is no official or universal definition of it. It means different things to different people, and meets different needs for different people. On an individual level, it is within families that we negotiate an urgent need for belonging with an equally urgent need for autonomy. On a social level, it is through families that we negotiate needs to be economic, moral, emotional and political actors. This book is about what these negotiations mean in current socio-legal discourse. It is about law's regulation of the intimate relationships we choose as well as those we do not choose, for even those of us who desire nothing more than to disassociate ourselves from our families, to shed any sense of belonging we may once have felt, or who have never felt that we belonged in any sense at all to a family of birth, most probably need to feel connected to another or to others with whom we share something in common, even if we choose to live alone. It is about what those connections mean in contemporary times to the individuals who comprise them and to the societies in which they exist. It is also about how those meanings change and the role of law in that change.

I suggest that family law has 'in mind' a particular image of the family and a clear picture of who family members 'are' and how they negotiate their familial lives and relationships. This image, implicated as it is in changing meanings of 'family', cannot be described simply, however. It is characterised by ambiguity. The policy expressed in the quote that begins this chapter makes it clear that for government neither a 'traditional' nor a 'modern' vision of family on its own is appropriate to describe family living in millennial Britain, and so law's families must accommodate them both. I suggest as well that this complicated normative family of law is also expressed as an ideal by family members themselves, even though it often clashes with their less-than-ideal lives. I am therefore setting up two conflicts: one between two parts of a normative family and one between that norm and experienced family living. I suggest that law has not found a way to reconcile the two parts of its ideal, and that this failure has meant a failure of justice for individuals whose family experiences are measured according to it.

I will examine trends in recent family law discourse that illustrate the constitution and regulation of these different families. Whether these trends represent deliberate strategies to manage family change or are simply examples of the 'normal chaos of family law' (Dewar 1998) is less important for me to observe than is their vitality and effect upon the men, women and children who comprise the families of today.

The first trend I explore is one towards the dejuridification of familial matters. Traditional forms of legal regulation have been replaced by forms that appear to rely less upon the formal adjudication of rules and direct coercion of norms than upon approaches that permit, or demand, individuals to take personal responsibility for organising their family lives in socially and politically 'acceptable' ways. It is a movement from law as 'command' to 'inducement' (Roberts 2001 p 265 n 4), and I examine recent policy and law reform initiatives in the substantive law of divorce (Chapter 3) and the procedural law of family dispute resolution (Chapter 5 and Chapter 6) that typify it.

The other trend I highlight is related to the first. It is the newly important place of the individual in society and, by extension, in families. The autonomous, free-willed individual, the paradigmatic legal subject in the spheres of the market and political and civil society, has now become a part of the sphere of the family, and family law has had to accommodate this intrusion. It thus asserts norms extolling conflict-free and altruistic relationships based upon love, at the same time as it acknowledges that individual family members have rights and may act in rational, self-interested ways to claim them. My discussion of divorce law reform

(Chapter 3), mediation (Chapter 5) and court management of financial disputes (Chapter 6) will also examine this trend, as will a chapter on child support (Chapter 7). Because formal law is an important but not exclusive regulator of behaviour, however, I also examine this trend in the context of normative cultural expectations in individual decisions to attach our lives with another (Chapter 2) and in how relationships with children are shaped (Chapter 4).

A variety of social or psychological regulatory practices impinge upon our intimate familial lives and selves and it is to these that I now turn. For we cannot, I suggest, easily separate them from direct legal regulation. If family laws and family policies are to achieve 'justice' through their regulatory practices, it makes sense that they evidence some understanding and appreciation of the lives and relationships with which they are concerned.

Sociologies of intimacy and the individual

Recent sociological perspectives on intimacy and relationships now report that negotiation and fluidity along with forms of individualism and feminism are key to many of the changes evident in contemporary familial expression. Davidoff et al (1999), for example, note how the 'self' is intimately connected with the characteristics of gender and age that are the basic elements of the family. To them, our 'self' is first of all gendered, differently for boys than for girls. They observe that language still casts male as the norm and female as the exception, so that 'the boy child has no difficulty in placing himself within this linguistic frame. But the girl child has to identify with "she", a form forced into the language and thus into her social being. She learns of dogs and "lady" dogs, poets and poetesses, bus drivers and women bus drivers, politicians and female politicians' (Davidoff et al 1999 p 53).

Our sense of self is also shaped by the culture of individualism, where the '"I" is set against the social' (Davidoff et al 1999 p 56). The 'I' we learn in families is thus an atomistic one, but one which must engage with the social according to the rules first tried and tested in the family. The rules are often different for boys and girls. The gendered nature of the autonomous self created in families, then, has implications for the political self in terms of citizenship and relationship to property (see Chapter 6), for the sexual and feeling self, and for the psychological self (Davidoff et al 1999 p 61–72 and see Chapter 3) that negotiates the world at large. The process is not only one-way, though. The world at large, in the forms of legal and cultural expectations of family and individual, also impact upon our selves and the families we make. So, at the beginning of a new millennium, we may be 'unique, yet multi-faceted' persons, 'free to make unlimited choices', but we still remain burdened by those assumptions, obligations and emotions, connections or disconnections that our 'family' experience has imposed upon us (Davidoff et al 1999 p 52).

Recent sociologies of intimacy and families attempt to make sense of these assumptions and impositions in the context of 'family' formation. They theorise a new form of individualism and the self that is rooted firmly in contemporary social conditions, including contemporary families. They approach intimacy and subjectivity from different sociological and theoretical perspectives, but have in common the idea that a person is now freer to choose or to recast her or his identity than at any time in history and that this freedom has vast repercussions for those relationships we choose as well as those we don't. These ideas have begun to inform socio-legal analyses of family law and family policy (eg Smart 1997; Smart and Neale 1999; Reece 2003), particularly in their efforts to understand the meaning and effects of legal and policy shifts (eg Day Sclater 1999a; Day Sclater and Piper 2001). As this is my project as well, I shall review here the main sociological perspectives that seem to me to have had the most impact upon the shape of socio-legal family law.

Anthony Giddens: a new self; a new relationship

In *The Transformation of Intimacy* (1992), Giddens explores shifts in the nature of the self and individual behaviour which he says have led to a dramatic change in the nature of modern intimate relationships. Noting first of all the emergence of what he calls 'plastic sexuality', he suggests that sexuality is, for the first time in history, fully autonomous (Giddens 1992 p 27). The 'romantic love' which became the foundation for the families of the nineteenth century was the first step towards this end: the 'pressure to have large families gave way to a tendency to limit family size in a rigorous way', which meant that '[f]or the first time, for a mass population of women, sexuality could become separated from a chronic round of pregnancy and childbirth' (Giddens 1992 p 26). Technological advances in, and moral acceptance of, contraception and assisted reproduction over the following century meant that sexuality became liberated entirely from reproduction;

in these conditions it 'can become wholly a quality of individuals and their transactions with one another' (Giddens 1992 p 27). This conclusion obviously has vast implications for heterosexually active women, but also has profound consequences for male heterosexuality and for gay men and lesbian women (Giddens 1992 p 28). Combined with his notion of the 'reflexive self' – an antidote to Foucault's constructed self – Giddens is saying that in modern society the self is an autonomous sexual being whose full complement of characteristics is constantly under negotiation.

The ongoing interrogation of self continues for Giddens into relations of intimacy, where it persists in respect of the relationship itself. He distinguishes between traditional marriage and what he calls 'the pure relationship' partially on this basis. Whereas the expectations, terms and meaning of marriage were clear, the expectations and meanings of today's 'relationships' are not.

'[A pure relationship] refers to a situation where a social relation is entered into for its own sake, for what can be derived by each person from a sustained association with another; and which is continued only in so far as it is thought by both parties to deliver enough satisfactions for each individual to stay within it' (Giddens 1992 p 58).

Further, and crucially, marriages traditionally were entered into on the basis of romantic love, whereas the pure relationship has as its basis 'confluent love':

'Confluent love is active, contingent love, and therefore jars with the "for-ever", "one and only" qualities of the romantic love complex. … The more confluent love becomes consolidated as a real possibility, the more the finding of a "special person" recedes and the more it is the "special relationship" that counts. … Confluent love presumes equality in emotional give and take, the more so the more any particular love tie approximates closely to the prototype of the pure relationship. Love here only develops to the degree to which intimacy does' (Giddens 1992 p 62).

The autonomy of the self is crucial to forming and sustaining a pure relationship based upon confluent love. 'Autonomy means the capacity of individuals to be self-reflective and self-determining', how they 'might determine and regulate the conditions of their association' (Giddens 1992 p 185). Autonomy of the individual in this sense is the foundation for democracy in the public sphere, and Giddens constructs a vision of that democracy in the sphere of personal relations (Giddens and Pierson 1998 p 125).

In his vision of the transformation of intimacy, Giddens sees the role of women as crucial. Women's successful claims to autonomy, equality and sexual emancipation, and the reinvesting of the autonomous individual with the traditionally feminine capacity for feeling and love instead of simply masculine-identified traits like reason and rationality, mean to him that '[w]omen became charged, *de facto*, with managing the transformation of intimacy which modernity set in train' (Giddens 1992 p 178).

There is much to draw upon in Giddens' work. First, he notes the importance of gender, both to the constitution of self, and to the constitution of relationships. Secondly, he sees an irreducible connection between changing social conditions, the changing idea of self and the changing nature of relationships. Indeed, he relates changes in modern intimacy to what he terms 'globalization', creating a world in which changes in tradition, custom and habit have affected day-to-day life as much as they have economic and the political life: 'globalization means not just economic, but wider structural and institutional change, having a profound impact on day-to-day life' (Giddens 1992 p 119 and see also Giddens and Pierson 1998). This view has profound implications for the blurring of previously perceived boundaries between the public and private self and the public and private worlds. Thirdly, he casts his ideas of modern intimacy in terms of equality and democracy and contrasts them with a history or tradition associated with inequality and hierarchy, adding a moral or political element to his 'transformation'. Finally, he hints at the implications for law of the radical democratisation of intimacy when he suggests that forming or dissolving pure relationships may have to affect their legal equivalents – marriage and divorce.

Giddens' work can be criticised, however, in his lack of attention to children and other dependants who are connected to the individuals he theorises. In other words, his model fails to account for the fact that many relationships may be triadic rather than dyadic (Smart and Neale 1999). Further, while he tempers the abstract nature of the 'pure relationship' by acknowledging that it may have a strong class factor (Giddens and Pierson 1998), he is less clear about its gender implications. In fact, the 'self' he assumes seems to be profoundly gendered: the free-moving autonomous individual resembles more closely the lived realities of men, who more easily than women are able to move from one pure relationship to the next in search of self-fulfilment (see Smart 1997; Smart and Neale 1999 p 11–13). His image of reflexive autonomy, therefore, is less a relational one than one that reflects a vision in which the acontextual individual enters and exits relationships on a consensual, negotiated basis (see Regan 1993). Finally, his focus upon individuals' personal responsibility for sustaining relationships feeds into a therapeutic discourse that downplays the importance of social structural factors that affect relationships on an experienced basis (Jamieson 1999; Crow 2002).

Ulrich Beck and Elisabeth Beck-Gernsheim: chaos and individual biographies

Beck and Beck-Gernsheim in *The Normal Chaos of Love* (1995) also write about transformations in love, family and personal relationships. They declare that it is no longer possible to pronounce what family, marriage, parenthood, sexuality or love mean; they vary from individual to individual and relationship to relationship. Further, their meanings depend upon negotiation between individuals who no longer have either 'standard biographies' or sets of rules governing status or behaviour that are determined externally, by church or community, for example. Instead, individuals have freedom to choose or to create their own biographies and their own rules. Beck and Beck-Gernsheim see this uniquely modern state of affairs as an opportunity to forge democratic love relationships, but also as problematic because the lack of external support systems binding to both parties leaves the difficult job of keeping the relationship intact entirely to the lovers themselves.

Beck and Beck-Gernsheim contrast pre-modern societies, where loyalties and identities were framed within strict boundaries and with strict rules, with the modern world that they see as a new, differentiated world in which individuals must create their own identities.

'Biographies are removed from the traditional precepts and certainties, from external control and general moral laws, becoming open and dependent on decision-making, and are assigned as a task for each individual' (Beck and Beck-Gernsheim 1995 p 5).

Significantly, this task is crucial for women as well as for men. Newly egalitarian roles and expectations in the public life of work, education and politics carry over into the private life of relationships, so that one cannot speak of personal biographies or of families without speaking of employment, income, schools or consumer activity, and in both public life as well as in personal biographies, the gender struggle is key. And a struggle it is. Beck and Beck-Gernsheim see a tension between attitudes to gender equality and social conditions. They see on the one hand great changes in some areas like formal law and education, but on the other a 'striking lack of change' in people's behaviour (Beck and Beck-Gernsheim 1995 p 14).

'This mixture of new attitudes and old conditions is an explosive one in a double sense. Better educated and informed young women expect to be treated as partners in professional and private life but come up against the opposite tendencies in the labour market and their male colleagues. Conversely, men have glibly *preached* equality without matching their words with deeds' (Beck and Beck-Gernsheim 1995 p 14).

While the desire and the need to create one's own biography, then, is universal in modern societies, the really innovative thing about relationships today may be the emergence of the new individual female biography (Beck and Beck-Gernsheim 1995 p 61). Both men and women may be free from prescribed gender roles, but it is primarily women who have taken up the challenge to manifest that freedom in shaping their individual biographies. Their struggle for individuality is new in the sense that it has not been possible before, but it is also a struggle for a new form of individuality, which previously was only available to men. It is an individuality that conforms to the demands of the global labour market – a traditionally masculine imperative. Beck and Beck-Gernsheim see a paradox, however, in the formation of modern individuality.

'Individualization means that men and women are released from the gender roles prescribed by industrial society for life in the nuclear family. At the same time ... they find themselves forced, under pain of material disadvantage, to build up a life of their own by way of the labour market ... So what appears to be an individual struggle to break free and discover one's true self turns out to be also a general move conforming to a general imperative' (Beck and Beck-Gernsheim 1995 p 6).

This is a struggle, then, where individuals must deal with the loss of old certainties of identity, but are caught up in global market forces beyond their control that result in new forms of identity. In their later work (2002), Beck and Beck-Gernsheim are careful to distinguish between a neo-liberal free market individual and this form of globalised individualisation that they see as creating new bonds of social and intimate cohesion. In other words, while we still seek love as the primary tie in our relationships, the meaning of love itself has changed. It is 'post- and a-traditional, and makes its own rules out of sexual desire now unhampered by moral or legal obligations' (Beck and Beck-Gernsheim 1995 p 194), and 'lacking any traditional restrictions, [it] becomes a radical form of personal responsibility … [in which] everything … is in the hands of the lovers' (Beck and Beck-Gernsheim 1995 p 194). As Smart and Neale (1999) observe, however, this 'new' form of love has almost a desperate feel to it, the more individualistic we become and the more fragile our relationships become, the more we yearn for love and for those relationships to fulfil us (Smart and Neale 1999 p 14–15). It is also why Beck and Beck-Gernsheim posit love for/of a child as the repository for the sense of permanence and certainty as well as for the irrational, natural side of our identity lost from the chaos of adult relationships: 'The child becomes the last remaining, irrevocable, unique primary love object. Partners come and go, but the child stays' (Beck and Beck-Gernsheim 1995 p 37). Our connection to our children is no longer communal or even familial in the traditional sense; it is ego-related and intense.

The ambiguous success of Beck and Beck-Gernsheim's process of individualisation has had profound consequences for the nuclear family. First, the 'traditional' nuclear family takes its form from prescribed roles. Once those roles become perceived as negotiable, the nuclear family loses its identifying characteristic. Secondly, an increase in the number of one's possible biographies leads to an increase in the possibility that negotiations will not, ultimately, be successful, permitting the parties simply to leave to try again elsewhere. Thirdly, if there are no external standards imposed upon the parties, they have to create their own new ones. This places them and the relationship under a pressure unknown in historical times. They must develop an ongoing dialogue of sorts, during which they continually seek and define common objectives, problems and solutions, but also during which they must find the happiness and fulfilment that only their relationship can provide. For a consequence of their individualised and continually revised biographies is the individualisation of their love and its constant negotiation. Finally, they must do this 'work' not in a social vacuum, but in a social and economic world which tends to segregate them rather than bind them together (Beck and Beck-Gernsheim 1995 p 95). It is not surprising in this light to see singledom as the archetypal existence behind a full market economy (Beck and Beck-Gernsheim 1995 p 143) or, in other words, to see the difficulty of retaining in this market-determined self some part of self that is rooted in relationship or family. To counteract this destructive form of individualism, Beck and Beck-Gernsheim say that we have adopted the ideology of love – our new religion.

Beck and Beck-Gernsheim's view of modern social, political and economic conditions thus sees little hope for a revival of traditional forms of family. We cannot, they say, return to old ways, and anyway, neither men nor women would want to. Sex equality and the global market economy have come too far: '[m]odernization is not a carriage you can climb out of at the next corner if you don't like it' (Beck and Beck-Gernsheim 1995 p 143). If the 'old' values of family included the likes of teamwork within separate spheres, obligation, duty, loyalty and allegiance, the new focus, according to Beck and Beck-Gernsheim, is on values such as 'self-awareness, sharing, loving people, bodies, nature and other creatures, finding the same wavelength, discovering oneself, spending time alone, arguing, and doing the chores; looking out for friends to accompany, support and criticize one's journey through life' (Beck and Beck-Gernsheim 1995 p 165).

If this is a realistic assessment of love and heterosexual adult familial connections at the turn of the twenty-first century, it is no wonder that these family relationships feel more precarious than they may have felt in times past, but it is also why we can say at the same time that they are based just as firmly on a form of commitment as they have ever been. It is, as Beck and Beck-Gernsheim say, the 'normal chaos of love' in an individualised, egalitarian and market-based society. And it is also why moral judgments based upon 'traditional' values may be at best inappropriate, and at worst destructive: 'when new family types emerge on a wide scale, there are probably good reasons for their emergence' (Nicholson 1997 p 37).

Selma Sevenhuijsen: connected autonomy

Dutch sociologist Selma Sevenhuijsen (1998) presents a new potential for individual subjectivity and consequently for intimate, social and political relations. Hers is a view, however, rooted in a non-liberal moral philosophy. She draws upon the work of feminist theorists such as Gilligan (1982), Tronto (1993) and Held (1993) to invest the individual self with a morality that is based upon considerations other than abstract justice or the exercise of autonomous rights. In particular she is concerned to add an ethic of 'care' to the normal components of human subjectivity. Her view takes issue with the prototype individual of moral philosophy and the liberal polity. Instead of the rational economic man, she argues we should adopt the paradigm of mother and child. In this way, care in the form of dependency, nurturing and connection would cease to be regarded as 'normal' only in the private sphere of intimate relations – for women – but dysfunctional or pathological in the public or civil sphere – for men. Instead, all individuals would be able to acknowledge in themselves what have traditionally been gendered ideas of connection and care, and the newly fashioned self and other would reflect a '"relational self", a moral agent who is embedded in concrete relationships with other people and who acquires an individual moral identity through interactive patterns of behaviour, perceptions and interpretations' (Sevenhuijsen 1998 p 55). Crucially, acquiring this identity involves the exercise of moral agency:

'This means that the definition of identity has shifted. Individuals are no longer seen as atomistic units with a pre-determined identity, who meet each other in the public sphere to create social ties. Identity, and with it the ability to engage in moral activity, is formed in specific cultural and historical situations, and thus it coincides with subjectivity, the ability to judge and to act. The self is not conceived as an entity, but as the protagonist in a biography' (Sevenhuijsen 1998 p 55–56).

Sevenhuijsen's approach, like that of Giddens and Beck and Beck-Gernsheim, rejects a predetermined and essential notion of self and emphasises the mutability, contestability and processual nature of the self. This preoccupation with a freedom or capacity to review and revise the self can be seen as post-modern in the sense that the certainties of either the pre-modern 'cosmos' or the modernist enlightenment no longer exist. In addition, like the others, Sevenhuijsen highlights the importance of gender in the reconstructive project, but unlike them she postulates the implications of acknowledging women's realities and experiences into a *new* moral imperative, which has profound consequences for the contemporary self:

'Human subjects do not arrive in the world as beings with a fully developed rational ability; they develop moral and rational capacities in connection and interaction with others, in the first instance with those who care for them and on whom they are dependent. ... The moral subjects in the ethics of care have not separated their experience of these things from the way in which they wish to understand social reality; rather they use it as a source of morally relevant knowledge' (Sevenhuijsen 1998 p 61–62).

The relevance of this knowledge and experience challenges 'the idea that the self-sufficient individual should remain the basis of moral existence and political regulation' (Sevenhuijsen 1998 p 27).

Sevenhuijsen's moral subjects are thus degendered and individualised in a different way than are Beck and Beck-Gernsheim's. While the latter observe the difficulty all 'new' individuals have in forging their subjectivity in a global market economy, in a way 'transcend[ing] the world of care on the way to "true" individuality' (Sevenhuijsen 1998 p 24), Sevenhuijsen suggests that women's 'experiences and considerations in relation to care' may instead transform definitions of the individual, the 'good society' (Sevenhuijsen 1998 p 24) and autonomy:

> 'In the liberal framework, autonomy and independency tend to be conflated, and autonomy, in the sense of autonomous judgment, is linked to an ideal of independence and self-sufficiency and to marginalization or even repression of the dependent dimensions of the self. This leads to a philosophical denial of dependency and interdependence as aspects of the "human condition" … In the ethics of care the quality of autonomous judgement can be regarded as enhanced, not only because the moral actors are better tuned to a diversity of moral considerations, but also because the illusion of a solipsistic subject is replaced by the idea of "being in the world with each other" … In such a vision, possessing an autonomous moral self does not rest on immutable assumptions about a uniform rationality, but rather on the norm of not approaching others in an objectifying or stereotyping manner' (Sevenhuijsen 1998 p 63).

Individuality in an ethics of care, then, embraces a differently constituted autonomy from that described by Beck and Beck-Gernsheim, or indeed by Giddens (Sevenhuijsen 2002). It follows also that love and intimacy will take on very different meanings. While all see the necessity for ongoing flux, negotiation and dialogue, it is only in an ethic of care that connection with and looking out for the interests of the other become a manifestation of autonomy[1].

Milton Regan: the communitarian self

Regan (1999) also sees room for a new form of moral autonomy in which the ability to foster and preserve relationships with others and sensitivity to persons in their particularity are important, and in which trust and obligation arise not only through consent between individuals, but also

---

1   For a review of other feminist conceptions of the self, see Reece 2003.

from a shared experience with one another (Regan 1999 p 11–12). To him:

> 'attention to the ways in which individual reflection depends on a social matrix leads us to appreciate that attachments are a predicate for meaningful personal freedom rather than merely an impediment to it' (Regan 1999 p 28)[2].

He attempts to reconcile a liberating individualism within relationships with community and connection. He thus does not so much re-imagine the meaning of individual autonomy as he re-imagines the liberal individual exercising that autonomy differently and contextually, with particular attention to connections with others.

Notwithstanding their differences, each of these conceptions of self and intimacy presents possibilities for new understandings of the foundations of, and thus the nature of, contemporary family life (Rodger 1996). They emphasise flux, reflexivity and agency in the constitution of the self and relationships. In many ways, they lie in stark contrast to traditional foundations for intimate adult relationships: the autonomous liberal self and romantic love.

The individual of classical liberal thought is one who has achieved an autonomy of self that is fixed and authentic. Autonomy is understood as independence, which allows the individual to negotiate its social, political and intimate choices according to a rational free will. It is curious that along with this form of individualism arose the tradition of modern, romantic love in which rationality seemingly plays little part. While I am tempted here to leave descriptions of romantic love to poets, lyricists or Mills and Boon, some mundane sociological or historical enquiry may be necessary both as a contrast to the above analyses of late-modern intimate connections and to provide some further insight into the relationships many people enter into today.

Traditional intimacy as romantic love

According to historians and anthropologists, it seems that love or infatuation has beguiled people from time immemorial (see Fisher 1992; Zeldin 1994).

---

2   For a review of other post-liberal and communitarian conceptions of the self, see Reece 2003, and for a criticism of the communitarian self in the context of a new reflexive paradigm for law, see Cohen 2002.

The physical, mental and emotional attraction it compels is thought to have emerged with the medieval troubadours who waxed lyrical about the simultaneous euphoria and anguish it caused, but others (Fisher 1992; Zeldin 1994) assert that romantic love is more widespread and ancient than that. But while romantic love, characterised variously as an affliction, distraction or disease, may be a timeless and universal part of the human condition, the idea of it legitimating family relationships is not. Stone (1990), Luhmann (1986) and Shorter (1975) all suggest that it was not until around the end of the eighteenth century that the idea and ideal of romantic love as the basis of intimate, and therefore marriage, relationships entered individual and public consciousness, at least for the middle and upper classes in Western Europe. Luhmann, for example, suggests that through a combination of socio-structural forces, love and marriage became connected, so that '[b]y the end of the eighteenth century the unity of a marriage of love and conjugal love was generally professed to be the principle of the natural perfection of humankind' (Luhmann 1986 p 146). Gillis (1985 ch 2) and Grassby (2001) write that love intruded upon some marriage choices and behaviour even earlier; although in the sixteenth and seventeenth centuries it was only one of many factors that influenced choice of marital partners. Nonetheless, Grassby notes that 'the power of romantic love was widely acknowledged and represented as a natural emotion' in the literature of the seventeenth century (Grassby 2001 p 37–38).

The ideal of romantic, conjugal love, the 'romantic love complex', beginning in the seventeenth or eighteenth century has been described as a 'social force' (Giddens 1992 p 44) or a 'revolution' (Shorter 1975 p 149) and the reasons for its emergence in Britain at that time have been linked in different ways with the 'modernization' of British society (Grassby 2001 'Introduction'). Mercantilism, contractarianism and 'enlightened' political theory (see Shanley 1989) contributed to a newly imagined individual separated from 'house' or kin group, with an increasing orientation towards the pursuit of worldly happiness.

Social historian Lawrence Stone (1979) describes that which he terms 'affective individualism' and the beginnings of the romantic love complex as arising in the eighteenth century. In the 'middle' and landed classes it meant a trend towards greater equality and warmth between spouses, greater recognition of children's freedom and special status and a greater separation of the nuclear unit from other kin and the community (Stone 1979 p 149–150). Stone saw the social conditions necessary for the move away from hierarchical duty towards affective individualism in bourgeois families in many spheres. There was, for example, a new interest in, and vision of, the self seen in the changing literary genres of the eighteenth century, which evidenced a desire for self-expression in the form of the diary or the autobiography (Stone 1979 p 154–155) or which told the stories of individual (male) adventurers or individual romantic or emotional struggles in the new romantic novels (Stone 1979 p 156). Further, a demand for autonomy and liberty of conscience was raised by religious sectarianism and 'secular ideas about natural law and the proprietary right every individual had in himself which could not justly be violated by anyone else' (Stone 1979 p 157), which became a part of the political orthodoxy after the Civil War in England. In addition, there was, as science and technology and the decline of religious beliefs changed the way humans viewed their place in the natural world, a 'progressive reorientation of culture towards the pursuit of pleasure in this world, rather than postponement of gratification until the next' (Stone 1979 p 159) because we believed we could master the natural world and use it to our benefit. Coupled with a possessive individualism which came to guide economic affairs, the selfish pursuit of happiness came to be seen both as a primary motivator of human behaviour and as in the public good. The quest for romantic love became the psychological and emotional equivalent of Adam Smith's economic individualism (Stone 1979 p 162; Regan 1993). As Regan states, 'romantic love is the purest form of individualism; it subordinates all familial, societal or group considerations to personal preference' (Regan 1993 p 23).

Shorter (1975) also relates changes in economic and political society to the revolution in sentiment he attributes to the eighteenth century. He suggests, however, that it was economics, more specifically the new capitalist society, that helped cause the 'romance revolution' (Shorter 1975 p 258).

> '[A]mong the common people whom the eighteenth century had forced into the marketplace, this egotistical economic mentality [of the free market] spread into the various noneconomic domains of life, specifically into those ties that bind the individual to the surrounding community. Egotism that was learned in the marketplace became transferred to community obligations and standards, to ties to the family and lineage – in short to the whole domain of cultural rules that regulated familial and sexual behaviour … ' (Shorter 1975 p 259).

These new rules created a 'wish to be free', which 'in the domain of menwomen relations … emerges as romantic love' – the desire to find personal happiness (Shorter 1975 p 259).

Grassby (2001) takes issue with both Shorter and Stone. His empirical history of the families of businessmen in the 'pre-modern' (1580–1740) period reveals that romantic love and romantic individualism 'existed long before the development of a sophisticated market economy' (Grassby 2001 p 394). Rather, 'it was the nuclear family that allowed individualism to develop, and it was individualism that created both capitalism and love' (Grassby 2001 p 394). It seems that marriages were made based upon individual choice in both 'pre-modern' and 'modern' times, but the degree of influence that romantic love had upon that choice changed from time to time.

The link between individualism, love and marriage recurs in Regan's (1993) work. Regan, however, writes of a later period in which he credits the Victorian form of the family with cementing what have come to be contemporary attitudes to love and marriage. He, like the others, suggests that individualism affected one's sense of self or identity and the intimate relationships one sought. He goes on to suggest, however, that the Victorians experienced 'acute anxiety' about the age's 'tendencies toward atomism' (Regan 1993 p 32) and so marriage became invested with traditional religious and other symbols of selflessness, particularly on the part of the wife, to offer a new version of connection to replace the old. On this view, the prospect of full self-realisation that preoccupied the Victorians could be completed by successful performance of a predetermined role in the family. The role-status of Victorian husband, wife, son or daughter, and the objective of adequately performing that role became linked to one's self-identity so as to domesticate the instability of personal feeling with the appreciation of more important duties toward one's family (Regan 1993 p 32). So, for the Victorians, family, familial status *and* individualism were crucial and contained elements of both reality and myth, serving important ideological functions related to what was assumed to be the optimal ordering of society.

Finally, Gillis (1997) also places the beginning of romantic marriage in the nineteenth century. His work shows that while few pre-modern marriages, apart from those of the aristocracy, were arranged, and young people enjoyed a large measure of choice of marriage partner (Gillis 1997 p 135), that choice was not usually based upon romantic love. 'Conjugal love was more feared than celebrated; it was viewed as too volatile and insubstantial to sustain either individual identities or the social order' (Gillis 1997 p 134). This changed in the nineteenth century:

'Eventually, the European and American middle classes would create a whole new ceremonial for themselves, but it would not be a continuation of but a break with all that had gone before. In the new rites that developed in the second half of the nineteenth century, conjugal love became a prerequisite rather than a consequence of marriage. ... Marriage was no longer a matter of stepping into new roles, but, beyond this, stepping into a new world' (Gillis 1997 p 143).

To Gillis, this was a time when marriage, specifically weddings, carried the burden of symbolising love (Gillis 1997 p 150), and we continue today to rely on the marriage ritual to sustain our faith in romantic love (Gillis 1997 p 151).

While the romantic love complex may have allowed individuals choice and the freedom to pursue happiness, it also contained elements that can be described as distinctly 'un-liberal'. In romantic love, that love which idealises the other and the love itself, the individual's link with the beloved is an irrational one; contrasted with reason, it is of the heart rather than of the head, and it is paradoxical because it requires at the same time an autonomous self, a fully reflexive self and a denial of self. Giddens describes it as follows:

'Romantic love presumes some degree of self interrogation. How do I feel about the other? How does the other feel about me? Are our feelings "profound" enough to support a long-term involvement? ... It provides for a long-term life trajectory, oriented to an anticipated, yet malleable future ...

It is incompatible with lust, and with earthy sexuality, not so much because the loved one is idealised – although this is part of the story – but because it presumes a psychic communication, a meeting of souls which is reparative in character. The other, by being who he or she is, answers a lack which the individual does not even necessarily recognise – until the love relationship is initiated. And this lack is directly to do with self-identity: in some sense, the flawed individual is made whole' (Giddens 1992 p 44–45).

The paradox within romantic love is also expressed as the 'simultaneous renunciation and affirmation of individual personality'; it is 'gaining self-consciousness only through the renunciation of independence' (Hegel 1991 s 158 p 199)[3], and it recurs in apparently timeless themes of love 'fulfilling'

---

3   I am grateful to Robert Fine for discussion on this point and for this reference. See also Landes (1982).

us as individuals, of 'losing one's self' in the other person and of it making us 'whole'. Finding 'true love' is still a quest for many, not only so that we can live out our days 'happily ever after' with our true love, but, more urgently, so that we can become whole human beings. Romantic love is both exclusive (as Luhmann says, how can you lose yourself in more than one person? (Luhmann 1986 p 97)) and eternal.

The dynamics of romantic love are also gendered. Though both men and women fall in love, women tend to be *responsible* for romantic love in way that men are not. Gillis notes:

'[Victorian] men were eager to "fall in love" but liked to think of love as something that happened to them rather than something they were responsible for nurturing. As with so many other aspects of Victorian life, the labours of love were unequally divided. Boys learned to expect love from women, and girls were trained to give and sustain it' (Gillis 1997 p 144).

Davidoff et al see the eighteenth-century romantic sensibility as arising in protest against 'cerebral rational individualism' and as almost a threat to it (Davidoff et al 1989 p 65). 'Romantic expression promoted a *feeling* self, created and sustained by relationships to others and to Nature' (Davidoff et al 1989 p 65). The connection of this feeling self with the home and the natural family, and the rational self with the public world had vast implications for men and women's engagement with romantic love. In many ways, romantic love was essentially feminised love (Giddens 1992 p 43).

Perhaps the point I am making here is simply the cultural and historical specificity of romantic love. Just as 'modern' love may be a part of a globalised, sexually liberated, individualised polity, romantic love may also have been a product of its time, of the newly liberated, *feeling* individual, or more prosaically, of cultural expectations, fashion or fad. In other words, people might never fall in love if they did not believe that their true happiness depended upon it. As Stone says, '[i]t is a product ... of learned cultural expectations which became fashionable in the late eighteenth century' and 'by becoming fashionable, ... inevitably also became much more common' (Stone 1979 p191). Interestingly, despite trends postulated by modern sociology, romantic love is still fashionable and still common; it is perceived as timeless and 'real'; it is, despite ideas about modern individualism, believed to be the cultural norm for 'healthy' adult individuals and the normal basis for those individuals' relationships. We expect (hope?) and are expected to fall in love, so that we can create a 'proper family' based upon this love.

Romantic love is not negotiable. It is out of our control, and when it is 'true' it lasts forever. It is not contingent, confluent love and it is not the love between individuated equals, all of which are thought to be crass impostors and to be the products of either our current, less than moral, 'valueless' society, or a throwback to less enlightened times. Although it was only a moment in the life of the early modern, and then nineteenth century, family, it gave that family, and that moment, an illusory but authoritative form that remains with us today.

If the more recent sociological analyses are correct, however, the illusion of our intimate connections and our families today may also demand a new type of individuality, choice and free will that mean flux and a kind of uncertain rationalism that potentially corrodes the romantic institution in which we, individually and collectively, have invested so much. So we struggle to cling to a 'true' and wonderful romantic moment at the same time as we negotiate our unromantic, individualised lives in the twenty-first century. In the next chapter I explore how these two apparently contrasting narratives of intimacy can exist together at both normative and experienced levels, and I develop this contrast as the theoretical framework in which I will examine current trends in family law, for it seems to me that it represents both perils and promise for achieving justice in the legal regulation of family lives.

Two families

This chapter introduces two different families: the families we live *by* and the families we live *with* (Gillis 1997). It is about how we are always and simultaneously a part of both, and how individual men, women and children negotiate this dual membership. The family we live by is responsible for 'representing ourselves to ourselves as we would like to think we are' (Gillis 1997 p xv). Unlike the families we live with, these families do not ever let us down: '[c]onstituted through myth, ritual and image, they must be forever nurturing and protective' (Gillis 1997 p xv). They are important to help us make sense of the messy and often disappointing individual family relationships we live with because they provide us with a needed sense of continuity and shared history and they assist us to help make sense of the broader social, cultural and political meaning of 'family'.

I suggest that the families we live by are constituted through a series of contrasting narratives about the nature of family relationships and the nature of the individuals who forge those relationships. I also suggest that law's ideal family shares this successfully contradictory framework and that this family has attained normative status in contemporary Britain. While the successful resolution of ambiguity is also a feature of the families we live with, however, the normative family reduces the messiness, uncertainty and complexity of lived experience into dichotomies. Further, and importantly, it sets up its dichotomous norm as the standard by which to judge the more complicated families we live with.

One of the contrasts at the heart of the normative family is that between the different narratives of love and intimacy outlined in Chapter 1. I suggest in this chapter that these narratives are linked to family types: romantic attachment is an important component of the image of the 'traditional family' and lies in contrast to a negotiated type of love said to bind the modern egalitarian family. I explore here how both the link and the contrast are sustained and the ways in which, indeed the degree to which, they can be managed in the day-to-day familial experiences that characterise the families we live with. I shall begin with the traditional family, an important part of the normative family.

The traditional family myth

A popular perception of family life in Britain at the beginning of the new millennium is that it is not like it used to be. There is a sense of loss, even if that which is supposed to be lost is difficult to identify. Some would say stability, some would say values and some would say morality, and many would simply say the 'traditional family', a term which to them captures all of the above. To these family traditionalists, this loss is cause for concern or worse. To others, it is cause for celebration, while for still others it is a neutral phenomenon: just another example of humans and historical conditions adapting to each other. On close examination, however, the traditional family that is so often eulogised is an elusive concept. Not only its meaning, but its location in time changes:

> '[f]or the Victorians, the traditional family, imagined to be rooted and extended, was located sometime before industrialization and urbanization, but for those who came of age during the First World War, tradition was associated with the Victorians themselves; today we think of the 1950s and early 1960s as the location of the family and community life we imagine we have lost' (Gillis 1997 p 4–5).

Gillis, and others, conclude that the traditional family is a myth, but it is a myth that we have always needed in order to make sense of the communities and families we live with and to give us a basis from which to face, indeed, to embrace the future (Gillis 1997 p 5).

Gillis' captivating work, *A World of Their Own Making* (1997), brings to light this traditional family and relates it to the families we live by. Gillis suggests that while families in times past may have found families to live by in tradition, in the 'cosmos or the community' (Gillis 1997 p xvi–xvii), contemporary families must carry the burden of creating and sustaining their own myths, rituals and images. Similar to Beck and Beck-Gernsheim's idea of the lovers' personal responsibility for defining and sustaining the terms of their love, Gillis sees families as personally responsible for creating and sustaining images of themselves. It seems to me, however, that these images take their shape, at least in part, from the values we feel we have lost from the community, from the 'traditional family'. They are both personal and universally 'traditional'. And so, the moral attributes we ascribe to the families we live by are also those we ascribe to the traditional family – romantic love, stability, loyalty and unity. They are important to us as individuals because they reflect the expectations or hopes we have for our relationships, and they are also important socially as they embody what we would like family life to mean in an uncertain and seemingly amoral society. That they may exist on only an ideal or mythical level is not important. Even though, for example, some of the characteristics we have ascribed to traditional families – a reverence of family history and ancestors, the multi-generational household, the sanctity of marriage and the stability of home as a physical place – were no more real for families of the past than they are for our present ones (Gillis 1997 p 1–19), we continue to idealise them as historical truth rather than acknowledge the possibility that the 'traditional family' never existed as a lived reality, but rather was always imaginary and is forever lost.

One imperfect version of the traditional family probably emerged with the romantic love complex and the nuclear family (see Grassby 2001; Chapter 1), first among the landed classes, but later among the emerging middle class in the eighteenth century. It was characterised by husband and wife, living apart from the parents of either, and 'geared to relations of affection as the household [became] less a unit focused on production and more on sexuality, intimacy and consumption' (Nicholson 1997 p 31–32). Partners were chosen on the basis of love and preordained roles within that love relationship complemented each other. The place of the mother became confirmed as guardian of the family's moral welfare and that of the father as distant, but secure, provider (see Regan 1993). The shift this family took to the 1950s version was only subtly different. Nicholson explains:

'While the Victorian ideal of domesticity included wife and mother at home, it portrayed her household activities in a very different way from the ideal of the 1950s. A notion of woman as moral guardian of the hearth who left her more practical tasks to servants gave way to an ideal of woman who was morally and psychologically fulfilled through housework and child-rearing. The family became seen as the site of leisure and consumption where, ideally, leisure activities were carried out together' (Nicholson 1997 p 33).

This version of the traditional family thus has its roots in a particular economic structure and could only be sustained by those with sufficient financial means. Just as the working classes of Victorian times could not sustain financially the new ideal domestic form of the bourgeoisie, the poor in the 1950s could not sustain the middle-class ideal of the self-sufficient nuclear family with wife at home. It seems that the traditional family is thus a 'classed' concept. Nicholson also points out that, at least in the United States, but arguably also in Britain with its associations of nation, nationality and family (Chambers 2001), it has racist origins as well. The economic expansion of the 1950s in the United States excluded a large number of people, most particularly those who were unemployable or unemployed, often due to the extreme racism which existed at the time. This meant that many African-Americans did not have access to the wealth created by the new service and professional sectors of the economy, and thus to the newly dominant middle class and the 'traditional family' that symbolised it.

The traditional family is thus classed and 'raced'. Perhaps more obviously, it is also sexed and gendered. Its heterosexual nature is simply taken for granted and the gender roles of the members strictly prescribed. All of this may be of historical interest only, until we remind ourselves of the 'belief in [its] universality and/or superiority' (Nicholson 1997 p 35). Thus, there may be an ideological function served by sustaining the myth of the traditional family (see also Barrett and MacIntosh 1991; Gittins 1993). It may have vanished or indeed may never have existed as a day-to-day reality, but it flourishes as ideal, symbol, discourse and powerful myth within the collective imagination (Chambers 2001). When we mourn the loss of the 'traditional family', therefore, we may be grieving for the loss of more than the values we ascribe to it like loyalty, stability, co-operation, love and respect; we must also remain aware of its underlying values of patriarchy, heterosexism and race and class hierarchy.

The traditional family is able to offer to its members a clear sense of their place within it, and consequently, their place in the world. It helps to provide one with an identity, a sense of self that is crucial to one's sense of continuity of place and time, and to negotiating relationships with others (see also Regan 1999).

'Human lives used to be determined by a multitude of traditional ties – from family business and village community, homeland and religion, to social status and gender role. ... On the one hand they rigorously restrict the individual's choice, on the other they offer familiarity and protection, a stable footing and certain identity' (Beck and Beck-Gernsheim 1995 p 45–46).

This certainty is important for social and individual, psychological reasons (see Chapter 4 and Hatten et al 2002). In mourning the loss of the traditional family, therefore, perhaps we also mourn the loss of the certainty of traditional identities and connections which, arguably, are rooted in the narrative of romantic love.

In mythical romantic love both the relationship and the beloved are idealised. (In this light, recall Baker and Emry's (1993) research finding that even law students believe that while 40 per cent of all marriages end in divorce, their marriages would be the ones that last forever). The beloved is 'the one' Mr or Miss Right and the love itself is idealised – it is real, and true, as opposed to previous relationships which become characterised as 'trial runs'. In romantic love the self is incomplete without the other – love makes one whole. Beck and Beck-Gernsheim (1995) describe it as person-related stability, which not only provides some accepted and acceptable structure to our lives (see also Berger and Kellner 1980), but also provides us with a new identity. 'We mirror ourselves in the other, and our image of a You is also an idealised image of I' (Beck and Beck-Gernsheim 1995 p 51). Berger and Kellner's view is that the 'identity of each takes on a new character, indeed, being typically perceived by people at large as being symbiotically conjoined with the identity of the other' (Berger and Kellner 1980 p 305). Further, the lovers complement each other so that the whole that is created from their unity is a 'perfect', complete, new individual.

The norms, rules and expectations of romantic love and the family it creates are either simply understood as one follows one's heart, or they emanate from cultural understandings of how one behaves and what it means to be 'in love' and to be a father, husband, wife or mother. In neither case are terms and conditions negotiated, negotiable or voluntarily chosen. Romantic love is out of our control – we 'fall in love', often against our better judgment. It is solely a matter of the feelings of the lovers, and thus can only be comprehended by the language of love. In this sense it is private – it remains in the realm of feelings rather than being contaminated by grubby material and social matters like money, employment or other worldly conditions. True love is thought to transcend such matters and will win out, so that structural conditions such as childcare, employment, transportation and education, and mundane matters like housework are irrelevant to it. Finally, romantic love, if it is 'true', is forever and exclusive and it creates a family that is similarly enduring, private and role-bound; one that looks, in other words, like the lost, traditional family.

The modern family myth

Late modernity may indeed require a reconfiguration of gender roles, both within and outside families, new ideas of a child's 'place' and indeed of what childhood is (see Chapter 4), and a revision of ties to intimates and to community such that we are now faced with uncertain and untested possibilities in creating our own new and changeable identities. The sociological perspectives outlined in the previous chapter are examples of how some see family connections and familial identities as having changed in recent years to cope with this uncertainty. Now, they seem to say, our intimate, family relationships are complex, often incoherent, and continually changing. These relationships and the ways in which we express them are manifestations of our substantive individualities at any given time, but because both our identities and our relationships are always works in progress and are inevitably bound up with social and structural factors, they have social and structural meaning as well as emotional and moral meaning. We relate to our family co-members in ways which would be inconceivable in the romantic discourse: as equal individuals, continually making and remaking our individual and joint biographies and obligations according to individualised and personalised moral economies. As lovers we remain always two separate individuals and the relationship as well as our individualities are subject to continual negotiation based on a form of equality that bears only a distant relation to the complementarity and symbiotic connection of romantic love. Both our subjectivities and the relationship are imbricated within social and structural conditions and thus can be said to be almost dependent upon them, rather than to transcend them[1].

In this narrative our family relationships are those we choose to define as such. We can identify ourselves as 'spouse', 'mother' or 'father' according to an idealised individuality which emerges through engagement with complex and changing social circumstances rather than as the result of predetermined and fixed identities. The self that we bring to our intimate connections is a

1   Rodger (1996) sees this form of relationship as defining contemporary marriages.

fluid, freely chosen one and thus we can define our connections in a fluid, freely chosen way.

Modern intimacy need not be either forever or exclusive; it is sustained only so long as it is mutually satisfying to the lovers. Confluent love is not perfect in its purity or in its creation of a unity, but is always unfinished, a work in progress. The relationship it creates is not ideal; it is open to change and its terms are therefore within our control. In this sense it is private, but in another, because it is firmly grounded in society, between two people with individualised biographies to which are relevant economic and social conditions (Beck and Beck-Gernsheim 1995), it is intimately connected with the public. The unit that it creates is not a Hegelian new individual, but something that is itself a constant work in progress. The self within that work at the same time embraces Beck and Beck-Gernsheim's equality and individuality and Sevenhuijsen's or Regan's moral, connected autonomy (see Chapter 1). This self is a continual work in progress as well, and crucially, it must not be absorbed within the other; maintenance of separate identities is crucial.

While this late-modern form of attachment and the self-conscious generation of identity and family is said to be an ongoing, universal project, Weeks et al (1999) suggest that it is in the gay and lesbian community that it can be discerned particularly clearly. Increasingly, gay men and lesbian women are asserting new positive personal identities and these in turn are shaped through both their social and more intimate worlds. Weeks et al use Giddens' work to suggest that for non-heterosexual men and women, the modern project of identity is actualised by answering day-to-day 'decisions about who to be, how to behave and ... who and how we should love and relate to' (Weeks et al 1999 p 84–85). The intimate relationship thus becomes the framework for everyday life as well as 'the focus for personal identity, in which the personal narrative is constructed and reconstructed to provide that provisional sense of unity of the self which is all that is possible in the conditions of late modernity' (Weeks et al 1999 p 85). The language chosen to express commitments and connections in these relationships is that of 'family'. Among the self-identified non-heterosexuals in Weeks et al's study, 'family' meant 'an affinity circle which may or may not involve children which has cultural and symbolic meaning for the subjects that participate or feel a sense of belonging in and through it' (Weeks et al 1999 p 86). Importantly, the language of choice and self-invention was also adopted, creating new 'narratives of family and of choice, of care and responsibility, of love and loss, of old needs and new possibilities, [and] of difference and convergence ...' (Weeks et al 1999 p 99).

This vision of 'modern' family life certainly lies in contrast to the romantic traditional family, but it is important to realise that it is just as aspirational (see Smart 2000). The individual equality we believe we have achieved in the public sphere may now be a meaningful part of our private lives such that we may indeed place a new importance upon self-actualisation, personal choice in partnering and creating and negotiating the terms of that partnership, but just as is romantic love, this pure relationship is an ideal. Both have as much to do with ideology as they do with social reality, yet together their mythic aspects, ritualised behaviour requirements and idealised statuses form the paradoxical basis of the families we live by.

Normative and experienced family life

Despite our idealisation of and desire for modern love's equality, reflexivity and fluidity, individuals seem also to love and idealise the security, stability, forever quality, unity and purity promised by romantic love, and we long for it because we feel that it and only it will fulfil us as individuals. This longing is expressed most clearly by those who lament the lost traditional family, but it is also reflected in narratives of romantic love offered by the popular media and in individuals' expressions of their expectations for intimate relationships. We understand romantic love to be the 'correct' kind of love on which to build relationships and families; it is a part of the foundation for the families that we live by. At the same time, as we urgently pursue a project of self, the other part of that foundation may be an idealised version of the individualised pure relationship.

The families we live with, on the other hand, embody the social, material and emotional 'messiness' that results from our experienced reality of trying to reconcile these two essentially irreconcilable forms of attachment. In them, we are engaged in an ongoing attempt to find ways of living with fluidity, insecurity, conflict and individualism, *and* with loyalty, altruism, stability and forever romanticism. Our lived relationships are thus complex and contradictory: they are moral, emotional, rational, sacred, reflexive and static. They often reinforce traditional gender and class stereotypes even while they attempt to democratise relationships (Jamieson 1999). Like the families we live by, they rely on notions of both predetermined and voluntarily assumed roles and obligations, but unlike those ideal families, they are not always successful in reconciling the two. They embody the tension between cultural ideals of equality, mutuality, stability and loyalty and the structural and personal inequalities and insecurities experienced on a day-to-day basis. I am thus adapting Gillis' (1997) characterisation of these two families, but I adopt his view that the families we live by are just as important to us as the families we live with. We are a part of both simultaneously.

The families we live with: 'doing' family

Morgan (1996 and 1999) uses the term 'family practices' to refer to modern family living (Morgan 1999 p 15). He is concerned with the 'family' quality of the interactions of everyday living so that activities which on their face seem immediately to be 'about' family are included in his term, but, importantly, so are activities which may not seem so obviously to be family matters. Accessing public transport, eating breakfast, working overtime and voting, for example, can all be studied as family practices. His approach also allows family to be seen as one of many 'foci of social enquiry' such as gender, work and stratification (Morgan 1999 p 16), so that all of the examples above can equally be seen as gender practices, social stratification practices or work practices as well as family practices. In his words, 'family [is] to be seen as less of a noun and more of an adjective, or, possibly, a verb. "Family" represents a constructed quality of human interaction or an active process rather than a thing-like object of detached social investigation' (Morgan 1999 p 16). To this extent, the concept of family practices characterises the families we live with, as it locates the individual and her or his family relationships within both public and private societies and recognises the importance of other discourses and social conditions in the making of that individual and those relationships from time to time. It embraces and helps us to understand modern changes in 'family structure' by refusing to see family in a structural way. As Silva and Smart say, it 'implies that individuals are *doing* family, instead of simply residing within a pre-given structure' (Silva and Smart 1999 p 5).

Interestingly, these academic views are presented more concretely by parents who responded to a survey by the National Family and Parenting Institute in 1999. Many of the people interviewed expressed frustration with policies explicitly stated to be 'family' policies, such as education, childcare or 'family-friendly' employment measures, but, significantly, they also recognised that issues about traffic, street lights, public transportation,

low wages, accessibility of shopping and business centres, and racism were
crucial to their everyday familial lives and to the 'connection between
outside realities and the quality of relationships within families' (National
Family and Parenting Institute 1999 p 16). Despite recent government
aims to 'Support Families' (Home Office 1998) by what it calls 'joined-up
government', the parents in this survey were unhappy that 'the message to
them was that they were on their own with their responsibilities' (National
Family and Parenting Institute 1999 p 19). The practices of the families
they lived with appeared to lack government support.

'Doing' family also occurs in the ongoing expression of responsibility to
others. Finch and Mason (1993), for example, explored this negotiation
between adult 'extended' family members. They found that extended family relationships are significant for most people; most people do rely upon
family as a source of support, advice and assistance, even if only as a last
resort. But the nature of the responsibility many felt to family members
was a negotiated one; responsibilities are created commitments rather
than rules of obligation based merely upon the 'fact' of family connection.
They are built within the history of the relationship and with a view to
its anticipated future. The idea, therefore, that 'responsibility is a natural
property of named relationships' (Finch and Mason 1993 p 178) does not
appear to be the reality of people's lives. Expectations regarding duties
and responsibility cannot be gleaned from social or legal norms, but rather
are individually negotiated in a moral and social context. In this way, they
represent the families we live with, but interestingly, the people to whom
Finch and Mason spoke often referred to the *ideal* of families working together, and were concerned to offer their perception that their families did
indeed *work* in this way. To them, giving and receiving help were seen as
a normal and unremarkable part of family life, even when that assistance
was a contingent, negotiated effect of individual and family histories and
biographies.

The people in Finch and Mason's study saw providing assistance to family members as part of 'the image of what constitutes "a family" and most
people in [the] study wanted to claim that they were part of "a family" of
this type' (Finch and Mason 1993 p 163). The image of a family as a unit creating responsibilities among its membership based on the 'natural' reality
of the relationships themselves is one that, historically, has been at the heart
of British social policy and law (Finch and Mason 1993), and it appears as
a part of the normative family that we live by in the image of many of their
interviewees, even while their behaviour and experience stressed the other

part, the importance of individual biographies, structural locations and negotiated reciprocities.

The modern/romantic same-sex family

Empirical studies are able to shed some light upon the factors that influence the way in which individuals constitute themselves as family. The conditions of late modernity have been said to influence non-heterosexual men and women in particular (Weeks et al 1999) and empirical research has also suggested that this may, in fact, be the case. At the same time, however, the 'families of choice' constituted by lesbians and gay men embrace a need for the same sense of security and continuity over time associated with the orthodox, traditional family, even while they remain rooted in specific, historic, non-heterosexual experiences (Weeks et al 1999 p 83).

The late modern views identity, including gender as an aspect of identity, as constantly being made and remade; it is something individuals 'do' daily, including in intimate relationships (Dunne 1999; Weeks et al 1999). In intimate, domestic relations even engagement in everyday tasks is about engaging in the production of gender and so in the context of a heterosexual norm, the intimate, routine gender practices of heterosexual individuals affirm gender difference on a daily basis; they contribute to a sense of who one is as a man or a women (Dunne 1999 p 71). Lesbian women and gay men, however, create their identities outside the norm, without the constraints it imposes upon gender expectations and gender practices, arguably rendering their partnerships and familial identities freely chosen in a way that would be impossible for heterosexual individuals. Dunne (1999) interviewed 37 cohabiting lesbian couples with dependent children and analysed the way they 'did' gender by dividing household tasks. She concluded that doing gender outside heterosexuality meant that:

> 'A lesbian's partner is usually her best friend, or at least one of them, and the operation of power is more likely to elaborate upon the rules of friendship (equality, support, balancing the differences, reciprocity) than the rules of heterosexual romance (the eroticization of difference, "intimate strangers" possessing different emotional vocabularies, institutional and sexual power imbalances)' (Dunne 1999 p 79).

She also concludes that 'the gender of the person one is doing gender with/for makes a real difference' (Dunne 1999 p 79). When we place these conclusions in the light of the following comment, which typifies the feelings of many of Dunne's respondents, we see some evidence of a lived version of the democratic, reflexive, *modern* relationship.

'I suppose because our relationship doesn't fit into a social norm, there are no pre-set conditions about how our relationship should work. We have to work it out for ourselves. We've no role models in terms of how we divide our duties, so we've got to work it out afresh as to what suits us ... We try very hard to be just to each other and ... not exploit the other person' (Dunne 1999 p 73).

Gay men often echo similar sentiments:

'I think there is ... less a kind of sense of possession, or property, in same-sex relationships, and more emphasis on ... emotional bonding ... that's not quite what I mean, but they're less ritualized really' (Weeks et al 1999 p 92).

Weeks et al (1999) and also Weeks (2002), however, highlight the importance of the narrative of family adopted by their respondents. Use of the term 'family' to describe intimate partners and close friends 'suggests a strong perceived need to appropriate the sort of values and comforts that the family is supposed to embody, even if it regularly fails to do so; continuity over time, emotional and material support, ongoing commitment and intense engagement' (Weeks 2002 p 218). So, while same sex families of choice exist within a narrative of self-invention, 'the story of creating your own life' (Weeks et al 1999 p 88), they also incorporate a narrative of traditional ideals. That they do so often without the social recognition afforded heterosexual families (see below) may mean that the rules, entirely rewritten in individualised scripts outside social norms, create new truths about intimate lives that subvert traditional ideals (Weeks 2002 p 219) and may provide an impetus for the increased convergence of heterosexual and non-heterosexual forms of intimate life (Weeks 2002 p 224).

'At the centre of this is the fundamental belief that love relationships and partnerships should be a matter of choice and not of arrangement or tradition. And the reasons for choice are quite clear: personal attraction, sexual desire, mutual trust and compatibility. The empirical evidence underlines the distance from actuality for very many people of this theoretical model. Yet the same evidence reveals an unprecedented acknowledgment of the merits of companionate and equal relationships among the same people, even as we fail to achieve them' (Weeks 2002 p 224).

There is a sense, in other words, that among the new truths discovered and created by non-heterosexual lovers is a new idea of commitment that can incorporate modern and traditional narratives. Men and women in the heterosexual community also express commitment to be an important part of the intimate partnership, but for them it is more difficult to rewrite what it means in a normative context where marriage remains its ideal expression (Gillis 1997).

The modern/romantic marriage

Much empirical work has been directed at ascertaining why people choose (or choose not) to marry. Hibbs et al (2001), in 1998 and 1999, asked 172 members of heterosexual engaged couples why they decided to marry: 30 per cent cited love as their primary reason with a further 13 per cent mentioning commitment and nine per cent saying marriage was a natural progression for the relationship. Further research on changing attitudes to marriage shows also that part of the attraction of marriage to young heterosexual men and women was the opportunity to make a commitment, not just to a partner, but to a way of living: by settling down to a stable family life (Reynolds and Mansfield 1999 p 6). At the same time, their attitudes to the meaning of marriage changed in line with general trends toward individualisation, so that mutuality, negotiability and equality were cited as important qualities in a 'successful' marriage. As the authors conclude, modern marriage seems to retain both institutional and relational elements[2]. The *idea* of marriage, in other words, seems to embrace both romantic and late-modern narratives.

Lewis' (1999) research also shows that mixed narratives of romantic and modern love may characterise the relationships of many 'modern' heterosexual couples. Her research affirmed recent sociological literature that describes a new culture of individualism based upon a utilitarian self-reliance, assertion of rights and expectations of self-actualisation, and suggests that this culture has invaded personal relationships. Pessimists, as Lewis observes, decry this innovation as a 'self-first disease' which has damaged investment in 'the family' and eroded commitment to partners

2　Cf Rodger (1996).

and families. These are the lamenters of the lost 'traditional' family. Lewis also describes, however, the more nuanced understanding of individualism, which, while it places a 'greater emphasis on individual autonomy, both economic and moral, [and] may result in different priorities being attached to the qualities sought' (Lewis 1999 p 29) in a partner, it does not necessarily make partners self-serving, or mean a decline in commitment between them.

Lewis et al (1999) interviewed married and cohabiting heterosexual partners in 1999 and found that while individualism did indeed exist in a different form from previous generations, so also did commitment. Commitment for their respondent couples was not quantitatively 'less' than that for previous generations, but rather its basis and its nature were different. Because relationships among their younger respondents existed or continued as a matter of choice rather than prescription, the nature of their commitment both to the other and to the relationship was different from that described by older respondents. Rather than being based upon expectations or norms from outside, modern marriages were based upon internal and subjective conditions that came from the individuals and their negotiations, so that while older married couples spoke of obligations, often stemming from the marriage vows, younger ones spoke of commitments. Rather than seeing the individualism that fostered this potentially more democratic form of relationship as heralding the downfall of families, however, Lewis postulates that family relationships may be based on a different rather than less firm moral foundation in which both individuality and connection need to be constantly balanced (Lewis et al 1999 p 90). We can discern here some negotiation on the part of the respondents of an emergent idealised late-modern type of individualism and connection that contrasts both with a 'traditional' individualism rooted in independence and with traditional romanticism in partnering. The romantic narrative was not entirely absent, however.

While younger married couples gave different reasons for marrying, for many of them cohabitation was seen as almost a stage in their relationship, which, when it was time to 'settle down' was converted to marriage; they 'either married or split up'. This response may indicate their acceptance on some level of the idea that marriage embodies the 'real' love relationship of their lives, and the marriage partner was their 'real' love with whom they were prepared to go the distance. Similarly, married couples more often spoke in terms of a joint identity than did cohabiting partners, and indicated their belief in the importance of the publicity of their commitment to each other. They, like the respondents in the attitude survey, experienced no tensions between prescriptive and forever notions of love and commitment and the ongoing and reflexive project of self; the two seemed to be able to co-exist in these intact and desired future relationships (Lewis et al 1999 p 89). Similar happily mixed messages have been obtained from other studies on attitudes and expectations of marriage relationships: at the same time as most couples enter marriage firmly believing it will be for life and a strong emphasis is placed upon companionate values, personal fulfilment and achievement and personal emotional satisfaction in marriage are also cited as important by a majority of European respondents (Walker, Timms and Collier 2001 p 7–8).

A reconciliation of traditional and modern roles in relationships is also evident from the research. Where formal equality was not manifest in their relationships, for example in the division of paid and unpaid work, Lewis' couples managed to 'reconcile expectations and reality', sometimes by inventing a type of myth of fairness to fit their experiences. This is not to say that overt misconstructions of their situations were apparent, but rather that an 'economy of gratitude' often existed whereby, for example, if men demonstrated an awareness of potential tensions and inequalities in the division of unpaid work in the home, and compensated with emotional support, their partner would be 'mollified' and both would accept that a type of fairness was achieved in the relationship (Lewis et al 1999 p 53–57). Here also we can see a successful reconciliation of two oppositions: the traditional family's status-based gender roles and the modern relationship's negotiated egalitarian ones.

Jamieson also argues compellingly that intimacy and inequality continue to co-exist in many personal lives and that the creative energies of the actors in those relationships are engaged more in coping with, minimising, disguising and thus necessarily sustaining old inequalities rather than in transforming them (1999). She reveals the many ways in which heterosexual couples generate a sense of themselves as mutually caring and equal, all the while reinforcing traditional gender-based inequalities, and thus provides empirical evidence for the difficulty, if not impossibility, facing heterosexual partners in transcending or transforming the gender norms that characterise the traditional family. The pure, democratic relationship may, in fact, be theoretically impossible for heterosexual couples who do and produce gender in their daily family practices (Jamieson 1999; Dunne 1999), but the myths and rationalisations they create to disguise this production are evidence of its idealised status.

Sometimes, however, reconciliation of the traditional and the modern is not possible. Smart's (2000) research illustrates the differences between the idealised image of families and relationships expressed in the expectations and hopes of young lovers and the experienced reality of the nature and type of commitment people make. Her respondents' reports are indeed of choice and agency, but it is an agency the exercise of which is clearly dependent upon an individual's stage in the life course, available alternative choices and economic and emotional resources (Smart 2000 p 49). She thus provides an account of people's everyday choices in attachments that counters the idealism and abstraction of either the pure relationship or of romantic love; it is an account in which one's social circumstances, crucially including gender, and consequent available opportunities are relevant to one's commitment and are not transcended by the idealised reflexive agency described by Giddens or Beck and Beck-Gernsheim, or by idealised, true love.

Investigating why people cohabit rather than marry, Smart found that relationships tended to fall into one of two conceptual models: reflexive versus risk relationships (Smart 2000 p 35), and that the model adopted was associated with the respondent's sense of self. In reflexive relationships, the speaker saw him or herself as a citizen and partner in spheres of both intimate and social life and valued democracy and equality in both (Smart 2000 p 36). While there were subtle gender differences in senses of self, these were not perceived as a problem by the couples (Smart 2000 p 39). The partners were committed to the relationship and there was a presumption that it would last. These relationships were more common among people engaged in professional occupations (Smart 2000 p 38). In risk relationships, concepts of the self differed more clearly according to gender. Women described a self that was self-reliant and resourceful and claimed no desire for autonomy or equality. Men, on the other hand, presumed an autonomy of self that they were reluctant to relinquish (Smart 2000 p 37). In these relationships, women spoke of interdependence and connection, men of freedom and independence (Smart 2000 p 45). Although women expressed a hope that the relationship would last, there was little expectation of this unless they perceived a change in their partner which would make him more 'marriage worthy' (Smart 2000 p 48). Likewise, men did not presume a lasting relationship, but did not appear to be waiting for any changes before committing, they wanted a door always to be left open (Smart 2000 p 45).

Smart concludes that the choices people make about their intimate attachments are not reducible to straightforward categorisation as a 'transformation of intimacy' (Smart 2000 p 51), and I would suggest that neither are they reducible to a search for romantic love. Her research demonstrates the way in which the idealism of these two narratives is negotiated in the families we live with, in which our individual circumstances make it difficult, sometimes impossible simultaneously to sustain both. The choices people make remain rooted in particular social and economic circumstances and are made by gendered rather than abstract individuals, each with his or her own differing capacity to negotiate successfully those circumstances. They are evidenced by family practices negotiated in the public as well as the private world.

Modernism, romanticism and law

What do these observations about individual and social expectations and behaviour mean for the law that regulates and governs them? Ambiguity and incoherence have always been a hallmark of law, albeit usually an unacknowleged one, and in family law in particular, they can be seen as part of normal 'chaotic' business as usual (Dewar 1998). Dewar, for example, characterises the ambiguity variously as anarchy, chaos or normative pluralism, and suggests that it is more than contradictory; it is antinomic (Dewar 1998). Trends in recent law reform, for example, particularly delegalisation, rights-talk, co-operation, formal equality and welfare, seem to reflect elements of both the individualised reflexive relationship and the obligation-based 'traditional' family. The mythical 'traditional' family founded on a type of romantic love may be at odds with its mythical 'modern' counterpart, yet family laws embody the illusion of their reconciliation. This conflicted yet (socially and individually) reassuring norm may be the result of happenstance, or it may be more purposeful. Law may reflect what appear to be antagonistic values in families in order to sustain a particular vision of society that embraces both traditional and modern values. In this vision, 'the family' can retain its iconic status, while a moral imperative is created for individuals to *choose* it and to assume personal responsibility for nurturing it.

Family policy and law do not, and indeed cannot, exclude either modern individualistic or traditional romantic relationships from their consideration. Prioritising traditional marriages resounds too strongly with previous, discredited, 'back to basics' policy and lies in contrast to current policy designed to 'modernise' British society. Pure relationships, on the other hand, are unregulatable, they are relationships which threaten the 'social cohesion' at the centre of that modernised society, and so marriage, the rules for which are prescribed by the state, is encouraged (Home Office 1998). At the same time, encouraging people to *choose* marriage allows the facilitation of the 'important social objectives' at the heart of government policy to restore social responsibility and self-discipline to their rightful places in society. Marriage thus begins life in the shape of a wilful contract between two independent persons, but the contractual element is soon superseded as the family becomes a 'single person' and its members become its accidents[3]. The unit that is created, as in romantic love, is greater than, in the sense of being of more social value than, its constituent parts.

At the same time, however, one can discern an underlying policy imperative to 'restore' a form of social responsibility that extols a new form of individualism. To this end, family law and policy seem to be concerned to legitimate a form of individualism and equality in marriage that contrasts with its traditional form. But this contrast may be more apparent than real in the light, for example, of marriage preparation classes to be imposed upon individuals and the new role of registrars as providers of information about marriage. These policies seem to imply that privately creating the *terms* of one's relationship is not to be encouraged, at the same time as the message is 'radiated' that if people are given enough 'information', they will be able to make their own rational, responsible choices about their marrying behaviour. Eekelaar (1999) has suggested that much of this political and legal activity is an exercise in form over substance. People are treated as though they have a choice, and if only they understood the issues properly, they will exercise that choice properly and rationally. We are reminded that we have rights, and we are encouraged to act responsibly in the exercise of those rights, at the same time as we are 'educated' to understand that 'responsibly' means conforming to received ideas about the desirability of marriage. It is interesting that despite research that indicates the modest effects of marriage preparation classes on marital stability and quality, usually because the two people are so convinced of their *feelings* for each other that trying to improve their *understanding* of the other will not have much effect (Simons 1999b), an information booklet on the 'rights and responsibilities of marriage' has been prepared for distribution through register offices, places of worship and marriage advice centres. It is interesting also

---

3   I am grateful to Robert Fine for discussion on this point and for this form of expression.

that public response to these proposals was positive and included providing this information also to those who cohabit[4] (Home Office 1999 p 22–23).

However, when another form of option is made available to people by law, they may not be entirely receptive to it. Half of the responses to the Supporting Families consultation document were opposed to a proposal to make prenuptial agreements binding, even where the court would retain jurisdiction to disregard it in a number of circumstances, including where it felt 'significant injustice' would be done. Respondents cited the negative expectations it would foster about marriage before the contract was entered into (Home Office 1999 para 4.6 p 23). Both Hibbs et al's (2001) and Lewis et al's (1999) research have indicated the same public antipathy for these contracts, with responses ranging from 'too cold' to 'we don't need one, we're not getting divorced' (Hibbs et al 2001 p202). It seems that while a freely chosen and negotiable relationship is valued both by law and by individuals, neither law nor those individuals want to be rid entirely of the enduring, obligation-based marriage at the heart of traditional relationships.

Law's family is thus one in which members assert their autonomy, take thoughtful decisions and conduct themselves according to these rational considerations, but at the same time it remains within the confines of a form of romantic love in which feelings, altruism, co-operation and self-sacrifice are the norm. It seems that the social, economic and political worlds are undergoing vast and turbulent change, particularly toward individualisation, and family law has embraced that change, but only on terms. Even the Civil Partnerships Bill before Parliament in 2002, which allowed (heterosexual or same-sex) couples over the age of 18 years to register their partnership if they lived together for at least six months, required that each sign, in front of witnesses, a declaration stating, inter alia, that he or she 'is fully aware of the gravity of the financial and emotional responsibilities of supporting and caring for the other partner that he [sic] is undertaking by entering into the civil partnership' (Civil Partnerships Bill clause 3(4)(d)), and prohibited any application for an order ending the partnership 'before the end of the period of 12 months' from its registration (Civil Partnerships Bill clause 31(4))[5].

---

4   The information booklet for cohabitants will be distributed through libraries and CABs.

5   Parliament has indicated its intention to propose further legislation validating some form of domestic partnerships, but as at April 2003, has not yet done so.

There is, however, an important level on which legal and social policy that aims to support the dichotomous ideal family is out of tune with day-to-day family experiences. Consider, for example, the strategy adopted to overcome stresses that were identified as affecting families from time to time. The Hart Report (1999, p 10–11) found that there are particularly stressful points in a marriage such as 'the birth of a first child, or during a period of unemployment' (Hart Report 1999 p 10–11). The strategy suggested to overcome these stresses is to ensure the involvement of counselling professionals (Advisory Group on Marriage and Relationship Support 2002). The problem in this way remains with the individuals and their relationship, and there is no suggestion that structural responses such as modifying employment policy, unemployment insurance provision, or childcare provision might be necessary to 'save' marriages at these stressful times. So, the Lord Chancellor's Department response to the Hart Report's recommendations champions the provision of marriage and relationship support to couples, but indeed goes further: government aims to 'foster a change in culture in which learning about relationships is seen as just as acceptable as learning about diet and physical health' (Advisory Group on Marriage and Relationship Support 2002 para 7.4).

Here, individualisation and communication, those elements of the modern relationship, are merged with status-based obligation. Education is key; people must be educated so they will see it is in their interests to involve professionals in saving their romantic relationships. This legitimisation of social work and therapeutic discourses in families not only prioritises the individual pursuit of a privatised well-being at the expense of a socially and structurally situated self and relationship, it also operates as a means of regulation of individuals and relationships (Rodger 1996).

Similarly, when youth disaffection or child neglect is identified as a social problem a policy of introducing parent-craft classes is promoted, again indicating that the problem and its solution lies purely within the bounded family. Constructing policy around this imagined family at the heart of British society allows government to divert responsibility for broader social issues and failures from its economic and social agenda, to its family agenda. It represents formal protection of 'the family' at the expense of family practices. Like counselling or therapy, this policy can be seen as an example *par excellence* of official protection of the families we live by: the egalitarian, dynamic families in which partners are able to talk, negotiate and change themselves, their behaviour and their relationships, and the romantic institutional families in which marriage and family behaviour remain private and personal matters, disengaged from matters of 'public' concern. If counselling or education does not help us to see how to mend our relationships, the failure remains ours – it is a failure of our love or our commitment. As one respondent put it in relation to marriage counselling, 'how can you make someone fall back in love …?' (McCarthy and Mitchell 2001 p 324).

The House of Lords decision in *Fitzpatrick v Sterling Housing Association*[6] is another interesting example of law's normative family embracing both change and tradition, yet remaining disengaged from familial experiences. In this case, Mr Fitzpatrick attempted, on the death of his homosexual partner, to claim a statutory protected tenancy provided for spouses and family members of deceased tenants. Despite Mr Fitzpatrick's self-identification as a member of Thompson's family, it took three courts and much legal machination for that identity to receive the authoritative stamp of the law. Even then the degree to which law allowed any deviation from the otherwise normative family model was questionable. Mr Fitzpatrick's non-heterosexual self was eventually recognised by law as being capable of forging a familial relationship with Mr Thompson, but the language in which the court framed its decision was a far cry from accepting new 'narratives of family and of choice, of care and responsibility, of love and loss, of old needs and new possibilities, [and] of difference and convergence … ' (Weeks et al 1999 p 99). Instead, Mr Fitzpatrick and Mr Thompson's relationship was constructed by the court to fit into a definition of family that accommodated individual choice, reflexive identity and the responsibilities flowing from that choice and identity, but which at the same time demanded altruism, privacy, sexual exclusivity and sacrifice (Diduck 2001a). If this case presents one legal definition of family, it is one that mirrors the families we live by, adopting both modern and traditional garb and setting up a difficult test for individuals to pass.

The familial subject

Adults[7] are thus held to be individually responsible for our simultaneously rational and irrational choices to form family connections and for the consequences of those choices. Sometimes those consequences are

---

6   [2001] 1 AC 27.

7   The child subject is viewed and constituted slightly differently. See Chapter 4.

non-negotiable, other times they are flexible. Where there is flexibility we see sometimes the image of a potentially modernised individual autonomy in which negotiations about conduct and connections take place within the framework of care, responsibility and interdependence, such as in Mr Fitzpatrick's case. More often the subject whose choices are coerced or encouraged by family law and policy is not the relational subject, but rather is the rational economic man (Barlow and Duncan 2000a; 2000b). He is the focus, for example, of child support provisions designed to 'encourage' lone mothers to reveal the names of fathers, those designed to discourage men from establishing 'second' families without the financial means to provide for the first (see Chapter 7), and he is the object of the New Deal for Lone Parents in which it is assumed that economic considerations are all that guide a mother's decision to work outside the home (Barlow and Duncan 2000a; 2000b; Chapter 6). His gender-neutral rationality is also at the heart of non-financial familial decisions, where it is assumed that on receipt of sufficient objective information he will make informed decisions about his marrying and divorcing (Chapter 3) behaviour.

Barlow and Duncan (2000a; 2000b) call this the 'rationality mistake' and found that people make moral economic decisions concerning their intimate connections based on a variety of factors that often have little to do with the morality or form of rationality assumed by law (Barlow and Duncan 2000b p 138; see also Dunne 1999 in the context of lesbian families). They conclude that in adopting the model of the 'rational legal subject' family law and policy fundamentally misunderstand how people make decisions about their moral economies (Barlow and Duncan 2000b p 141).

> '[P]eople seem to take such decisions with reference to moral and socially negotiated views about what behaviour is accepted or expected as right and proper and this negotiation, and the views that result, varies in particular social contexts. Thus people make decisions in a different and arguably more sophisticated way, giving different results to those anticipated by the purposive policy-makers using conventional economic and legal models' (Barlow and Duncan 2000b p 141).

The rational legal subject also expresses other tensions. On the one hand he is gender neutral. Law 'speaks' of parents and spouses rather than of mothers, fathers, husbands and wives, and relies upon that subject exercising a form of free will in determining his or her course of familial action. At the same time, however, law plays an important part in constructing or reflecting clearly gendered familial subjects, through whom, for example, 'spouse' *is* gendered and mothering is expressed differently from fathering (see Chapter 4 and Chapter 7). Again, it does not acknowledge its incoherence or inconsistency in this respect, and it is often only the family practices of individual subjects that reveal the extent to which gender does or does not make a difference to justice and the process by which subjects are both situated and abstracted by law.

We thus see a tension in law's familial subject that mirrors the tension in its family. The men and women in law's families on the one hand remain fixed as gendered mothers and fathers, husbands and wives, who must conform to the predetermined obligations that flow from those identities, and on the other hand are assumed to be subjects who exercise agency and choice about family responsibilities according to rational calculations. We also see a tension between this conflicted legal subject and the more frequently experienced subjectivity of family members who tend to express their individuality and their family practices in more complicated and sophisticated ways.

Conclusions

The conditions of late modernity, including globalisation, a form of sex equality and a new prioritisation of personal growth and self-actualisation, have meant that individualism has become an important element in narratives of political and intimate engagement. It is a form of individualism that offers, indeed often requires, an ongoing exploration of the self and of commitments resulting in a sense of contingency in both. At the same time, however, narratives of stability, tradition, loyalty and bounded gender-identity are called upon by individuals and by law to constitute normative familial identities and relationships expressed in an idealised discourse. Mr Fitzpatrick, for example, whose acceptance in law as family to his non-heterosexual lover appears most dramatically to embody the ideal reflexive and contingent self and relationship, was required to style himself within the paradigm of sexual and romantic exclusivity, altruism, self-sacrifice and privacy before he was so recognised by law (Diduck 2001a). Heterosexual couples, with the collusion of law and social policy, profess to be in love and to be bound to the institution of marriage at the same time as they profess equally strongly to be in negotiated, equal and reflexive relationships.

What can we make of these apparent contradictions? The antinomies between the conflicting ideals within law's family sustain social norms through which families remain discrete, identifiable, moral and regulatable units, the members of which are encouraged to believe that they are the makers of their own destiny, whether that be as 'success' or 'failure'. They instil in individuals an ethic of personal responsibility for maintaining political and social values of family stability, tradition and obligation, *and* free will and individual choice. On this view, our family practices, rooted as they are in more complicated negotiations of these values and in particular social economic conditions, and which have the potential to destabilise those polarised ideals, are estranged from family law; we will always have difficulty living up to law's ideal. There are indeed, as Collier said, 'tensions inherent in the reconfiguring of heterosexual [and non-heterosexual] attachments presently taking place' (Collier 1999 p 268) in the twenty-first century, and it is crucial that laws not merely reproduce or obfuscate these tensions, but begin to engage with them in a meaningful and realistic way.

In the next five chapters I will examine the degree to which families and family law and policy succeed in this engagement. It seems to me that 'good' family law, 'good' family law professionals and 'good' family law clients are defined as such according to the degree to which they advance the normative dual vision in the contexts of divorce, forms of dispute resolution, childcare and financial matters, and that this definition may too often work injustice for the families we live with.

Chapter 3

Divorce: saving the family

The tensions between the families we live by, those that are legally privileged, and the families we live with often become most acute on divorce. Day Sclater (1999a), for example, found that the ideology of the romantic, companionate marriage was a major theme within which divorcees constructed their experiences, whether they were through victim or survivor narratives. The fairy-tale ending did not happen for these people, and they struggled to make sense of why it did not. Further, the prevalence of their feelings of loss, not only of a partner or of a relationship but of their very self on divorce, seems to reveal that the nature of the investment they made to the fairy tale was one of giving up their entire self. Simultaneously, however, they often also expressed a 'rediscovery' of self, a newly found independence or freedom that may also reveal their 'need' for expression and re-evaluation of that self. As Collier (1999) notes, 'the way in which the divorce process is itself now negotiated and experienced has been seen as just part of the development of a broader "project of the self" over the life course' (Collier 1999 p 263). Divorce seems to be a moment, then, for the simultaneous disruption and endorsement of the normative family and the subjects who embody it.

Laws regulating divorce contain many contradictory assumptions about the nature of the marriage relationship and about the individuals in that relationship. They assume and are designed to protect a type of traditional romantic family while at the same time importing elements of individualism that are antithetical to that family type. The 'new' family law promotes a norm that extols altruistic morality, legal rights, co-operation and individual responsibility, and divorce law and policy in particular seem to be directed toward preserving the complicated family that embodies it.

Divorce in law – morality, stability and marriage saving

As statistics and personal experience tell us, just as we 'fall' in love, we also 'fall' out of it. While neither of these two emotional states connects necessarily with the legal statuses conferred by marriage and divorce, the cultural link between love and marriage means that heterosexual partners are expected to marry when they find true love (Chapter 2). When that love ends, though, it is not quite so simple; falling out of love is neither morally nor legally a legitimate ground for divorce. Yet increasing numbers of people do divorce and much research energy and money is spent on attempting to discover why their marriages, or their love, 'fail' in this way. It is often not mere intellectual curiosity that fuels this research. If the married family lies at the foundation of a stable and moral society then any suggestion that it may be in danger means that the society that it upholds may also be in danger. We see, in fact, throughout the history of divorce law reform and indeed the history of family law reform in general, a preoccupation with, verging on anxiety about, stable society's dependence upon stable marriages. The social and legal context in which divorce law reform is investigated has consistently reflected this anxiety and reform proposals reflect it as well by declaring their aim to be as much about marriage as about divorce.

Whether divorce law is the best place to advance a marriage-saving agenda is a matter of debate, and indeed the way in which law is useful at all in influencing people's behaviour, particularly their intimate, sexual and affective behaviour, is also questionable. But policy on reform has consistently adopted the position not only that law can be utilised to influence behaviour, it should be so used.

Divorce reform – history

The idea, at the beginning of the nineteenth century, of removing divorce from its historic and traditional ecclesiastical jurisdiction faced powerful moral opposition not only from the church, but also from many politicians who believed that by secularising and democratising divorce, the state would be abandoning its role as moral guardian and social protector. And so, while access to divorce was seen to be important to the newly expanded middle classes of nineteenth-century English society, there were reservations about complete equality of access; it seems that the moral rectitude of the poor and labouring classes was always suspect.

Prior to the Divorce and Matrimonial Causes Act 1857, marriage was upheld by the church and state as indissoluble, with the exception that bills of divorce could be passed by Parliament on the proof of one's wife having committed adultery. It was seen as important for a nobleman to be able to rid himself of his adulterous wife, and the Lords felt morally as well as legally justified in effecting the severance. Before Parliament would grant the bill of divorce, however, the petitioner was required to prosecute a successful action of criminal conversation in the common law courts against his wife's lover, and then to pursue a successful petition to the ecclesiastical courts for a divorce *a mensa et thoro* (from bed and board), in effect, the equivalent of a modern judicial separation. While Parliamentary divorce was originally a prerogative of the male aristocracy only, its use did filter down to the merchant class (Anderson 1984), and occasionally wives were granted relief, but women were required to prove that their husband's adultery was aggravated by incest, rape or bestiality. Only four wives were ever successful in obtaining a Parliamentary divorce (Stone 1990 p 360–362). The poor and the working classes were also excluded from this expensive and lengthy process, and if they wished to bring their marital unions to an end had recourse to informal means of divorce, including desertion, wife sale, or other public ceremonies (O'Donovan 1984; Stone 1990). In this context, a movement for reform rooted in ideas of secularism and liberal equality brought the establishment of a Royal Commission on marriage and divorce in 1850 (for further details see Finer and McGregor 1974; Stone 1990).

The Commission, chaired by Lord Campbell, reported in 1856. It looked in detail at the consequences for marriage and divorce of the Reformation and it discussed the public policy of allowing divorce at all against the backdrop of a demand for reform championed by the middle classes and their representatives, the common lawyers. The commissioners clearly did not want to encourage divorce, but did wish to appear to respect the growing ideology of liberal equality and individualism. As Stone says 'after 1832, the principle of extending political privilege further down the social system to the ranks of the middling sort had been accepted' (Stone 1990 p 366), but in reality, complete gender and class equality was paid only lip service. Stone goes so far as to call it 'hypocrisy' (Stone 1990 p 372).

While some of the debates on the bill that came from the Report favoured full equality between the sexes, for example, there remained a strong feeling, based on biblical passages interpreted as warning against the danger of admitting spurious progeny into families (Stone 1990 p 379), that although marriage was an indissoluble union created by God, divorce should be allowed to men on the grounds of their wives' adultery. Further, the idea of equality of access by women to divorce on the grounds of their husbands' adultery struck at the very heart of the double sexual standard (Stone 1990 p 374) and the strict divide between public and private society (Shanley 1989). Because husband adultery posed no threat to the smooth intergenerational transition of property interests or the husband's property interest in his wife's body, it was thought not to cause the wife, or indeed, society, any 'very material injury' (Cornish and Clarke 1989 p 379).

Extending the right of divorce to the poor was also suspect. Despite government arguments that the bill would bring divorce to 'the doors of the humblest classes' (Stone 1990 p 371), it is arguable that there was never any intention on its part to allow the poor equal access to divorce. In Stone's words, '[t]o virtually all legislators, the poor were seen as a threatening, immoral dissolute mass of people to whom it would be extremely dangerous to extend the facility of easy divorce' (Stone 1990 p 374). For whom the danger lay was not always clear. One MP cited by Stone thought that it would create 'one of the greatest social curses that this country has ever been visited with' (Stone 1990 p 371) and Lord Redesdale, dissenting with the majority of the commissioners who favoured reform, thought that to give the poor this 'door for escape' was not in their best interests. Just as women's sexual morality was foundational even to an increasingly liberal society, the morality of working-class families was also seen as the foundation for a stable society, and both remained 'protected' from easy access to divorce even in the bill that became the Divorce and Matrimonial Causes Act 1857. The Act did not change the old ecclesiastical grounds for divorce and its major change provided simply that divorces were to be heard only in the High Court in London. It therefore removed governance of divorce from the church and Parliament to the common law courts, but effectively excluded women and those who could not afford the cost of the suit in the London High Court and thus ensured that the sexual morality of women and the poor remained in check (Shanley 1989).

After the secularisation of marriage with Lord Hardwicke's Act of 1753 and the Marriage Act 1836, and of divorce with the Divorce and Matrimonial Causes Act 1857, the state assumed control over the morality of private relations of 'family' and, in the area of divorce, took its responsibility seriously. Initiatives designed to reform the laws of divorce further were met with claims that to make divorce easier would undermine the stability of marriage and thereby of society. The minority report of yet another Royal Commission on marriage and divorce, the Gorrell Commission of 1912, expressed its concerns in this way, and even those who advocated divorce reform did so by arguing that allowing for the legal mopping-up of spiritually dead marriages would promote and strengthen rather than undermine marriage. The preamble to the Matrimonial Causes Act 1973, which extended the grounds for divorce beyond adultery, for example, stated that its aim was to 'offer true support for marriage'.

In the period of reconstruction and attempted restabilisation after the 1939–1945 war another Royal Commission on marriage and divorce was struck. The Morton Commission had the specific mandate to inquire into the causes of divorce, as well as the much broader one to consider matrimonial proceedings generally, the property rights of husbands and wives and 'the need to promote healthy and happy married life and to safeguard the interests and well-being of children'. The spiralling rate of divorce after the war, partially due to the introduction of legal aid in 1948, revealed that divorce had become available to more women and members of the working class and anxieties linking the welfare of society with the divorce rate, which had lurked beneath the surface of previous reform agendas, became overt in the Morton Commission's enquiries. '[T]heir paramount consideration therefore was the wellbeing of the community and the Commissioners *knew* that the bedrock of this wellbeing was stable marriage. Moreover, they presumed that the law could be utilised to this end' (Smart 1984 p 37).

The introduction to the 1956 Report of the Commission surveyed the causes of divorce over the first half of the century and identified a number of social, economic and legal factors which contributed to higher rates of divorce. It highlighted as primary factors the instability caused by the 1914–1918 and 1939–1945 wars, the extension of legal grounds for divorce, a housing shortage and the sexual, social and economic emancipation of women, along with a vague but presumptively dangerous idea of changing attitudes to modern psychology which encouraged 'self-expression' and a 'dangerous' tendency to take the responsibilities of marriage less seriously (Royal Commission 1956 para 43–49 p 8–10).

It may thus be in the 1950s that the first recognition of an individualised yet romantic marriage (and divorce) could be seen in law and policy, although Regan (1993) suggests that this tension first faced the Victorians who coped by investing marriage with 'traditional' symbols of selflessness and strict gender role identification with status. Discourses surrounding marriage and divorce in the 1950s, however, were not palatable in the Victorian moral language of religion and patriarchy, and so theories of family stability and morality became couched in 'modern' languages of child welfare and psychology[1], which proclaimed one's individual responsibility for the well-being of children and the community, indeed for the well-being of England's post-war reconstruction, and therefore of the 'nation'. In this context, the 'romanticised' notion of the Victorian family (Smart 1984 p 50), based on 'true marriage', or 'marriage as an institution for life' (Royal Commission 1956, para 70(ix)), existed simultaneously with law's complacent and arguably misguided belief that it promoted equality between the sexes, the welfare of children and an individual's need for self-expression.

The incompatibility of these characteristics, as well as their import to society, is illustrated by the commissioners being unable to reach any majority conclusions about how best to use divorce law to promote and support marriage. They split in their recommendations, with nine members of the 18 favouring abolishing matrimonial fault as grounds for divorce and replacing it with one ground only: marriage breakdown. This, they thought, would heighten respect for 'true marriage' (Royal Commission 1956 para 79(ix)). The other nine members thought that such a reform would mean divorce by consent and provide an 'easy way out' (Royal Commission 1956 para 69 (ii)); 'people would then come to look upon marriage less and less as a lifelong union and more and more as one to be ended if things began to go wrong' (Royal Commission 1956 para 69 (ii)). Above all, they said, 'the State must be concerned in the maintenance of a marriage and in its dissolution, because the state has an overriding responsibility to ensure, in the interests of the community, that the institution of marriage is upheld' (Royal Commission 1956 para 69(vii)); to do otherwise 'would be disastrous for the nation' (Royal Commission 1956 para 69(viii)).

Using divorce law to support marriages continued to be a theme throughout subsequent reform initiatives. In 1966, both the Law Commission and a group convened by the Archbishop of Canterbury (Putting Asunder 1966) agreed that irretrievable marriage breakdown should be the sole ground for

---

1   For example Bowlby (1953).

divorce, but again framed this conclusion in the rhetoric of marriage saving. The Law Commission concluded that 'the objectives of a good divorce law should include the support of marriages which have a chance of survival' (Law Commission 1966 p 53) and that 'something more' might be done to encourage reconciliation of troubled spouses, although, interestingly, they allowed that 'little is to be expected from conciliation procedures after divorce proceedings have been initiated' (Law Commission 1966 p 54).

On the other hand, removing fault from divorce law spoke volumes about a revised idea of the marriage relationship. It was a concession to the idea of individualised, voluntarily assumed conjugal obligation (see Regan 1993; Rodger 1996). Ultimately, though, this modern view did not prevail. The Divorce Reform Act 1969, which allowed divorce on proof of one of five 'facts', three of which were the matrimonial offences of adultery, cruelty and desertion, to evidence the only ground for divorce, irretrievable breakdown of marriage, was the compromise piece of legislation that reflected both a traditional, obligation-based marriage *and* a modern, individualistic one. Crucially, though, the new Act was proposed and passed in the language of marriage saving. Proponents argued that divorce based upon marital breakdown rather than matrimonial fault did not undermine marriage and the family so much as it strengthened both by allowing illicit unions to become legitimate, while maintaining some concept of the matrimonial offence in the 'facts' required to prove marriage breakdown supported the moral duty and externally imposed obligations inherent in romantic aspirations of marriage and family. So it straddled two different moral ideals of marriage and divorce: a fault-based divorce system that reflects a duty-based view of marriage (Eekelaar 1991 p 16) and a no-fault system that reflects a consensual, choice-based view[2] (also see Regan 1993).

In making divorce 'easier' the 1969 Act appeared to liberalise the law and to succumb to the modern allure of individualisation, sexual permissiveness and self-actualisation at the same time as it confirmed marriage as a moral institution. What it also did, however, was find a way to manage increasing numbers of people who cohabited outside the regulatory net of marriage. The potential economic disruption to the public coffers caused by cohabiting women and their children was thus controlled by a divorce law which 'facilitated a shifting of persons around different family groups and ... in the process averted a large-scale dissent from legally controlled marriage'

---

2   See Bainham (2001), who reviews these arguments in the context of debates in the UK on FLA 1996 and in the US about a return to fault-based divorce.

(Smart 1984 p 56). In this way, it was as powerful a social regulator of the public morality as was Lord Hardwicke's Act 1753 and the Divorce and Matrimonial Causes Act 1857 (see on this Parker 1990; Rodger 1996).

The Divorce Reform Act was incorporated with other pieces of legislation into the Matrimonial Causes Act 1973, and remains the law today. Substantively then, the law in 2003 proclaims the values and idiosyncrasies of the 1960s. Procedurally, however, divorce has changed probably beyond the recognition of the original reformers, with the special procedure for undefended divorces appearing to reduce the fault aspects of the divorce to mere rhetoric and the mediation revolution appearing to undermine the state's role in the management of relationships and ultimate decision-making about them[3].

Indeed, Smart suggests that as early as the 1970s there was a shift from the state utilising divorce and family law to enforce a moral union, to it using law to enforce an economic one (Smart 1984 p 100). She cites cases which demonstrate that judges tended to preserve the support obligations of husbands, at least to maintain wives until another husband took over responsibility for her. She says that adjusting the financial situation of divorcing parties rather than adjudicating upon moral notions of fault, blame or desert became the court's preoccupation. The 1970s are culturally and popularly known as the 'me' decade, though, and the individualism and desire for self-expression and actualisation that the Morton Commission feared in the 1950s could not be expected to go away in these times. From then, into the 1980s, and coupled with the changing political and economic rhetoric of Thatcherism, the psychology of the 'I' took on a new resonance to become economically as well as morally and psychologically revered in a way in which previous law reformers could not have envisaged.

Divorce reform in the 1990s

While the increase in divorce rates in the 1980s probably had more to do with the special procedure for undefended divorce actions introduced in 1977 than with a real increase in the number of relationships breaking down, a destructive individualism was said at this time to be at the heart

---

3   See Chapter 5, however, in which I argue that mediation is an important means of regulating families and family relationships.

of the destruction of families. But while a suspicion of women's role in the process was always present, this time it became more overt, as newly financially independent women were held to blame for exercising their new 'freedom' irresponsibly. Smart quotes the Campaign for Justice on Divorce, a men's rights group, as follows:

'There can be little doubt that the general movement towards economic equality for women and the high divorce rate are not independent events. Indeed the very institution of marriage and its former stability have been rooted in women's dependent status' (Smart 1984 p 134).

This analysis is probably correct, as financial independence is certainly a factor in allowing one to exit from an unsatisfactory marriage. The question is whether women's independence *and individuality* was something policy wished to encourage or discourage.

In the light of the failed 1990s Conservative 'back to basics' campaign, which could be seen as an attempt to reimpose a 'traditional' morality on the public, government had to find other ways of managing marriage and divorce behaviour. It was faced with pragmatic and financial concerns about the cost of divorce to the legal aid budget and the courts, promoting a policy of individualism and financial self-sufficiency and, at the same time, it needed to respond to the 'same old story' of moral panic about the damage divorce does to society, which emerged again in political debate in the 1990s. The new 'truth' that emerged was that divorce harmed children[4], and this harm was in many ways more horrific than were previous moral violations caused by divorce. Children of divorced parents were positioned either as the vulnerable and innocent 'victims' of their parents' irresponsible divorcing behaviour (Piper 1996a) or as dangerous members of the delinquent, drug-taking, pregnant underclass. The moral panic, and the responsibility for it of women particularly, remained the same, but now was expressed in a discourse that was virtually unchallengeable – the discourse of child welfare (see Chapter 4).

New Labour embraced this discourse and its communitarian vision of tying a form of individualism to social responsibility has meant that the recent story of divorce reform begun by a Conservative government in

---

4   Interpreting the results of the Rowntree study, the *Daily Mail* proclaimed in 1996: 'Now the figures that prove what common sense always told us: CONFIRMED – DIVORCE DAMAGES CHILDREN' (p 1).

the 1980s has embraced the economic imperatives Smart identified in the 1970s, the moral imperatives of the first half of the last century *and* the new and differently autonomous individual of the *fin de siecle* whose moral autonomy is rooted in a form of responsibility and self-interest.

Discourses of responsibility fill the pages of government policy documents. Responsibility to children, to partners, to the community and more generally to the state (usually identified as the taxpayer), is called upon to balance the 'me-first disease' that is seen to be a part of modern relationships. And so, just as in previous reform investigations, the goal for new legislation about divorce was identified as marriage saving and also as in previous times, a disproportionate moral responsibility for attaining this goal was placed upon women and the poor. What was new in the 1990s was that it was conceded that sometimes the goal would not be achieved. If it was not, and people must divorce, an alternative goal was identified: to ensure that people divorced responsibly, so that even if the marriage could not be saved, the 'family' could be.

Responsibility to society – the problematisation of divorce

The problem of divorce has taken on different shades or nuances historically, from the earliest problematisations based on patriarchal and property concerns, to moral ones rooted in Christian theology, to more recent concerns about the welfare of children. At the most basic level, though, one can identify a fundamental 'truth' and that is that divorce is 'bad' for society and marriage is 'good'. Why do we collectively and individually agonise so over marriage and divorce? What stake do we have at the personal, psychological, emotional, political and social levels to these forms of attachment and detachment?

Day Sclater says that we – individually and collectively – have an investment in a notion of family as comforting, stable and enduring (Day Sclater 1999a p 4). In other words, this family we live by, reflected in the investment and evidenced by people's attitudes, is a 'traditional' one and is expressed as an ideal. It is being in love with someone who provides that comfort and stability and with whom we share an identity and a world. Or, it is belonging, if not to someone, at least to an institution that is perceived as timeless, morally unassailable and clearly identifiable. Even if that ideal increasingly includes 'non-traditional' values of individual autonomy and gender equality, this family we live by does not let us down. It provides roots, permanence and safe boundaries as well as a space for personal growth, self-exploration and self-actualisation and is not cognisant of any tensions in these aims. That this ideal is just that, an aspiration, is clear, however, from the research that consistently illustrates a discrepancy between it and the realities of people's family practices, including particularly their marriage and divorce behaviour (Day Sclater 1999b).

Socially and politically, the allure of the stable, comforting and enduring marriage may have much to do with material matters such as control over public resources and finances, control over unruly populations and their sexual behaviour, and the facilitation of private enterprise in a market economy. It is a form of government *through* the family in the classic Donzelotian/Foucaudian sense. So, government spends money on attempting to discover why people divorce, or why they cohabit without marriage, in an attempt to curtail a massive exodus from the regulatory familial net. Recent research commissioned by the Lord Chancellor's Department concludes that people divorce for a variety of reasons, and that certain socio-demographic factors such as young age at marriage, teenage pregnancy, previous partnership breakdown and low income may be predictors of divorce (Clarke and Barrington 1999). The research also found that economic incentives to marry or to stay married were only marginally influential on people's behaviour, and that this was so only in a few cases (McAllister 1999), and that the content of divorce legislation itself has had only a slight effect on divorce rates (Mansfield, Reynolds and Arai 1999). Further, neither relationship therapy (Simons 1999a) nor marriage preparation courses (Simons 1999b) were found to be particularly helpful to 'save' distressed or otherwise precarious relationships. In fact, it seems that people divorce because of their changing attitudes to marriage and divorce in the context of changes in social values and the material environment. They experience a conflict between the competing narratives of traditional marriage and confluent love:

> 'While most people place a high value on stable marriages, the progress of individualism, especially among women, has resulted in diversification of family and relationship forms, and has imposed new stresses involved in negotiating roles and responsibilities. The meaning of marriage has changed; the quality of the relationship between the partners has become more important, the institutional aspects of the union less so. As a consequence there is now more pressure to leave a relationship if its quality falls short of expectations' (Mansfield et al 1999 p 6).

Policy changes cannot stem the tide of individualism they began, but they can make that individualism work for socially 'productive' ends. I hope I am not painting a picture here of government as overly Machiavellian, so much as I am acknowledging that there are always complicated and ambiguous goals, methods and outcomes of any legal or policy provision, and attention is not always paid to this ambiguity. In an attempt to illuminate it, I now turn to a recent but unsuccessful proposal for further reform of divorce law. Like those before it, Part II of the Family Law Act 1996 was designed as an exercise in morality and marriage-saving as much as it was a law about divorce. Unlike those before it, however, it also seemed to concede the reality of the new 'individualism' and thus tried to address itself to both imperatives. Perhaps it was this unrealistic dual aim, as much as it was other factors, which contributed to its downfall.

The Family Law Act 1996: ambiguous moralism

Part II of the Family Law Act 1996 (FLA 1996) will not be implemented, but its vision of the good divorce and the good divorcing subject looms large in government and public consciousness. It cannot be ignored for that reason. It contains the policy and legal aspirations which may yet come to pass in different form. It is an interesting document. With its idea of divorce as process, it adopts the late-modern idea of fluidity, of continual construction and reconstruction of life's subjects and contingencies; with its sole ground of irretrievable marriage breakdown it rejects the idea of the matrimonial offence firmly and clearly and thus appears to reject a traditional duty-based view of marriage and acknowledge the 'confluence' of love; and in its administrative rather than judicial process it eschews externally imposed rules for conduct and encourages continual reflection, communication and co-operation on the part of its subjects. Its moral imperative is rooted in a new idea of morality as the exercise of a responsible *choice* (see Reece 2000a and 2003) after careful consideration of all the consequences of that choice. In this way, it coheres with Bauman's (1993) idea of morality in late- or post-modernity, in which the lack of straightforward rules to follow means that people are in fact 'more' moral than they were before, because there is now an authorship and actorship or reflective agency involved in the moral choices we make. The Act appears, in both its substantive and its procedural aspects, to accommodate this reflective, connected and situated individual and to facilitate movement between his or her pure relationships. Yet, with marriage-saving as its aim and with its clear preconceptions of what responsible behaviour looks like, it also preserves the traditional individual's traditional marriage.

While the FLA 1996 appears to eschew the moral language of fault or blame and to reject a moral absolutist position, it cannot be said to demonstrate the state's abdication of responsibility for public morality. Smart and Neale (1999), Finch (1989) and Sevenhuijsen (1998) claim that decisions to divorce are profoundly moral, but not in the way that moral absolutists would characterise them, as 'right' or 'wrong'. To them, moral decisions are ones made in their particular context, after weighing all the consequences and considering connections with others and the implications of the decision for the self and others. They may change from situation to situation and therefore cannot be assessed against abstract right or wrong. In this sense, the 1996 Act required actively moral decisions to be made at various stages of the divorce process and thus remains a profoundly moral document in this more modern sense. But, because it is also so clear about the manner in which decisions should be taken and indeed about the content of the decisions themselves, it is also a moral document from the moral absolutist perspective.

The dual vision of morality was not lost upon Parliament. Both proponents and opponents of the legislation adopted the language and the rhetoric of individual responsibility and morality to make their cases, with opponents adopting a moral absolutist position and proponents a more 'modern' one.

'The removal of fault undermines individual responsibility. By removing it, the state is actively discouraging any concept of lifelong commitment to marriage, to standards of behaviour, to self-sacrifice, to duty, to any thought for members of the family. It declares that neither party has any responsibility for the breakdown of marriage' (Baroness Young Hansard (567 HL Official Report (5th series) col 733 30 November 1995) Reece 2000a p 67);

and:

'[i]t is a mistake to believe that the present law [the Matrimonial Causes Act 1973] underlines in any way the idea of responsibility by the use of fault in the ground for divorce. Using fault as a basis for divorce enables a quick exit from marriage, leaving the responsibilities of that marriage behind. Under the new system, couples will consider the responsibilities of their marriage [and, he might have added, the consequences of their divorce] in the period of reflection and consideration' (Lord Mackay (Hansard 567 HL Official Report (5th series) col 701 30 November 1995) Reece 2000a p 68).

It seems that whatever other message was to be 'radiated' from the legislation, one that was certain was the message of the individual's moral responsibility for marriage and divorce and for their personal as well as social consequences.

The responsible divorce

Government may be less convinced today of law's ability to influence individuals' behaviour on a micro level, but may yet remain convinced of its capacity to do so in a more general way (Dewar 1998). Both Dewar (1998) and Eekelaar (1999) remark upon the almost proselytising nature of both FLA 1996 and its 'spin'. Dewar sees the Act as 'best understood as setting out general aspirations about how to divorce well: adults should be reasonable, self-denying, conciliatory, and fully conscious of the implications of their actions for themselves and for others' (Dewar 1998 p 483), and Eekelaar sees the spin in official explanations of FLA 1996 as designed to keep us 'on message' about how to divorce responsibly and 'properly' (Eekelaar 1999).

These messages relate to and call into being variously a good divorce, a good society and a good divorcing subject. The marriage-saving premise means not only that individual marriages could and should be saved, but also that the institution of marriage could and should be saved. Where it cannot, the good divorce is harmonious, it promotes the best interests of children, it is considered rather than rash, and by staying out of the courts it will save public money (Collier 1999 p 260). The good divorcing subject is one who acts reasonably and responsibly by acceding to these imperatives in his or her divorcing behaviour. That many of these imperatives or aspirations may conflict is not considered.

The mechanics and the message of FLA 1996 have been discussed at length by many socio-legal scholars[5]. Its unique aspects included prohibiting divorce until sufficient information was provided about it and its consequences so as to encourage rational decision-making and responsible behaviour on the part of the actor, and this responsibility was to be buttressed

5   See, for example, Dewar (1998), Eekelaar (1999), Collier (1999), Day Sclater and Piper (1999).

by a period of reflection and consideration to require further deliberation and calculation. Provision for marriage counselling was inserted into the procedure so that potentially divorcing parties could be offered assistance in understanding themselves, their partners and their relationships more fully before taking any decisions about the fate of their marriages. Let me examine some of these provisions now in some detail.

Divorce as process

Mandatory information meetings were designed to provide information to those contemplating divorce in the light of the objectives of saving marriages, promoting a conciliatory approach to divorce, reinforcing continuity in parenting, and providing protection from violence and abuse (Walker 2001 'Summary' p 2). Although unarticulated, part of their object was also to encourage use of professionals other than solicitors, perhaps by diverting to mediators those determined to divorce. Solicitors, it was thought, unduly encouraged an adversarial relationship between the parties and thus promoted conflict and litigation (see Eekelaar et al 2000). Yet in this way government perhaps underestimated the importance to people of acknowledgment of their moral position, the relation of this position to vindication of their perceived rights, and awareness of rights generally among the population (Genn 1999 p 254–255). Genn's research showed that among people with divorce- and separation-related problems, solicitors were overwhelmingly cited as the most popular source of advice and assistance (Genn 1999 p 115 and 118). Coupled with her other conclusion that there exists 'across all social-educational, and cultural boundaries and for all types of justiciable problems' a 'profound need for knowledge and advice and information about obligations, rights, remedies and procedures' (Genn 1999 p 255), policy designed to provide this information is not misplaced. The difficulty with the information meetings designed in Part II of FLA 1996 may have been, at least in part, their evangelical tone in the imposition upon people of moral imperatives not of their own choosing around their obligations and rights (see also Collier 1999).

FLA 1996 was intended to do more than simply provide a new framework for divorce. It was intended to effect a cultural shift in how people view marriage and divorce, and also to effect behavioural change. Results from the information meeting pilot project research indicate, however, that effecting behavioural change requires more than the mere provision of information (Walker 2001 p 833), as respondents indicated that they were just as likely, if not more so, to seek the advice of a solicitor after attendance at the pilot information meetings than they were before. One view, then, may be that the information meetings were a resounding success in that they focused people's minds upon their rights, obligations and responsibilities on divorce and on the importance of law in protecting these rights. Another view, however, was that in failing to deter people from lawyers, the information meetings failed in their task of shifting moral responsibility for regulating behaviour from law to individuals.

While the 'vast majority of those attending an information meeting described it [as] useful' (Walker 2001 p 829), and, following the statutory objectives, 'some attendees ... reflected carefully on the decision to divorce and some took steps to save the marriage; messages about reducing conflict and being conciliatory were understood and respected; and parents were helped to consider the needs of the children' (Walker 2001 p 829), these impacts were not necessarily translated into the crude behavioural changes anticipated or hoped for by government. 'There are', the researchers found, 'no simple links between increased knowledge and understanding and the increased use of services such as counselling and mediation' (Walker 2001 p 832).

Further, the research highlighted that the tensions in the statute's aims were reproduced in the results of the project. The researchers, for example, 'became increasingly aware that saving marriage is an objective distinct from securing civilised divorce' (Walker 2001 p 830) and that 'expectations of the extent to which people facing divorce will behave in socially approved ways need to be modest' (Walker 2001 p 833).

One of the clearest messages from the pilot study was the need for particularised information relevant and important to the families we live with that is often missing from the relevancies of the ideal families of law for whom the standard information was designed. Violence in the home, difficulties arising from cultural differences, the special circumstances of senior citizens and those coping with ill health or disability are not a part of the normal or normative family of law[6] and thus were not adequately addressed in the information meetings, rendering attendees with these experiences extraordinary or marginal.

And yet, while the information meetings will not now be implemented, government retains its faith in the ability of information to influence

6   See, for example, Bridge (2001); Bridge and Mitchell (2001); Kaganas and Piper (1999); McMullen and Kain (2001); McCarthy, Stark and Walker (2001); and Collier (2001a).

people's behaviour. The newest proposal for the provision of information recognises that people need and trust law and solicitors, and the Legal Services Commission is currently piloting a project whereby accountable service providers (solicitors' firms and not-for-profit advice agencies) – Family Advice and Information Networks (FAINs) – will provide a range of services and information through a single point of reference through the Community Legal Service. The FAINs will 'provide tailored information and access to services that may assist in resolving disputes and/or assist those who may wish to consider saving or reconciling their relationship' (Legal Services Commission 2002 para 2.1). The lessons of the pilot projects have been learnt, it seems, but the objectives enshrined in Part I of FLA 1996 remain current. Advice will be flexible to recognise individual circumstances and it will be provided by solicitors, but the content of the information will likely remain familiar.

Marriage counselling

The pilot projects also studied the 'Meeting with a Marriage Counsellor' provided for in the legislation. This provision was included as a part of the marriage-saving agenda, but marriage counselling services have a different agenda. They market themselves as helping people to end, as well as to save, relationships (McCarthy 2001 p 390). Indeed, respondents in the pilots shared this view, as less than half of them went to a meeting with a marriage counsellor hoping to save their marriages. About 15 per cent wanted help in ending their marriages, and almost a third wanted help to come to terms with the end of their marriage (Walker 2001 'Summary' p 36). Rather than interpreting these findings as evidence of the importance to individuals of emotional rehabilitation on divorce, government interpreted them as part of the overall failure of the system to 'save marriages' (McCarthy 2001 p 396). It seemed in this way to disregard the experiences and needs of divorcing subjects, but its commitment to counselling as a way of encouraging married subjects to reflect upon saving their marriages remains strong (see Chapter 2).

The period of reflection and consideration

The theme of personal responsibility continued in the period of reflection and consideration required by FLA 1996. It was thought that if only people would think hard enough and long enough, they might realise the folly, or at least the seriousness, of their actions. The period of reflection was to meant to encourage individuals to consider the effect of their actions upon others, particularly their children, and thus to take decisions about their divorcing behaviour in a profoundly moral and personalised way. It seemed, in this way, to provide legislative approval of the late-modern reflective and connected self.

Reece (2000b), however, likens it to a 'time out' imposed as a form of discipline by parents upon recalcitrant children. While reflection and personal choice are approved, they are approved reluctantly and with an air of paternal *disapproval*. The seriousness with which a decision to divorce is imbued is captured in the Act's objectives and in the information about the process and consequences of divorce with which individuals were to be provided. The discourse of harm to children was prevalent and the overall marriage-saving tone of the legislation seemed to encourage parties to use the time to *re*consider their decision to divorce as much as to consider the financial and residential consequences of their decision.

The whole experiment that was Part II of FLA 1996 reflects a policy concern to protect the idealised romantic relationship – to save marriages – at the same time as it attempts to shift responsibility for this to an individual's choice. It seemed to be the conflicting legal expression of Beck and Beck-Gernsheim's idea of love being the exclusive responsibility of the lovers at the same time as it proclaimed the sanctity and institutional importance of the relationship they were supposed to preserve. We can see a tension between a process that appeared to allow people to choose the routes their relationships would take and to allow them autonomy and agency in manifesting those choices, and to encourage or coerce a particular form for the ultimate decisions to take. That form is rooted in the 'two become one' image of the enduring romantic family and is based upon co-operation and altruism expressed through the discourse of child welfare and the conciliatory and harmonious divorce. In this way, the ideal divorce strikingly parallels the ideal marriage, each containing elements of the modern intimate relationship and the romantic forever one.

Its effect upon individuals was potentially damaging, however. At the same time as it normalised divorce, FLA 1996 pathologised many of the normal *experiences* of divorce such as anger, conflict and the need to assert rights (Day Sclater 1999a). Further, the information meetings, marriage counselling and period of reflection and consideration that it provided to accommodate modern, reflexive relationships were revealed as all too clearly designed to fit the standard (or ideal) couple in the standard (or ideal) marriage, one which could and should be saved, if only the parties put enough emotional effort in to do so. Finally, the families people lived with, which recognise situational and structural factors to be important to their family practices and to their senses of self and other seemed to be disregarded at each stage. It remains to be seen whether the FAINs will continue the 'message' of FLA 1996, albeit in a more user-friendly form.

In general, the pilot research on Part II of FLA 1996 found that in choosing a path after the initial information meeting, people underwent a constant weighing-up of what was happening to them and whether they felt they were active participants in the process. The importance they attached to individual agency can be linked to the control that is assumed to be a part of the pure relationship in which the parties themselves determine the terms and outcome of the negotiations. And so when the Lord Chancellor announced that Part II would not be implemented because, in effect, too many people were exercising this control, their choice, he was also saying that the morality of reflective consideration was not adequate for divorce. Perhaps we were not yet ready to exercise our choices responsibly. Perhaps only after the education measures planned and recently begun, outlining the responsibilities of marriage and the damage divorce does to children, we shall be ready and sufficiently educated to exercise our moral selves in this way. Perhaps we have been infantilised not only by the legislation (Reece 2000b), but also by its repeal.

Individual responsibility continues to be the focus of changes to divorce law. These changes have now been restricted, by and large, to procedural innovations tied to the more pragmatically traditional Matrimonial Causes Act 1973. It is to experiences of divorce pursuant to this legislation that I now turn.

Divorce experiences

The experience of divorce is lived through more than its legal manifestations, and even the social or collective experience of divorce lies 'at the intersection of legal and extra-legal discourses, practices and institutions' (Collier 1999 p 259). Divorce is a phenomenon which has a multitude of aspects; it is a social, psychological, emotional, moral and political, as well as a legal, matter, and the men and women who experience its legal manifestations experience them at all of these levels, with all the tensions that exist among or between them. Collier points to an example of the tensions between the normative divorce and individual negotiations of it:

'the social processes of individualisation, and the dominance of what we might call a form of "rational, self-seeking confluent love" would appear to run counter to, if they do not fly in the face of, the normative model of the "good divorce" … The dominant saving marriages [and reducing conflict] agenda points to – indeed it requires – a focus on the "we" at a time when, psychologically, many spouses are concerned primarily, for a host of complex reasons, with a project of (re)development, (re)assessment and defence of the "me", of the divorcing self' (Collier 1999 p 261).

In other words, 'divorce strikes at the roots of identity' (Day Sclater 1999a p 175) and coming through it is as much about creating a new individual identity as it is about creating a new family form. Divorce law and process are preoccupied primarily with the latter concern, however, and may therefore do a profound disservice to divorcing individuals when they fail adequately to acknowledge parties' emotional and subjective needs related to the former. In other words, while it appears to incorporate aspects of a late-modern concern for reflective choice in individual behaviour, divorce law seems to evidence little concern for the late-modern reflexive individual who engages in that behaviour.

Where divorce law does demonstrate concern for the individual divorcing subject, it tends to abstract and fix rather than to particularise that subject. On the one hand, the normative divorcing subject has no gender, no age, no ethnicity nor class; it is autonomous, free-willed and capable of both reflection and foresight. It is both disembodied and decontextualised, with the capacity, indeed the drive, to choose its own roles, attachments and identities, and to rethink, from time to time, these choices. It is an inherently unencumbered and unsituated complete self whose encumbrances and situations accrue only by choice. On the other hand, law is cognisant that the choices that individual makes contribute to its *gendered* subjectivity as husband or wife, but in assuming those choices are voluntarily and rationally undertaken, it does not disturb the inherent completeness of the subject while it fixes that subject with a gender identity. Divorce law thus both abstracts and genders its subjects, but leaves little room for any ongoing project of self, which would disrupt that process and its outcome.

In its post-liberal garb, the self is situated, in fact is constituted in part by its situation and the decisions it makes in regard to those situations from time to time. When the post-liberal individual reflects on a decision, then, it is reflecting not only upon different actions and potential consequences, but also upon different modes of being, upon its very identity (see Reece 2000a and 2003). It is this agency that means the post-liberal subject is reflexive, is 'always open to growth ... and transformation in the light of revised self-understandings' (Reece 2000a p 78). It is this self that Giddens and Weeks, for example, see as the individual who forms modern intimate attachments.

Every decision taken by that individual contributes to its project of identity and decisions to attach or detach from another are thus life-changing in more than the traditional sense. But because the self is situated, its place in the gender order is crucial to its identity. While this is true in all moments of the life-course (see Smart 2000; Fineman 1995), divorce is a particularly important moment for 'doing gender' (Collier 2001a p 696). It is on divorce that the project of self becomes particularly urgent and particularly salient and law's part in, or absence from, that process more pronounced. In this context, the tension between the 'we' and the 'me' of divorce law takes on different meanings for women and men.

Gendered selves

Recent socio-legal studies on people's divorcing behaviour shed some light on the gendered individual who goes through the process and on the nego-tiations of power that are critical to remaking or rediscovering a self that was bound up or submerged within another during marriage. Smart and Neale (1999) suggest that different forms of power in relationships relate to different ideas of the self.

> 'Debilitative power occurs when one's partner takes more than s/he gives or puts obstacles in the way of personal growth and autonomy. ... Debilitative power was seen as an attempt to stop the other from becoming a new self or from rediscovering their old selves' (Smart and Neale 1999 p 139).

'Situational power', on the other hand, is depicted as one having control or mastery over one's situation; it is other-focused, and can be expressed through economic or physical domination of others. It is a form of power that, in the marriage relationship, has its roots in 'traditional' marriage (Smart and Neale 1999 p 138), unlike debilitative power whose roots lie in the confluent love relationship. Smart and Neale argue, however, that while the exercise and balance of both kinds of power are important during one's life-course and with one's partner and frequently must be negotiated on divorce, divorce *law* takes seriously only the balancing of situational power, and fails to understand or recognise issues of debilitative power (Smart and Neale 1999 p 146). Because they also state that it is more frequently women who experience a loss of debilitative power on divorce, this tendency on the part of law affects women's experiences of the *justice* of divorce law. Concurrently, men's more frequently expressed losses of situational power are at least comprehended, if not always redressed, by law.

These observations mean that at the same time as it appears to accommodate individual reflection and choice, divorce law does so with respect to choices made by the liberal individual at the expense of the post-liberal one. It prioritises the concerns of the traditional marriage and family and usually men by its preoccupation to reorder the relationship between the idealised and fixed (soon to be ex-) husband or wife over the concerns of the individual struggling to remake her new, perhaps non-familial *self* on divorce.

There is a paradox created by the primacy accorded in divorce law to the rational liberal subject. At the same time as his rationality is foregrounded, divorce discourse also foregrounds the welfare and harmony of his family (Day Sclater 1999a). It states that the rational course of action in divorce is to be self-sacrificing rather than self-serving. Creating this curious form of rationality can thus allow divorce law successfully to protect the altruism of the ideal family, while marginalising the intense feelings also assumed to be associated with it. This paradox also can have profound emotional and psychological consequences for individuals (Day Sclater 1999a). Day Sclater's research on the psychodynamics of divorce demonstrates that emotions, conflict and anger are normal psychological parts of coping with loss, separation and reconstruction of identity, yet divorce law and process reject the relevance of feelings, or at least assume they are 'manageable', and submerge conflict (Day Sclater 1999a). Further, while an opportunity to revisit, reinterpret and understand the past – to revisit all one's perceptions of the past – cannot be overestimated in the process of building a new identity, a new 'world', or a new future (Day Sclater 1999a p 175), the process allows only a focus upon the future.

Again, attention to gender is important. Day Sclater found subtle differences in the way in which men and women 'recreated the emotional intimacy in their memories of the marriage' (Day Sclater 1999a p 178). Women identified a need for reciprocity and emotional closeness, while men focused more on their wives' physical availability and the need for centrality of their wives' lives. Gender differences in this part of the project of self may have implications not only for the work and outcome of that project from time to time, but also for the individual's psychological well-being during the divorce process and for his or her feeling of the justice or fairness of that process. While law is interested in contending with the past purely in terms of the pragmatics of rearranging money, housing or welfare of children as 'scientifically' understood, it denies a gendered need for coping with loss by reconstructing a new self through engaging with the intimacies of that past.

The ideal divorce manages families, it brings new forms of families into the ideal family net – in this case a post-divorce family which must take up where the pre-divorce one failed and be forever, stable, co-operative and harmonious. It is a non-threatening family (Day Sclater 1999a p 15) and it can only be achieved by the 'good' divorce which is 'harmonious and characterised by rational appraisal and behaviour which plans properly for the future. … [it] keeps families together' (Day Sclater 1999a p 177). It is the bad divorce that tears families apart – it is 'conflict ridden, accusatory, costly … and associated with the legal process' (Day Sclater 1999a p 176). Divorce as the creator of the good family reflects a strategy for survival on both individual and social levels. It sustains the dual imperatives of family stability (Day Sclater 1999a p 179–80) and changeability.

Psychological and emotional experiences of divorce may thus be at odds with a process that denies them while paying them lip service. People do not experience divorce in isolation, though. Many have friends, family and professional support and advice at their disposal.

Divorce and solicitors

Professional support is most frequently obtained from solicitors, although many divorcing people also seek the assistance of counsellors or mediators. I will look at mediators in Chapter 5, but now I wish to turn to the role that lawyers play in individuals' experiences of the divorce process. Research on the information meeting pilot projects and Genn (1999) both observe that clients overwhelmingly still go to solicitors when they contemplate divorce. King (1999) states that this shows that the perception remains of divorce as a legal rather than psychological or emotional problem and, importantly, that solicitors must collude in this perception.

The ways in which they collude are interesting, though. In the US, Sarat and Felstiner (1995) found an attempt by divorce lawyers to maintain an ideology of separate spheres that was characterised by their consistent attempts to distance their clients' emotions from the rationality of law, alongside clients' equally consistent attempts to speak in the discourse of fault, blame, emotions, anger, love and hate. Even in the no-fault legal world of the US, clients evidenced that which they call a desire for moral vindication, but which may also be characterised as the necessary reconstruction of identity explained by Day Sclater. Whatever one terms this process, Sarat and Felstiner suggest that lawyers and clients may be occupied with two different but fundamentally necessary divorces: lawyers with a legal divorce, clients with a social and emotional divorce (Sarat and Felstiner 1995 p 50). Lawyers' conscious or unconscious belief that law has no place for the sphere of the 'social' is troubling, as this means that often they refuse to engage with clients' efforts to give meaning to the past (Sarat and Felstiner 1995 p 51) and they marginalise clients' attempts to 'expand the conversational agenda to encompass a broader picture of their lives, experiences and needs' (Sarat and Felstiner 1995 p 144).

Piper (1999; see also King 1999; Neale and Smart 1997a) suggests, however, that the 'good' family lawyer in England is one who is successful precisely in moving between the legal and 'non-legal' discourses that are the stuff of family law in order to control and motivate the client (Piper 1999 p 107). He or she is an expert in 'client handling' who takes on a multidisciplinary role as a 'rather odd and expensive social worker', a 'lawyer-psychologist' and a legal advisor (Piper 1999 p 102). While family law specialists, perhaps more than other specialist solicitors, may see a place in their practice for traditionally non-legal discourses such as welfare and morality, however, they also seem to have internalised these discourses and operationalised them in legal terms when constructing themselves as good lawyers and their clients as good or sensible clients (Piper 1999; Bailey-Harris et al 1998; King 1999). This is to say that family law, like other specialist areas, is composed of legal procedural rules, legal doctrine and professional codes of conduct, but unlike other specialist areas it is also composed of norms expressed through psychological and medical discourses of welfare, and political discourses of common sense (Diduck 2000) and responsibility

(Piper 1999). It 'potentially has within it conflicting ideologies of seeking the greater good of families and of individual justice and self interest' (Piper 1999 p 107). While the law may deliberately invoke this mixed vision of its normative family – it is the conflicted family we live by – it leaves it up to the individuals concerned to reconcile the conflict on a day-to-day basis. Dewar observes:

> '[L]aw more and more becomes the context in which those contradictions or oppositions that cannot be resolved politically are worked through ... legislators have in fact created a set of inconsistent principles and commitments ... while at the same time using law to give the appearance of having created shared values; and then have offloaded the detailed working out of those contradictions to the legal system' (Dewar 1998 p 484).

Dewar emphasises the burden placed on the legal system, but it seems that much of that burden is actually taken up by family law professionals and their clients. Piper's research indicates that one way in which lawyers have successfully managed the role of 'worker-out' of political contradictions is to internalise government policy both on responsibility and welfare in the context of the conflict-free divorce and post-divorce child-rearing, and then to transfer these values, in the form of legal advice, to the 'soon-to-be-separated-but-continuing family' (Piper 1999 p 106). 'They endorse particular client problems and not others, they construct particular suggested arrangements as "good" and not others, they refer to particular types of solutions as the "real solution" and they do all this through a particular construction of parental responsibility' (Piper 1999 p 106 n 85), and we might now add the 'responsible divorce'. They must do this while maintaining the trust of the client, however, and so are able to move in and out of the client's realm of the social, albeit not always to an individual client's advantage. Piper notes:

> 'The "good" family lawyer ... uses a language of involvement and responsibility – concepts which have taken on particular meanings ... [Good solicitors] have reconstructed the political and social meanings of these terms for use in a legal discourse. "Involvement" in an every day [sense] where practical "doing" would be indicated is not what the solicitors mean. Indeed if parents had indicated they had disputes over the "real" practicalities of continuing parenting – laundry, taking the child to medical appointments during working hours, sending or taking food and other items to school at the ap-

propriate time – then they would have been labelled as childish. The law is not concerned with such "trifles" and nor are specialist family lawyers, though their use of hybrid terms often gives the impression that they are' (Piper 1999 p 108).

Individuals' family and gender practices are rendered trivial or childish in law and solicitors collude in this trivialisation. They, like divorce law, are only concerned with the ideals and abstractions of the normative family.

Also included among the elements of recent divorce rhetoric is that a part of the individual's responsibility for her or his own good divorce and for the consequences thereof is the displacement of law. Perhaps surprisingly, solicitors' collude in this rhetoric by providing norms to suggest that law/litigation is likely to do more harm than good, is legitimate only in exceptional cases and is able to help out in the case of an unreasonable parent/spouse (King 1999 p 257) while at the same time managing to foster clients' dependency upon them and their legal expertise. While solicitors diverged in most ways in King's (1999) study, 'one thing that did unite them was a consistent confidence they expressed in their ability to help anxious, emotionally distressed and often initially intransigent clients to realise the importance of taking ownership of and resolving their own disputes' (King 1999 p 266).

In the light of this research, it is somewhat surprising that the Lord Chancellor's Department took it as given that lawyers disrupt harmony, are litigious and adversarial, and inhibit communication and settlement. Eekelaar et al (2000) also found that this image of lawyers is far from accurate. They reviewed the sociological and empirical work, which confirms the multitude of tasks and skills performed by solicitors and the many roles as helper and advice-giver they adopt (Eekelaar et al 2000 p 46–56). In their own study of family lawyers they identified the difficulty in separating the different roles a divorce solicitor adopts: information blends into advice, which blends into negotiation, which blends into help and support (Eekelaar et al 2000 p 78–79). In general, it seems that family solicitors have accepted themselves as the embodiment of the paradoxical divorce: they are at the same time the protectors of rights and the facilitators of co-operation and harmony.

Conclusions

Divorce may be a *problem* for individuals because it implies a responsibility for personal failure. Not only have we let ourselves down, we have also failed in our social responsibility to sustain a 'stable' family. We can be redeemed, however, if we divorce responsibly. To do this we must deny any psychological need to feel angry, hostile and selfish or to reconstruct our autonomy or our self in the light of this psychological work. We must become the paradoxical individual husband or wife of liberal law whose actions are guided by principles of formal equality, rationality, self-sacrifice and harmony. Neither our welfare nor our feelings are important in the good divorce, both are of concern only about our children. It is no wonder that our family practices fall short of the ideal.

The paradox within divorce law captures the current paradoxical problematisation of divorce for society. In an effort to accommodate both reflexivity/confluence/individualism and morality/stability/unity, divorce law is both modern and traditional. Divorce has become acceptable, it is a reflection of our changing selves, changing needs and changing duties, yet it is traditional because to do it responsibly reflects the morality of the classic, enduring family.

'The very concept of divorce itself has been a battleground between the pursuit of individual self interests and the interests of other parties and communal values. [Divorce is made up of a series of dichotomies that] reflect the inherent conflict between the individualistic values of the contemporary Western world and an aspiration for protection and cultivation of the benefits of caring, cooperation and communality' (Eekelaar et al 2000 p 187).

Chapter 4

Children: constructions and connections

At this point I may be accused, like Giddens, of ignoring the importance of children to intimate and familial relationships. But the ideal family, both in law and in the collective imagination, includes children, and much of our intimate behaviour, many of the choices we make and a good deal of the policy and legal 'knowledge' that informs those choices is created and sustained in a context in which children are the primary concern. In this chapter I suggest that sociological enquiry that has begun to explore the changing nature of individualism in the context of intimate adult relationships also has important insights to offer the study of childhood and adult-child relations. The child, in this approach, is not so much an object of study but a subject in his or her own right with a capacity to exercise a form of agency. It is an approach with which parents and the law have an ambivalent relationship, however, as it requires recognition of children's individuality and agency in a social and policy context that also reveres and demands their 'romantic' dependence.

In this chapter, I explore how these two ideas of childhood are expressed both normatively and through family practices and I conclude that, like the normative family, the child of law is conceptualised through an amalgamation of two distinct and polarised narratives, but that the child's experiences and expressions of self, attachment, responsibility and relationship integrate those narratives in more complex and nuanced ways than does the ideal.

Conceptualising childhood

Let us recall here recent ideas of individualisation that claim that an individual's embeddedness in, and engagement with, political and public society have shifted. Beck's (1992 and with Beck and Beck-Gernsheim 2002) idea is that individualisation liberates or 'disembeds' people from traditional roles and constraints so that 'the individual must become the agent of his or her own identity making'; 'individuals have to develop their own biography and organize it in relation to others' (Beck and Beck-Gernsheim 2002 p 203). In the context of intimate relationships, just as in the public political realm, this means that the sources of traditional obligations and the rules of establishing and maintaining connections are no longer taken for granted. It also means that the individual rule-making required to negotiate one's economic, occupational and political biographies cannot be kept separate from the formation and ongoing project of one's personal and intimate biography; as Beck says, 'modernity does not hesitate at the front door of family life' (Beck and Beck-Gernsheim 2002 p 203)[1].

On this view, the individual, rather than the couple, the family, the class or political party, is the foundation of society, but Beck contrasts this individual and the ethics of this individualism with the form of individualism that emerged in the eighteenth and nineteenth centuries, the 'first' modernity (also see Chapter 2):

'The late-eighteenth and early-nineteenth centuries witnessed the emergence of subjectivity and romanticism in everyday life. It was a dramatization of romantic love which created not only an individual biography, but also a moral and emotional complex that helped to create the couple and their history, as opposed to society. ... The first impression one might have of individualized subcultures today is that they are similarly centred on the dramatization of their own egos. But research ... has challenged the idea that we are living in a "selfish society".... Being an individual does not exclude caring about others. In fact, living in a highly individualized culture means you have to be socially sensible and be able to relate to others

---

1   Lee (2001) attributes much of this change in the 'standard' adult individual to the economic changes created by a post-Fordist global economy in which the traditional model of the stable, completed adult is no longer appropriate. Instead, 'the flexible "new economy" means that one's geographical location, one's employment status, one's range of skills and, above all, one's self-identity now remain open to change' (Lee 2001 p 17).

and to obligate yourself, in order to manage and to organize your everyday life. ... Thinking of oneself and living for others at the same time, once considered a contradiction in terms, is revealed as an internal, substantive connection' (Beck and Beck-Gernsheim 2002 p 211–212)[2].

This work is crucial for men and women from all nations and classes; indeed the experience of globalisation is central to his thesis. Let us consider, however, how children fit into this analysis. In his earlier work with Beck-Gernsheim (1995), Beck postulates that in the second modernity's uncertain world of negotiation, contingency and individualisation, where relationships based upon choice no longer provide the lifelong support and self-actualisation that the old rules promised, it is to our children that we look for grounding, existential security and unconditional love.

'The child becomes the last remaining, irrevocable, unique primary love object. Partners come and go, but the child stays. Everything one vainly hoped to find in the relationship with one's partner is sought in or directed at the child' (Beck and Beck-Gernsheim 1995 p 37).

Beck and Beck-Gernsheim imply here that relationships with children do not have to be 'earned or renewed' (Smart, Neale and Wade 2001 p 44), that they have somehow escaped the phenomenon of modernisation. Indeed, Ribbens McCarthy and Edwards (2002) argue that this intense connection with a child represents the *reality* of the mother-child connection and that it is therefore inappropriate to use (changing) adult-adult intimacy as a model for adult-child intimacy. In this and Beck and Beck-Gernsheim's views, the adult-child bond seems to have some objective, predefined meaning and import that transcends the transformation that is taking place in all other social relationships. This late-modern parent-child relationship thus resembles nothing so much as a more intense version of romantic love and seems to hold the same revered place in the public consciousness.

Yet, if children *are* included in the phenomenon of individualisation, their subjectivities and the nature of their familial attachments must be revised to take account of their disembeddedness and individual rule-making as much as it does their parents', but must also be understood to exist alongside

---

2   This view is similar to Sevenhuijsen's (1998) discussed in Chapter 1.

more traditional accounts. Classical philosophers[3], psychologists[4], sociologists[5] and historians[6] have all contributed to current understandings of what childhood means, and consequently where children can be situated both conceptually and empirically in terms of both citizenship and the democratic ideal and dependency and the romantic ideal. These ideas have influenced legal and political understandings of children's identities and attachments that create and contain childhood as a special status and children as individuals in apparently paradoxical ways. This observation should be neither surprising nor unsettling, though, especially in the light of the 'normal chaos' of identity-making, loving and law discussed in the previous chapters. Legal and social policy-makers, welfare experts and advocates of rights advance theories which appear to set up then balance contradictions between dependence and autonomy or welfare and rights for children, while at the same time professing the integrity of childhood as a condition that is qualitatively different from adulthood. Perhaps, however, the claim to, or indeed the search for, ontological integrity is misguided. In other words, while the mythological or idealised child, like the mythological or idealised family can be theorised neatly, the child constituted through everyday family practices, the one protection of whose welfare, dependencies, individuality, rights and citizenship is important, may not be so easily categorised or coherently understood.

Enlightenment's children – the child as 'becoming'[7]

Perhaps the apparent coherence of childhood as a 'condition' has its epistemological roots in the Enlightenment thinking of that which Beck calls the 'first modernity' (Beck and Beck-Gernsheim 2002). With the rational

3 Archard (1993) observes that John Locke's ideas of children and childhood can be discerned from remarks he made in various texts. He mentions particularly *An Essay Concerning Human Understanding* (1689) and *Some Thoughts Concerning Education* (1693). Jean-Jacques Rousseau's *Emile* (1762) exemplifies the later romanticism of childhood.

4 Such as Sigmund Freud (in Strachey 1959) and Jean Piaget (1952).

5 Such as Emile Durkheim (1973) and Talcott Parsons (1951).

6 Such as Phillipe Aries (1962).

7 Obviously, the following synthesis of two hundred years of thought must be simplified and summarised. Detail and nuance clearly are sacrificed, yet I hope what remains provides an accurate, if somewhat crude, picture of traditional understandings of childhood. Similar, if perhaps more comprehensive, reviews of these and other approaches to childhood can also be found in James, Jenks and Prout 1998; Smart, Neale and Wade 2001; Archard 1993; and Jenks 1996.

individualism that emerged at that time came a refutation of pre-ordained status and of non-consensual bonds, but crucially this idea applied only to certain segments of the population. Children, even more obviously than women, were omitted from this 'universal' emancipation, and were, in effect, excluded from the public sphere of political and civil society. Radical ideas of individual autonomy, equality and democracy were applicable only to rational subjects, and only upon reaching adulthood was this capacity for rational thought deemed to be achieved. Children were not legal, political or social subjects as much as they were objects of their parents or the state's concern. They were incomplete adults, always in the process of 'becoming', rather than simply 'being' (Smart, Neale and Wade 2001), or as Lee (2001) says, 'human becomings' rather than human beings.

Locke's important contribution to political theory is 'his insistence that legitimate political authority is founded upon the freely given consent of those individuals over whom authority is exercised' (Archard 1993 p 7) but that it is only adults who have the full rationality to exercise this choice and give consent. Children, while born with reason and the capacity for rationality, have not yet achieved it and it is only age and experience that can bring about its exercise. Locke's idea of the child as a blank slate, his empirical developmentalism, can be contrasted with the moral developmentalism of Thomas Hobbes, who theorised children as innately evil and therefore in need of taming and saving on their way to adulthood, or that of Rousseau who thought children were born with a natural goodness, clarity of vision and innocence. These conflicting ideas of 'immanent childhood' (James, Jenks and Prout 1998) remain in modern policy and 'common sense' concerned to control Hobbes' evil or anarchic child, and in policies of child-centred education, provision of resources for special needs and concern for welfare designed to guide Rousseau's idealised, kind and innocent child and Locke's child as potential citizen (James, Jenks and Prout 1998).

Other models that accept childhood as a 'natural' and universal category of becoming originate in developmental psychology. The leading developmental psychologists of the first part of the twentieth century assumed that all children progress through an inevitable process of maturation on their way to becoming 'finished products', and because the stages through which they progress sequentially are natural, rather than socially constituted, children 'become a unitary category from which any variation is perceived as deviance' (Smart, Neale and Wade 2001 p 4). There was, however, little consensus about the number or requirements of each stage. Freud's theory, for example, attempts to account for the development of personality; it is a theory of cognitive and psychosexual development. He claimed all humans passed through three stages of personality development – the id, ego and superego – and five stages of psychosexual development, beginning in infancy with the oral stage and culminating with a healthy adult in the genital stage. Erikson (1980), drawing on Freudian concepts, postulated a theory of psychosocial development in terms of eight sequential stages, each of which is described as a basic conflict which must be resolved by the healthy individual before he can progress to the next. Piaget (1952) identified six stages of cognitive development from the sensorimotor, in which the child is said to have no notion of objective reality, to the final stage of formal operations characterised by an ability to deal with the hypothetical and by development of strong idealism. Kohlberg (1984) delineated six stages in the development of moral judgment, beginning with punishment and obedience orientation and culminating in the morality of individual principles of conscience.

Despite their diversity, these developmental theories have had tremendous impact on 'generations of educationalists, paediatricians, child-rearing experts, and public policy-makers' and on legal understandings of child welfare (Smart, Neale and Wade 2001 p 4). But as many have noted, they can be criticised on a number of bases. The insistence on grading children as they progress through a predetermined sequence of stages gives scientific credibility to the idea that children are not yet something – they are in a state of transition to completion, and therefore cannot be understood as simply being what they are (Smart, Neale and Wade 2001 p 4). Further, developmental stage monitoring, or being 'evaluated against a "gold standard" of the normal child' (James, Jenks and Prout 1998 p 19), has significant possible repercussions for individual children who appear to deviate from the standard, and these repercussions are multiplied if the standard itself fails to take account of cultural and structural gender and ethnic diversity.

Feminists, for example, have criticised these theories on the basis that they universalise the masculine experience as the human experience and so postulate the male child as the universal 'normal' child. The work of Nancy Chodorow (1978) was among the first to reveal a masculine bias in Freud's developmental theories. Chodorow suggests that the sex differences Freud found in children's development toward individuation and relationship were not examples of female deviance or pathology whereby women develop 'weaker' ego boundaries than men. Rather they could be understood as consequences of early childhood experiences of being parented by a mother rather than a father and the effect this has on masculine gender identity, defined by individuation and separation, and on feminine gender identity, defined by attachment. She thus criticises the 'standard' child and adult both as asserting a masculine norm. The influential yet controversial work of Carol Gilligan also illustrates this point.

'The quality of embeddedness in social interaction and personal relationships that characterizes women's lives in contrast to men's ... becomes not only a descriptive difference but also a developmental liability when the milestones of childhood and adolescent development in the psychological literature are markers of increasing separation. Women's failure to separate then becomes by definition a failure to develop' (Gilligan 1982 p 9).

Gilligan was concerned that the universalism of psychology, developmental psychology in particular, persistently treated women and girls as though they were men or boys, misunderstanding the differences that emerged between the sexes as immaturity or deficiency in women. Kohlberg's theory of moral development, for example, locates women's traditional traits of care and sensitivity to the needs of others at stage three of his six-stage sequence, while his final stage of maturity reflects the importance of individuation in the traditional development of boys and men (Gilligan 1982 p 18).

'When one begins with the study of women and derives developmental constructs from their lives, the outline of a moral conception different from that described by Freud, Piaget or Kohlberg begins to emerge and informs a different description of development. In this conception, the moral problem arises from conflicting responsibilities rather than from competing rights and requires for its resolution a mode of thinking that is contextual and narrative rather than formal and abstract' (Gilligan 1982 p 19).

These feminist critiques render it difficult to imagine childhood as merely a stage in the progress to a universal adult subjectivity by problematising both the stages and the ultimate 'destination'.

Developmental theories that comprehend children essentially as universal, natural, unfinished beings thus fail to account adequately for the effects on individual children and their carers of social structures and systems as well as their individual agency and competence to affect those social conditions. Theories of socialisation advanced in the 1940s to 1970s replicated many of these problems, but from a different perspective.

Socialisation

Socialisation can be defined as the process through which one incorporates the norms, behaviours, codes and values of a social system. It is the process by which an individual develops an identity, or self-concept. It is about internalising conformity and is an ongoing project on the completion of which the child has been transformed from a 'savage' (Jenks 1996) or an asocial being to a fully social and autonomous adult (Smart, Neale and Wade 2001 p 5). Socialisation is achieved not so much through formal learning processes, but by the child absorbing norms, values and expectations from experiences, school, religion and community, although the primary socialising agent was indisputably believed to be 'the family'. It was through 'the family' that girls learned how to be women and boys to be men. It was through the nuclear family idealised in the 1940s and 1950s that that ideal model of the social and cultural order was said to be reproduced. While all socialisation theories tend to treat children as passive mounds of clay to be shaped, stretched or compressed into finished socialised products, and thus are more about what adults do to children than about how children experience their social space (Smart, Neale and Wade 2001 p 6–7; Jenks 1996 p 8–22; James, Jenks and Prout 1998 p 22–25), in the structural functionalist theories of Talcott Parsons that dominated 1950s and 1960s family sociology, 'socialization assumed the character of a totalitarian system of control that gradually engulfed the child through the psychological process of "internalization" and moulded it for its own ends' (Smart, Neale and Wade 2001 p 6).

Parsons saw society as an organism concerned to ensure its continued perpetuation through time, and socialisation as the process through which this was accomplished. He begins from 'a presumption of binding central consensus values [that] trickle ... down to an anticipated conformity at the level of the individual personality' (Jenks 1996 p 15). His is a profoundly conservative theory that simply accepts as axiomatic the functionality of replicating a given and particular social and cultural system. It successfully disarms the potential threat that 'difference and divergence within childhood' pose to that system by treating childhood as a universal and 'residual category to be incorporated through theories of socialisation' (Jenks 1996 p 12). While Parsonian functionalism may now be out of fashion, socialisation remains a dominant theme through which both childhood and parenthood are regulated (see Day Sclater and Piper 2001; '10-year-old offenders to be sent to foster homes' Guardian 15 November 2002 p 1).

Enlightenment and romantic developmentalism

In one or a combination of forms, the 'child as becoming' thesis dominated sociological and psychological theorising until recently, and indeed it is consonant with an Enlightenment idea to view children in this way (Jenks 1996). The idea of social evolution or progress from the primitive to the civilised corresponds with ideas of individual development or maturity from the elemental to the complete. That children are projects that adults shape to completion also fits with Enlightenment ideas of mastery over the natural by the rational. Finally, there is an optimism in this vision of children that is central to the Enlightenment ideal: proper education, socialisation or 'illumination' of the 'darkness' that is the unfinished child will complete him or her into the enlightened, rational, functional, *good* citizen; it will turn 'disorder into order' (Lee 2001).

The optimistic Enlightenment view of the child that I call 'romantic developmentalism' integrates a curious amalgam of the innocent child, the evil child and the child as blank slate. There is a sense not only of the child as project or as a human becoming, but also of the child as qualitatively different from the adult (Diduck 1999a). Criteria from developmental psychology and socialisation theories are imported into what becomes the 'truth' about our children: that the paradigm child is dependent (versus autonomous) and is innocent, both in absolute moral terms and in terms of an impeccable ignorance of worldly matters such as citizenship or production and consumption (Diduck 1999a; Hendrick 1990; Cunningham 1995). Children must grow or mature into independence (individuation), being taught or guided (socialised) by loving carers attentive to their welfare so as to ensure they do not reach this state prematurely and thus become corrupted. Until this time, they lack an appreciation of their interest or will and are not capable of expressing it. Jenks describes this modernist view of children as 'futurity' (Jenks 1996 p 97); James, Jenks and Prout (1998 see also Smart, Neale and Wade 2001 p 9–10) explain that it is the reason why the study of children has traditionally been subsumed under the umbrella of 'family studies'; and Smart, Neale and Wade conclude that it explains why children have been viewed as 'marginal' and 'invisible' in contemporary social studies (Smart, Neale and Wade 2001 p 8–10). There is some evidence to suggest, however, that recently this romantic developmentalist view of children as 'becoming' has had to make room for alternative conceptions.

Late-modernity's children – children as 'being'

Recently a 'new sociology of childhood' has begun to take seriously both social-structural contingency in understanding childhood and the child *as being*, worthy of study in and of him or herself. It has begun to see childhood not as a natural or universal category, but as a socially constructed space or as a variable concept (Archard 1993) and ascribes a kind of late- or postmodern idea of individualisation, reflexivity and agency to children which recognises that they 'inhabit a world of meaning created by themselves and through their interaction with adults' (James, Jenks and Prout 1998 p 29). Crucially, this world of meaning is firmly rooted in, and particular to, a time and space. According to leading proponents of what is termed this 'social constructionist' view, 'childhood does not exist in a finite and identifiable form' (James, Jenks and Prout 1998 p 27).

'New' childhood studies thus attempt to understand the contingency and particularity of childhood, and importantly seek to do this from children's perspectives rather than simply from the perspectives of their teachers, parents, social workers or psychologists. In it children are important in the here-and-now, rather than only as future persons; they can be conceptualised as 'active and interactive practitioners of social life' (Smart, Neale and Wade 2001 p 12). In this way, research about children and childhood has left its customary home in 'family studies' and has begun to explore children's agency in negotiating their autonomy and (inter)dependence in contexts other than merely the familial (Smart, Neale and Wade 2001 p 12).

In the context of the family, empirical research has taken on board the new sociology of childhood by engaging directly with children as research subjects. Whether it aims to examine how children construct close relationships or 'family', how they negotiate trauma or personal information sharing, how they experience the legal system, or how they fare in post-divorce families, these researchers recognise that children themselves are meaningful contributors to their subjectivity (see Smart, Neale and Wade 2001; Brannen and O'Brien 1995; Douglas 2001). This approach empowers children to an unprecedented degree; it acknowledges the dignity of their autonomy, accords respect to their views and attributes value to their individuality. In short, rather than treating them as objects of study and concern, this approach treats children as competent and reflective subjects who have much to offer, not only to an understanding of their social worlds, but also to an understanding of ours. Indeed, there is a point at which the dichotomy between 'theirs' and 'ours' become specious. While it is important to recognise that children are dependent in a way in which many adults are not, and are subject to degrees and mechanisms of control to which many adults are not, children are a component of all societies and social structures[8] and the boundaries between 'theirs' and 'ours' must also be recognised as socially constructed. On this view, 'children are "knowers" of the same social world that sociologists have sought to describe and explain, and they offer a novel perspective on that world' (Smart, Neale and Wade 2001 p 13).

The new sociology of childhood fits comfortably within late-modernity's individualisation. The ideal late-modern self, as we have seen, is always a work in progress and so today's child may be an unfinished product, but unlike his or her state of incompleteness in the 'first' modernity, the process is now seen to be unfinishable. Beck applies this idea to older children:

> 'young people no longer *become* individualized. They individualize *themselves*. "Biographization" of youth means becoming active, struggling and designing one's own life. … A life of one's own is becoming an everyday problem for action, staging and self-representation. … [Individualization] becomes taken for granted, perhaps the core of one's self-image. … [S]ocialization is now possible only as self-socialization' (Beck 1997 p 163).

Autonomy and agency are also different in the late-modern view. Autonomy now is said to incorporate (inter)dependency: 'being a self while being with another' (Sevenhuijsen 1998 and see also Beck and Beck-Gernsheim 2002); and agency is seen to be achieved and exercised through dependency rather than to be something a person possesses (Lee 2001 p 130–131). On this view, the ambiguity produced by late-modernity's uncertainty means not only that we are *all* human 'becomings' now, but that becoming must be understood from outside the dominant framework. It is no longer opposite to, or developing toward, being, but has a new meaning: it is 'becoming without end' (Lee 2001 p 82).

Obviously, it is as naive to suggest that this view represents a consensus about the nature of children or childhood in late-modernity as it is to say that it is any more than one sociological approach to adult subjectivity. But just as many (adult) individuals are struggling to find alternative strategies

---

8   James, Jenks and Prout call this view the 'social structural approach' to childhood, in which both the constancy and the essentiality of the child is acknowledged (James, Jenks and Prout 1998 p 32–33).

for understanding their identities and attachments, it is not unreasonable to believe that children may face the same existential demands.

Indeed, the new childhood theorists suggest that, like adults, even younger children have a need to 'design' their lives; they have a perspective or an insight about themselves and their relationships and a need to feel some meaningful influence over their social and material conditions. Williamson and Butler (1995), for example, found that children of around age ten felt that 'like it or not, *only they* can sort things out for themselves' (Williamson and Butler 1995 p 306). Children who were experiencing difficulties at school or in their homes did not wish to refuse any adult support whatsoever, but the type of support they were offered was critical.

'[They] want adults to provide them with ideas and information on which they can make *informed* choices ... They want to feel that they have actively influenced and directed the courses they are taking in their lives' (Williamson and Butler 1995 p 306).

These studies have found that children also see themselves with a degree of autonomy in their construction of family and relationships. They negotiate care and support in a democratic way within their families. Smart, Neale and Wade (2001) found that the blood tie or 'natural' relationship was not sufficient for children to define someone as a 'proper' parent; rather the quality of the relationship was crucial. Mutual and reciprocal provision of care, love, support *and respect* were all-important to measuring that quality. 'They viewed themselves not simply as children needing care but as young people who wanted to talk to others and be listened to, trust others and be trusted, and engage in open and meaningful communications. ... In other words, children value a democratic style of family life' (Smart, Neale and Wade 2001 p 58) in which they are active participants.

We cannot, of course, take even nuanced ideas of children's autonomy to the extreme, as there are significant social, material and physical vulnerabilities that remain specific to them. But if we accept that the phenomenon of late-modern individualisation applies to children as well as to adults, we are conceding at least that children have some part to play in constituting their worlds, including their identities and their relationships, and we are already radically reformulating traditional ideas of the romantic developmental child. First, we are adopting a non-deterministic view of development, seeing it as a lifelong and ongoing process rather than as a linear and finite one in which early stages of the process are viewed as deficiency or inadequacy. Secondly, we recognise the value of children's agency in affecting and influencing their environment, conditions, attachments, detachments and self-identity. Children are no longer conceived of as inactive mounds of clay to be formed by socialising agents or nature or structural forces over which they have little control. Thirdly, we accord value and respect to that agency instead of simply assuming childhood incompetence or irrationality.

It is my contention that both this late-modern autonomous child and the romantic developmental child reflect the ideal child of law, and that this may have as much to do with political choices as it does with ambivalence and 'normal chaos'. Further, the tensions created by this polarised and often paradoxical view of children may remain hidden in the normative construct, but often are revealed in children's family practices. Finally, not only does the ideal reflect a 'standard' based upon white, middle-class children (Ribbens McCarthy and Edwards 2002 p 203), it also makes a profound statement about its adult 'other' and about relationships between adults and children.

Parent-child relationships: the romantic connection

In the traditional, romantic family relationships between husband and wife and between parent and child are assumed to be based upon the irrationality of ever-enduring love or upon timeless and universally understood *duty*. They assume coherent and fixed familial identities. In contrast, relations in the ideal modern family are said to be based upon choice, flux and freedom, where not only the rules, roles and obligations, but also the identities of its members are always negotiable. The myth of the families we live by sustains both these idealised forms of connection, demanding individual agency, (a form of) democracy *and* obedience to traditional, romantic relationships and duties. Let me turn first to the romantic part of the ideal.

The romantic parent-child connection is first and foremost gendered. It calls into being children who are dependent upon mothers and fathers in very specific ways. It is given expression through a version of the traditional family in which clearly defined gender roles contribute to stability in the concepts of childhood, motherhood and fatherhood as well as to social and economic structures that rely upon that stability. We see, for example, in traditional understandings of the mother-child connection, and in empirical research that confirms mothers' and fathers' beliefs in those understandings

(Hatten et al 2002), a reliance on nature (see Bowlby 1953), and a trust in the maternal bond to fulfil our dreams of lost altruism and unconditional love.

'Mother is perceived as "natural" nurturer, or "natural" caretaker who bears a relationship with her child which seems to be explicable only in terms of "maternal instinct" or mystical or biological bonds forged in the womb or early infancy. In this view, mother and child are not quite a unit, but neither are they quite separate (Diduck 199[8]). They are a unit/not unit with a subjectivity which contrasts with the legal [and social] subjectivity of the autonomous individual. Their relationship is based upon "love" or "maternal bonds", and this is antithetical to the liberal legal relationship based primarily on relations of rights or of exchange (Diduck 199[8]). ... [Childhood and motherhood] are therefore protected through a moral discourse of caring (Smart 1991) or welfare rather than a legal discourse of rights and exchange' (Diduck 1999a p 124).

This mother-child dyad resides firmly in the romantic, private domain of instinct or love and lies in contrast with the rational legal world, and the late-modern reflexive world of choice, individualism and equality (also see Ribbens McCarthy and Edwards 2002). The romantic 'good' mother is self-sacrificing in her care for her child. She is, most fundamentally, a nurturer, because nature (or God) has made her that way.

Many feminist scholars have identified this 'ideology of motherhood' in law and popular discourse[9] as socially constructed: quite literally, as 'man-made' (Diduck 1999a p 124) and as implicated in women's economic and political subordination. They suggest that there is nothing intrinsically female about mothering (eg Fineman 1995) and that mother-child relationships are no different from other intimate relationships based upon commitment and interdependence. But such a liberal or post-liberal framework in which parenting is deemed to be equal and obligations are deemed to be consensual may also provide an inappropriate point of reference from which to understand the very real, material, physical and emotional complexity of the mother-child bond. It is often by reducing mothers to abstract parents or by explaining maternal connections by reference to individual autonomy and choice that the worst injustices can be done to mothers and children (Ribbens McCarthy and Edwards 2002). Again, it is the polarisation of these two views that is problematic because it fails to account for

9　See Collier 2001b and sources cited therein.

complexities arising out of irrational and rational choices, structural and internal constraints and contingency and flux over time and place.

In contrast to the naturalised maternal bond, the father-child connection has traditionally been grounded in sociality and legality; its roots lie in a notion of paternal proprietary rights over children and it thus sits more comfortably in a realm of rationality and choice. The intention, or choice, to be a parent fits more closely with men's experiences of procreation than with most women's (Douglas 1994 p 638). Notwithstanding this potential harmony with late-modernity, however, it is a romantic connection because it carries with it clearly understood and predetermined ideas of both filial and paternal obligations. The traditional father figure is, in this way, as inflexible as the traditional mother figure. Fathers, mothers and teenagers alike, for example, report that the central role for fathers 'these days' is the provider role (Warin et al 1999) and even those families who deviate from the norm of breadwinner-father/homemaker-mother tend to confirm this role as the ideal. In Warin et al's research 'there did not seem to be an ideological commitment to changes which would offset the "breadwinner" imperative' (Warin et al 1999 p 17; see also Collier 2001b; Hatten et al 2002).

Ruddick (1997) also suggests that in modern Western societies the ideal father is defined by the functions of provision, protection and authority/legitimation (Ruddick 1997 p 207). Crucially, however, while she recognises that mothers also fulfil these functions, they do so in a more immediate way, so that fathers provide 'distantly' – away from home – mothers more closely and intimately; fathers protect against physical intrusion or 'an uncertain and dangerous world', mothers adopt an additional focus on daily dangers or emotional suffering; and fathers represent the reality of the 'world' and its authority to judge and punish while mothers represent the comforts of home and 'soft love' (Ruddick 1997 p 207–211). Her observations have been confirmed in empirical research which shows that these gendered roles for parents are deeply entrenched in peoples' ideals of family life (Warin et al 1999; Hatten et al 2002). She states, of course, that there is nothing inherent about these characteristics, and indeed images of the 'new' caring, sharing father who changes nappies and experiences emotional intimacy with his child have abounded in the last decade or so. That men *can* 'mother' in this way is not disputed (see also Fineman 1995) and presumably this means also that women can 'father', but social and economic conditions and ideologies of motherhood, fatherhood and childhood conspire to make this type of degendered parental work difficult, reinforcing the virtual inevitability of the romanticised roles.

The idealised obligations and relationships of parenthood are also expressed in other, traditionally gendered, ways. Smart (1991), for example, observes the difference between 'caring for' children and 'caring about' them. Both law and parents tend to reward fathers for caring about their children, while mothers' caring for them is unremarkable, taken for granted and thus unrewarded. And so, separated mothers whose plans for children are based upon years of caring for them, often without direct paternal input, often find themselves characterised as selfish because fathers' expressions of care about the children are valued more highly than mothers' actions of caring for them.

Ribbens McCarthy et al (2000) also discern gender differences in how parents and step-parents internalise the moral imperative to 'take responsibility' for children in their care and put the needs of children first. While both mothers and fathers positioned themselves as moral agents in this way, and constructed children as *outside* moral agency (Ribbens McCarthy et al 2000 p 800), 'mens' moral tales, as biological or step-fathers, were often concerned with being a provider and also with authority' and some centred on ideas of providing guidance or a good role model. Women's moral tales of accepting responsibility focused on accepting what to them was the inescapable responsibility for children by creating a stable family environment for them, usually requiring considerable emotional work, mediation of relationships and organisational skills (Ribbens McCarthy et al 2000 p 793).

Whether we are considering romantic maternal or paternal connections with children, the expectations and duties that arise from the connection are certainly not negotiable; they remain unspoken and understood by parents and children alike. But modern conceptions of childhood and of individualisation may now be creating new ideas of motherhood and fatherhood.

Modern attachments

Individualised parent-child relationships can never be completely freely chosen and negotiated, of course, and so an unqualified form of the pure relationship cannot apply to them. But that is not to say that individualisation, equality and democracy have not made some ideological impression even upon these potentially most profound of familial relationships. As the new studies of childhood tell us, children, if not able to choose their parents, are at least capable of forming views about 'proper' parenthood, about the exercise of power in their family relationships, about the importance of openness and communication and about their demands for respect for their personhood. In Giddens' view of family democratisation children are included as equal individuals with important contributions to make to family decision-making (Giddens and Pierson 1998). There is some evidence not only that these demands and these ideas are resulting in changes to the way in which parents conceptualise their children, but also that they have affected men's and women's identities as parents.

Ribbens' (1995) study of mothers' images of children found that mothers expressed their child-rearing practices according to three main typifications of their children: children as natural innocents, children as little devils and children as small people. The first two categories of responses correspond to a romantic developmentalist view of children and the last corresponds to a late-modern view[10]. Although it was expressed by Ribbens' respondents the least frequently of her three typifications, and often was mixed with the other typifications, this last perspective assumes the child is an individual, their 'own person', worthy of respect as such (Ribbens 1995 p 66).

The implications for relationships of this late-modern perspective are considerable.

> '[T]here is less explicit ideology which lays down pre-determined guidelines as to how mothers and children should interact. This is because mother and child are construed as different individuals of equal standing, without reciprocal obligations centred on the dependency needs of childhood. ... There are less clear-cut implications for relationships within the family unit, since age status is not construed as the basis for hierarchy, either of power or dependency ... There is thus less scope for a guiding framework of beliefs about how older individuals in the household should respond to younger ones. Instead, there may be a focus on responding to the individual natures, (or "person"-alities), of those involved, with scope for

---

10   This view might also be said to correspond to a 'pre-modern' view of children in which they did not merit special treatment, but also had no legal or autonomous power. I am grateful for Christine Piper for this observation.

negotiations about how best to meet the needs/wishes of the different family members' (Ribbens 1995 p 72).

Individualising the child seemed to create a mother-child relationship that lacked the institutional framework of 'naturalness' and reciprocal, but predetermined, obligation. It created a type of negotiated relationship, or at least one where the rules were flexible, untried and untested. Importantly, it also seemed to create a 'new' image of mother.

'If we typify children as small people, we emphasise the significance of individuality regardless of age status, and can be correspondingly construed as freeing mothers from the obligations to meet those needs, providing more scope for their own individuality. If we typify children as *different*-from-adults, then mothers who pursue their own individual preferences may be described as "selfish", since they are perceived as failing to meet their obligations' (Ribbens 1995 p 74).

There is evidence also that fathers' views are changing. If motherhood is becoming more social, fatherhood may be becoming more 'naturalized'[11]. Recent evidence suggests that fathers' attitudes toward 'family life' and parenting are dominated by ambiguity and uncertainty and mean that many men are working fatherhood out as they go along: '[t]heir own experiences are not adequate or sufficient in many new types of situations which they face as fathers but which their own fathers were not confronted with' (Bjornberg 1995 p 34). The erosion of traditional patriarchy, traditional roles and traditional images of children mean that respect for all individuals in the family, negotiation and meeting emotional needs becomes work that all family members must do. Men are therefore developing different relationships with their children, and are doing so in different ways than their fathers did (Hatten et al 2002).

Empirical evidence confirms these views. Warin et al (1999) found that in addition to 'providing', the other part of a fathers' role was said by mothers, teenagers and fathers to be 'involvement' with his children. Fathers, in turn, recognised that they were expected to 'be there' for their children, even though they were often unable to define what that meant. In fact, none of the respondents was able to articulate what they meant by 'involvement' – it was simply something to be accomplished by the ideal father. Hatten et al (2002) also found that providing financially was important to fathers and

---

11   Ruddick (1997) suggests, for example, that men's natural procreativity offers a rich source for further study and exploration.

to the meaning of fatherhood, but that 'being there' for children was also crucial to being a good father. 'Being there' was undefined and unclear for their subjects as well. It ranged from spending 'quality time' with children, to being physically present in the home as much as possible, to simply being there to call upon in case of emergency (Hatten et al 2002 p 7–9).

Thus, it seems that parents and children alike tend to see mothers' and fathers' roles and identities differently, even while they aim for an egalitarian, negotiated ideal. These empirical studies provide some evidence of the resilience of the romantic parent-child relationship as well as of the challenge made to it by the late-modern one, and also provide evidence of an ideal child who straddles the romantic developmentalist and the late-modern individualist paradigms.

This normative or ideal childhood is also reflected in law as a duality in which the child embodies both the romanticised, dependent and unfinished project and the reflexive, autonomous, rights-and-responsibility-bearing individual (cf Neale and Smart 1997b; Day Sclater and Piper 2001). In the family law context, the tension is most clearly expressed by dual aims to protect children's welfare and their 'rights', or at least some form of autonomy, agency and intentionality. While there may not be an inherent conflict between these aims (see below and Diduck 1999a; Day-Sclater and Piper 2001; Smart and Neale 1999; Smart, Neale and Wade 2001; Lee 2001; Bainham 2002), law tends to express them as conflicted.

Law's children: the romantic developmentalist child and the paramountcy of welfare

Legislative attention (Children Act 1989; Adoption and Children Act 2002) to children's welfare evidences law's romantic developmentalist child, relationships for whom remain in the moral realm of care, love and connection rather than the legal realm of objective and free choice, even though it purports to provide 'objective' criteria by which welfare can be ascertained and measured (Children Act 1989 s 1(3); King and Piper 1995). In this way it corresponds to the romanticism of the traditional family in which parental altruism is assumed to protect children's vulnerability. It also corresponds to this model in its concern for the welfare of a paradigmatic child (Diduck 2000, Piper 1996; Day Sclater and Piper 2001) over the welfare of individualised children, and in its confidence that it knows what that child's welfare entails, despite part of children's welfare including their 'ascertainable wishes and feelings' (Children Act 1989 s 1(3)(a)) about a proposed course of action. In the paramountcy principle, there are, in other words, preordained, objective and authoritatively assessable duties owed to children.

Law has applied scientific truths about child development, socialisation, harm and risk (Kaganas 1999) to its 'desubjectified' child subject to paint a picture of that child's welfare. In that picture, harmonious, co-resident, biological parents are the ideal carers for children, but when the ideal is not achievable, it is to be approximated as closely as possible by the child's continued contact with non-resident parents (Cretney et al 2002 and cases cited therein; Eekelaar 2002).

These goals are met through formal[12] and informal[13] law when parents separate, and importantly also through less coercive means of informal regulation when they co-reside. Government has identified both parental conflict and parental absence as harmful to children (Advisory Group 2002), and has received public support for initiatives designed to promote goals of co-operative parenting. It has created a National Family and Parenting Institute, a National Parenting Helpline, and an expanded role for health visitors and schools in providing 'parenting education' (Home Office 1999 p 8–13). It intends to provide education about counselling to parents and children so they will seek help in conflict management and relationship support (Advisory Group 2002). Apart from living in an intact marriage and 'managing' conflict, however, there is little indication of what co-parenting or co-operation means. On the normative level, it means parents 'being there' for their children and acting selflessly, rationally and in harmony when taking decisions about their children's upbringing. It reflects, yet abstracts, the day-to-day care of children, including managing meals, bedtimes, finances, employment and childcare and masks the gender dimensions of the experience of parenting.

As was the case with marriage and divorce, responsibility for achieving the welfare ideal is meant to be internalised by the parties, so that any difficulties they may encounter are regarded as personal deficiencies. Even after they separate, parents are expected to subsume their own interests, needs and rights to the welfare of their children and to be 'reasonable'

---

12   See *Re D (Care: Natural Parent Presumption)* [1999] 1 FLR 134; *Re M* [1996] 2 FLR 441; *Re L, V, M and H (Contact: Domestic Violence)* [2000] 2 FLR 334.

13   By informal law I mean mediated agreements (see Chapter 5 and Bailey-Harris 1999).

(King 1999; Neale and Smart 1997a) in negotiating the details of the co-parenting arrangements that law has already decided is in their children's welfare. There are problems with this expectation. First, it denies parents any legitimate expression of their own individual needs or rights (Reece 1996) and assumes that their only individual responsibilities are to their children (and thus to safeguarding the post-divorce family). It thus denies adults expression of any ethic of care of *self* (Ribbens McCarthy et al 2000 p 800).

Secondly, it imposes upon mothers and fathers, who may not have desired or experienced it before separation (Smart 1999 and Neale and Smart 1997b), the duty to achieve a particular style of child-rearing after separation. It also disregards the possibility that, even if they had achieved some sort of satisfactory accommodation before separation, many may find it impossible to continue it after, when separation has meant the loss of the former 'joint project'. Smart observes that on divorce the co-parenting ideal means, for example,

'[t]he father must become a "proper" father for which he may be ill equipped. But if he tries, he must encroach on the sphere of mothering which was his wife's main source of self-respect and purpose – as well as an important site of emotional satisfaction. If she is to remain a "good mother", she will relinquish her special place in relation to the children' (Smart 1999 p 112).

Thus, parenting arrangements that may have 'worked' – at least to the extent that they sustained the 'good parent' myths – during the relationship are no longer adequate when measured by law. Finally, the welfare imperative demands a form of idealised parenting that depends upon, yet fails to provide, institutional structures and cultural resources that would facilitate it (Smart 1999).

Welfare and wishes and feelings

Law does take account of the wishes and feelings of children, and in this way does recognise a 'person'-ality in them. But, locating the importance of their wishes and feelings in the welfare discourse means not only that they can be 'trumped' by welfare, but that wishes and feelings are heard, and filtered, through that discourse (Day Sclater and Piper 2001). Whether it is by courts or welfare professionals such as family and children reporters (formerly court welfare officers), the weight attached to those wishes and feelings when they are solicited also depends upon adult constructions of children's degrees of competency and understanding, which are in turn linked to their welfare[14]. This tends to mean that a child's wishes and feelings are more likely to be respected if they conform to adult (and universal normative rather than individualised) ideas of welfare and suggests that law here takes the romantic developmentalist view of its child.

The discourse of family autonomy and privacy, itself a part of the traditional romantic family, also conspires against listening to the children's wishes and feelings. While children are undoubtedly part of families, if parents choose to exclude them from consultations, the law can do nothing about it despite its claim to value their views. Where parents agree arrangements for children after divorce, for example, the non-intervention principle, an important link between family privacy and welfare, means courts usually investigate neither the wishes and feelings of the children about those arrangements (Douglas et al 2001), nor whether they promote the children's welfare at all (Bailey-Harris 1999). When the arrangements are disputed but proceed to mediation, mediators rarely seek to ascertain children's wishes and feelings (Piper 1999; Day Sclater and Piper 2001; and see Chapter 5). Where residence or contact matters become the subject of litigation, judges have a discretion to consult the children directly but they do so only rarely (Piper 1999; Douglas et al 2001; Day Sclater and Piper 2001; Freeman 2001), and solicitors representing parents rarely seek to ascertain the child's wishes and feelings. They do not ask the parents about what their children may want; they tend to assume the parental view is self-interested (Diduck 1999a; 2000), and they do not ask the children directly, believing that to do so would be to place the children in an invidious position contrary to their welfare (Diduck 2000; Piper 1999; Day Sclater and Piper 2001; Douglas et al 2001). Children are in this way seen to be universalised objects of parental or other adult concern.

The usual way for children's wishes and feelings to be heard is through the children and family reporter, who is obliged to interview all people she or he considers relevant, notify the child of the contents of the report as she or he considers appropriate to the age and understanding of the child, and to consider whether it would be in the child's interests to be made a party to the proceedings (Family Proceedings Amendment Rules (2001)). Indeed, the creation of the Children and Family Court Advisory and Support Services

14 See, for example, *Re M, T, P, K and B (Change of Name)* [2000] 2 FLR 645.

(CAFCASS) was intended to concentrate focus in family proceedings upon children, but difficulties with the reporters' engagement with children may not have been 'solved' by the new service.

While CAFCASS may result in more children than previously being seen by child and family reporters[15] we must remember that these professionals work within the same welfare and child-saving discourses that militate against them taking children's views seriously (Piper 1999). Trinder (1997) found, for example, that welfare professionals engaging with children tended to categorise them according to one of two approaches:

> 'children are classified as either subjects or objects, competent or incompetent, reliable or unreliable, harmed by decision-making or harmed by exclusion, wanting to participate or wanting not to participate. The various adult perspectives on hearing "the child's voice" were based on idealized and stabilized conceptions of childhoods, with no distinction between "children" as living beings and "childhood" as a shifting set of ideas' (Trinder 1997 p 301).

It seems, therefore, that even those who are trained specifically to 'listen' to children operate within the dichotomy that expresses law's ideal child.

Finally, there is a presumption that in most cases the child's interests will be sufficiently safeguarded by the children and family reporter, and separate representation or separate party status for the child is seen as an exceptional measure (Sawyer 1999; Freeman 2001; CAFCASS Practice Note 2001). Although the Children Act provides for circumstances where children can initiate their own applications, circumstances where leave is given to them to do so have been narrowly construed (Roche 1999; Freeman 2001).

Autonomous children – no room for welfare?

The above examples of family law's engagement with children and their parents illustrate a legal conception of childhood that rests in the 'child as becoming' or romantic developmentalist paradigm and represents an important part of the normative child of law. The other part of the legal child in late-modernity, however, is the one that recognises his or her autonomy as a rights-bearing, reflective and reflexive legal and moral subject. The

---

15   In contrast to family court welfare officers, who saw children less than half the time (Piper 1999; see also James and James 1999).

Gillick decision[16] was perhaps the watershed that consolidated and legitimated this view, and it, along with the UN Convention on the Rights of the Child, the very creation of CAFCASS, recent changes to conceptualisations of children in criminal law (see, for example, Piper and Day Sclater 2001; Fionda 2001; Vaughan 2000) and changes to procedures for children giving evidence in court (Lee 2001), demonstrate a commitment on some level by law and legal institutions to create a child subject who bears some degree of legal and social subjectivity. In other words, there are images of autonomous and responsible children from which law can and does draw to invest children with the capacity for social and legal agency (Day Sclater and Piper 2001). While it may appear that these images conflict directly with the romantic child, the conflict is managed by law in order to constitute almost a 'hybrid' child who embodies that which law and policy consider to be the best of both worlds. In other words, law's autonomous child exists, but only on law's terms.

Law tells parents and children, for example, that contact with a non-resident parent is the *right* of the child[17], but only enables that right to be exercised meaningfully with the aim of furthering already established ideas of welfare. It tells young offenders and their parents that children are legally responsible for their anti-social behaviour from the age of ten (or younger in the case of a Child Safety Order – see Piper 1999; Fionda 2001), but does so in a punitive, moralising way that also incorporates ideas of family or parental failure; and it tells children that their wishes and feelings are important to decisions made about their care but attends to those wishes and feelings only when they correspond to preconceived ideas of welfare.

The issue of a child's contact with his or her non-resident parent after separation is a good example of the ambiguities I have asserted thus far. The presumption that contact is in the interests of the child, even where there is a history of violence in the relationship, is difficult to displace[18]. The presumption relies upon beliefs in the importance of parental role models; importing Parsonian ideas of socialisation, it creates the norm of the good mother who cares immediately for her children but who encourages and

---

16   *Gillick v West Norfolk and Wisbech Area Health Authority* [1986] AC 112; [1985] 3 All ER 402.

17   *M v M (Child: Access)* [1973] 2 All ER 81; *Re R (A Minor) (Contact)* [1993] 2 FLR 762; *Re W (A Minor) (Contact)* [1994] 2 FLR 441.

18   See, for example, *Re L, V, M and H (Contact: Domestic Violence)* [2000] 2 FLR 334 and Kaganas (2000).

facilitates contact with the absent but caring father, of the good father who cares about and distantly provides for his children and of the good child who is able to rely upon these relationships with parents differently. It also, however, imports ideas of rationality and individual responsibility into its subjects. Parents are encouraged to 'choose' and to negotiate this ideal, and increasingly they are also encouraged to include children in the process.

The Lord Chancellor's Department's report 'Making Contact Work' (2002) illustrates this ambivalence (Diduck and Kaganas 2002). It refers throughout to the paramountcy of the child's welfare in contact cases and recommends ways in which that welfare is best to be promoted and protected, but some of these methods identify the child him or herself as a crucial player in the process rather than merely as the object of concern. Not only, for example, are parents to be educated and informed so that they can communicate with each other and with their children so as to make rational decisions about their child's welfare, children are also to be educated, advised, consulted, informed and listened to about contact with their parents. Respondents, members of all disciplines working within the family justice system and members of post-divorce families themselves, were asked, for example, whether children should have access to 'age-appropriate information' and whether they should be given 'advice about their rights and about how they can make their voices heard in any dispute between their parents' (LCD 2002 para 4.1). Almost all answered in the affirmative (LCD 2002 para 4.3). CAFCASS was thought to be the best provider of that information (LCD 2002 para 6.12), which, it was thought, ought to include advice on practical strategies to manage problems arising in relation to contact (LCD 2002 para 3.22). It was recommended that children be told that contact can be difficult and be encouraged to talk to parents about their views (LCD 2002 para 4.5).

The image of the children with whom this document is concerned is one of children who are fragile and in need of protection but who are also potential actors, participants in the ongoing negotiations about contact. These children have not only an interest in the way post-divorce family life is organised, but also some responsibility for it. Children *and* their parents must internalise the normative message that contact is desirable and good for them and that they are responsible for achieving this 'good' so as to ensure that the post-separation family functions as it should. Not only do we see, therefore, images of 'good' post-separation mothers and fathers as both traditional and modern, we also see in this document a particular image of the 'good' post-separation child as both. He or she is vulnerable and in need of protection, but also embodies the potential to disrupt the normative post-separation family by his or her resistance to contact. Information and consultation is not only necessary to protect children's best interests, it is important to secure their co-operation (Diduck and Kaganas 2002).

There is an air of familiarity about this proposed treatment of children and their parents. Like the divorce reform proposed and then abandoned in the Family Law Act 1996, these proposals treat children and their parents as rational actors who simply must be sufficiently educated in order to appreciate their welfare and exercise their rights and choices responsibly. Despite its clear support for the paramountcy of welfare, it seems also to be important in this document not to subsume children into their parents and to recognise their individuality, partly as a way of protecting them, but also perhaps to create in them and their parents some sense of individual responsibility for maintaining a social project that is also expressed in other policies. Mandatory citizenship classes are now a part of the national curriculum, and the government's vision for a new strategy for children and young people includes giving children 'the chance to contribute to their local communities – feeling heard and being valued as responsible citizens – shaping their lives and their futures' even though it still wishes to give them 'the opportunity to grow up in a loving, stable environment' defined as 'families' – 'the foundation of society' (Childright 2002 p 3).

Finally, the Joint Select Committee on Human Rights in 2002 became the first parliamentary committee to take evidence from individual children. The chair indicated that the committee was anxious to hear what children had to say about human rights in the UK, particularly their evidence on the case for a commissioner for children's rights (HC Press Release 30 May 2002). We may, therefore, be witnessing a shift in the discourse of childhood generally, which corresponds with the recent political imperative to create 'active citizens' of us all (Vaughan 2000).

Suggestions that the attention paid by family law to children as individuals is 'mere rhetoric' because the welfare and 'children as becoming' discourses are so powerful may miss an important ideological message. While the 'children as becoming' framework is dominant and its power resides in romantic notions of families and childhood that we are unable to live without, we are also witnessing the emergence of a powerful discourse of individualisation, rights and democracy. We may, in other words, be witnessing the beginning of a paradigm shift, or at least a paradigm muddle, in which competing sociological and historical ideals are affecting the legal and the social worlds.

Family practices

The current focus of research and policy on children may be part of a politicised problematisation of *families* (Collier 2001b), and we must examine closely the effects of that problematisation on families themselves. Despite, for example, emphasis on the ideals of the 'new man', his cosy intentions, increased focus on 'family' and his struggle with the ideals of heterosexual masculinity played out in the public and private spheres, it is to his family practices that we must look to see if fatherhood has indeed changed. In other words, masculinity is not 'a thing-in-itself'(Collier 2001b p 539); gender and the role it plays in constructing identities is not something that floats free from that which men and women do (Collier 2001b p 538). The same can be said for ideals of childhood. How closely do those ideals reflect individuals' daily lives of *being* a child or a parent?

Few children would want either complete autonomy or complete dependence in their family relationships (Smart, Neale and Wade 2001) and few parents could claim always to promote either individuality and democracy or status-based hierarchy in family decision-making. In a way, the successful give-and-take that characterises our family practices represents the ideal relationships of the families we live by. Where, for example, both parents enter into parenthood with the idea of sharing childcare responsibility equally – living the co-parenting ideal – most settle into what has become the 'typical' pattern, where mothers gave up employment to become primary caretakers and fathers take less day-to-day responsibility for children (Hatten et al 2002). The 'work' of child-rearing is more than the physical labour involved, however, and on this level, too, that work is differentiated by gender. The important point is that this way of organising family practices is not intrinsically problematic for parents; fathers do not have to do equal amounts of caring in order to be regarded as 'good' fathers (Neale and Smart 1999 p 47–48); 'being there' for their children could include that which Ruddick calls 'distant provision' (Ruddick 1997 p 48) or what Smart might characterise as 'caring about' (1991). In Smart, Neale and Wade's study, '[b]asically fathers were one step removed from their children and their relationship with them was sustained via their relationship with the mother' (Smart, Neale and Wade 2001 p 47). Bjornberg (1995) also reports that often the time spent by men with their children is spent in play rather than in organising day-to-day matters, and Hatten et al (2002) also report parental satisfaction with a gender-based division of childcare work. These families demonstrate an ability to combine respect for individuality and for the traditional collective enterprise. Sometimes, however, the ideal was more difficult to sustain.

Neale and Smart's (1999) research with parents demonstrates that while many family members were successful in reconciling tensions to sustain the myth of their ideal family, many could not do so. Some mothers in the study, for example, did express disappointment with the fact that their partners did little of the physical work of childcare, especially after what they termed a 'promising start' of equality, while others were satisfied with the division of physical labour, but felt that fathers 'rarely seemed to be "in tune" with the children or that they did not notice or anticipate emotional states' (Neale and Smart 1999 p 49)[19]. They quote one mother:

'I think I had this vision of the new man that I'm now very sceptical of. Although they may wash up, they don't see the thousand and one other things that need doing. I remember we once had a big argument because I'd been out at college all day and it was half-term and I came home and he was very upset that I didn't say "Thank you" for looking after the children. I couldn't get across to him that I didn't see why I should. I said "You don't say Thank you to me every day for the work that I do"' (Neale and Smart 1999 p 50).

Women's double burden and the difficulty they have in reconciling their identities as workers and mothers has been well documented. But fathers also express frustration with their inability to reconcile the role of new father with that of traditional father (Warin et al 1999; Hatten et al 2002; O'Brien and Shemilt 2003). Their inability to define the details of 'involvement' with their children, for example, means that many simply felt a gap between the dual (and competing) ideals and the lived experience of fathering.

Children's subjective experience also mirrors both halves of the ideal; they speak of parenting as a central experience in their lives in which they participate with mum and/or dad, but they also make a distinction between the type of care that is provided by mothers and fathers (James 1999 p 190).

---

19   This may be part of the traditional masculine view that sustaining intimacy and being emotionally attuned to others is family 'work' usually left to women (Duncombe and Marsden 1993).

Citing Morrow's (1998) study, James states 'mothers are often seen as the parent who is the main source of physical and emotional care … fathers may be seen as caring through their adoption of a more task-oriented stance towards their children – as someone to do things with' (James 1999 p 192; see also Smart and Neale 1999 p 60).

Because children's reports also emphasise their agency in the parent-child relationship, they also represent an important attempt to sustain the late-modern part of the ideal. Children, for example, often take the lead in forging relationships with non-resident parents and in caring for and supporting their parents and they do not regard this activity as onerous or anxiety-laden (Smart, Neale and Wade 2001 p 71–75). Rather, they 'regarded it as an everyday family practice and expression of relatedness' (Smart, Neale and Wade 2001 p 75). Where they could influence decision-making, children exercised a moral agency based upon ethics of fairness, care and respect for all members of the family (Smart, Neale and Wade 2001 p 103) and often expressed disappointment when not offered the opportunity to participate in family decisions. Children did not always want to be responsible for decision-making, but they were equally clear that they wanted the opportunity to decide this for themselves. They simply wanted a voice (Smart, Neale and Wade 2001 p 122). In general, children seem to work hard to sustain close and mutually respectful relationships with both parents, and while they may have different expectations of their mothers and fathers in meeting this goal, their attempts to negotiate conflicting ideals of their parents and of autonomy and dependence are clear, if not always successful.

It seems then that family practices can accommodate the normative family *up to a point*. 'While there is an ongoing joint project individuals are often prepared to put up with quite jarring incongruencies in order to sustain their emotional and ethical investment in a joint past and a joint future' (Smart and Neale 1999 p 70), but in the absence of that project, strategies designed to sustain the myth of the ideal mother, father or child may cease to be desired or desirable. The families we live by, those that include dual images of the child as individual and not-yet-individual, and images of mothers and fathers who are both socially and naturally connected to their children, are difficult to sustain, particularly when structural conditions militate against them (Hatten et al 2002; O'Brien and Shemilt 2003) and laws so polarise them.

Conclusions

It is important in any society committed to liberal principles of equality, justice, fairness and the rule of law, that the rights and autonomy of all of its members are respected. Equally, domestic legislation and the UN Convention on the Rights of the Child proclaim that children's welfare ought to be promoted. This slippage between unreconstructed ideas of rights and welfare can be problematic for individual interpretations of justice for families. In determining the residence of and contact with children after separation or divorce, for example, fathers wanted 'measurable objectivity', a 'rational rule-bound approach to measuring welfare' (Smart and Neale 1999 p 168), while mothers focused more upon responsibilities than upon measurable rights (Smart and Neale 1999 p 171). Further, both parents articulated fathers' relationships with their children in a language of rights (either the father's or the children's) while mothers' relationships were described in a language of care or responsibility (Smart and Neale 1999 p 166). Studies of this type suggest that too often, neither (usually) mothers' voices of immediacy and care/responsibility nor (usually) fathers' of distance and rights, are satisfactorily accommodated in a law that appears to value both.

It is also important in a society in which individual and social responsibility are expressed by the making of responsible choices that all are imbued with the capacity to do so. The 'rhetoric' of children's agency and individuality encompassed in ratification of the UN Convention on the Rights of the Child and in the government's strategy for young people, the policy attention paid to their wishes and feelings and recent concerns to consult and include them in family decision-making and parliamentary procedure, all testify to a commitment to include children in this ideal.

Law thus operates within both a 'children as becoming' paradigm and a 'children as being' paradigm. In both, families are key to addressing a 'social problem' of childhood, and the duality allows responsibility for it to be attributed both to children and to parents. So the 'problems' of youth crime and of underachieving 'socially excluded' children require official attention to parents and parenting, but also to imbuing a sense of individual responsibility in children themselves. Maintaining the responsible post-divorce family is the responsibility of parents upon being adequately educated and informed about their children's welfare, but it is also up to the children themselves to choose this form of family. Further, making claims to acknowledge children's participatory rights, rather than merely their rights to protection, means that the onus can then fall upon children themselves actively to make rights claims and to participate in the project of citizenship, and shift much of the responsibility for life choices and the making and taking of opportunities to them from the structural conditions that may otherwise direct or restrict them (Brannen 1999).

Law's part in sustaining the myth of family democracy is vital, therefore, but so also is its part in sustaining the myth of the romantic family in which we have invested so much. By empowering children *on terms,* law sustains its image of the paradoxical normative family. Empowering children otherwise (Sawyer 1999), or ignoring them altogether, would each entail a reconstruction of the family, the individual and the 'good' society within the legal imagination that belies its dualistic ideal.

Law's dualistic ideal remains rooted, however, in competing rather than integrated narratives of welfare and rights. While aiming to respect both, it tends still to conceptualise these discourses as mutually exclusive so that children and their parents sometimes come to law as autonomous, rights-bearing subjects and other times as a unit over which the irrationality of love and welfare prevail. It has yet to accommodate a childhood subjectivity and a parent-child relationship that integrate these discourses. Importantly, it is research conducted by the 'new' childhood theorists that demonstrates that such an integration is precisely how children themselves experience family life. When children engage with the legal process, for example, they claim and assert agency in the same way they do in their everyday family practices: they neither want complete autonomy in decision-making nor to be treated as objects (Trinder 1997; Smart, Neale and Wade 2001; Bretherington 2002). They seem to be frustrated by the disconnection of welfare from rights and autonomy from dependence. To them, agency does not equate unequivocally and immediately with autonomy nor welfare with dependence. They appear to be trying to articulate a subjectivity that can accommodate dependence and independence, but to be frustrated by idealised legal and social visions that try to force together the neo-liberal ideas of autonomy, connection and developmentalism within which they are constrained (Douglas et al 2001; Bretherington 2002; Smart and Neale 1999; Smart, Neale and Wade 2001; Trinder 1997).

We have not yet grasped the opportunity to achieve a nuanced view of rights and welfare for which the families we live with may be struggling – Smart, Neale and Wade call it 'citizenship-in-context' (Smart, Neale and Wade 2001 p 122) and Lee (2001), dependent agency for all 'human becomings'. It is, perhaps, in this way that law's ideal child fails individual children and their carers most acutely. Taking genuine account of children's family practices, however, may help us to collapse the dichotomy and destabilise the polarised ideals, not only of childhood, but also of other normative constructs on which childhood depends, such as the responsible mother, father or family.

Chapter 5

The mediation revolution

The 'stories' of private family law that I have told so far reveal a variety of themes, including privatisation, co-operation, responsibility, rights and welfare, and I have argued that there is a coherence beneath the apparent disparity of these themes. That which has been described as perhaps the 'main "story" of private family law over the past two decades' (Davis et al 2000 p 1), also reveals this coherent disparity. Mediation has become the officially sanctioned method of resolving family disputes when adult partners separate, and in the light of the themes identified above, its revolutionary impact is not surprising: mediation represents private, co-operative decision-making by responsible equals concerned to promote the welfare of children and families. It is about reasonableness, compromise and maintaining, indeed, ideally strengthening, enduring obligations and familial relationships through the development of enhanced communication and communication skills. Most importantly, it is about an individual's personal responsibility for doing just this.

The principles and practice of mediation are ideal for the normative twenty-first-century family. They confine disputes, conflicts and problems within a private arena and rather than decisions about obligations and norms being imposed upon families by an authoritative decision-maker based upon preordained abstract principles, the parties appear to be left to negotiate and allocate responsibilities according to their individual needs and circumstances. Yet party autonomy is not exercised too freely, however, as a clear set of normative guidelines exists to steer their negotiations in the 'correct' direction toward the separate but continuing family.

Mediation is extra-legal in the traditional sense and so is ideally placed to deal with emotional, irrational, intimate conflict, but it resides firmly within the legal process so as to formalise and legitimise both the processing and outcome of that conflict. If, as Luhmann says, love only understands the language of love, mediation may be one way in which law can manage legitimately the irrationality of intimate attachments and detachments.

There are three stories of mediation that I wish to present in this chapter. The first is the official story told by mediators and government policy-makers, which constructs mediation as the 'civilizer' of family disputes. The second is the unofficial, more subversive story that reveals issues of power and manipulation in the privatisation agenda behind the official version. The third is the story told by users of mediation services, those men, women and children who have tried to integrate the mediation ideal into their everyday familial lives. By examining these three stories together I hope to demonstrate that in this area of family law *process or procedure*, just as in the more doctrinal or substantive areas of divorce and child welfare, and in the more culturally or socially regulated areas of commitment and marriage, there is a dualistic normative family at the heart of the family we, and particularly law, live by.

From reconciliation to conciliation to mediation

'Mediation is a form of intervention in which a third party – the mediator – assists the parties to a dispute to negotiate over the issues which divide them. The mediator has no stake in the dispute, and is not identified with any of the competing interests involved. The mediator has no power to impose a settlement on the parties, who retain authority for making their own decisions' (Roberts 1997 p 4).

This rather clinical definition of mediation was offered in 1997 by a leading practitioner of family mediation. While it provides basic descriptions of the scheme and role of the mediator, it does not capture fully the premises underlying mediation which have been described elsewhere as follows:

'that family disputes should be approached in a spirit of restraint rather than antagonism; that those in dispute should retain responsibility for decision-making rather than surrendering this to third parties; that there are advantages in informality of process; that the focus of third-party intervention should be upon relationships rather than specific issues and vice versa; that outcomes should be founded in agreement and compromise rather than coercion; that the handling of disputes should be taken out of the hands of specialists; that there should be a move from state ordering to private ordering, from a legal to a non-legal world' (Roberts 1983 p 538).

'Official' policy on family mediation captures both the detached objectivity of the first definition and the sentimental spirit of the second, from the government's original proposals in 1995 to promote the widespread use of family mediation to the information for the public published on a government web page in 2002:

'Family mediation is a process in which an impartial third person, the mediator, assists couples considering separation or divorce to meet together to deal with the arrangements which need to be made for the future. ... Mediators are trained to help couples talk about what they each want for the future and to focus on protecting the best interests of their children, even when talking together may be difficult and painful because they are hurt, angry and confused' (Lord Chancellor's Department 1995 p 37–38);

and:

'When you divorce or separate, it is generally better if both of you can sort out together the practical arrangements for the future. The aim of mediation is to help you to find a solution that meets the needs of all of you, especially those of your children, and that you both feel is fair. At the end of mediation, you should feel that there is no "winner" or "loser" but that together you have arrived at sensible, workable arrangements. Mediation can help to reduce tension, hostility and misunderstandings and so improve communication between you' (Lord Chancellor's Department website April 2002).

These views of mediation, coupled with its depiction as a 'civilised and civilising procedure' (Walker et al 1994 p 1) present mediation as the desirable outcome of progress in the development of family law over the years. The idea of evolution from 'primitive' adversarialism to 'enlightened' co-operation in family decision-making resonates with ideas of social progress from the tyranny of authoritarianism to the freedom of social and familial democracy. But this vision of mediation is different from that advanced by law and policy in mediation's early days. Divorce mediation as a legal process was born in policy to promote the reconciliation of separating spouses (Eekelaar and Dingwall 1988)[1].

It was not until 1971 that some separation of the concepts of reconciliation and conciliation was made. In that year, the President of the Family Division of the High Court issued a practice direction providing for courts to refer contested cases to probation officers for 'conciliation' where it 'might assist the parties to resolve the issues or any part of them by agreement' (Eekelaar and Dingwall 1988 p 12). As Eekelaar and Dingwall note, this provision did not have any significant effect on divorce practice, but may have been the precursor to the Finer Report on One Parent Families (1974) which began to change thinking about the practice and the effects of divorcing.

Since the 1970s the value of conciliation (as mediation was then known) – 'assisting the parties to deal with the consequences of the established breakdown of their marriage' (Finer 1974 para 4.288) – has become accepted wisdom among family law policy-makers and attention has thus shifted from marriage-saving to facilitating the settlement of matrimonial disputes with a minimum of conflict. While marriage-saving remains on the agenda (see Chapter 3), it is now acknowledged that some marriages cannot be saved, but that a version of the ideal family that marriage represents can be continued nonetheless. Mediation is now seen as the best way to achieve this post-divorce family.

In the 1970s and 1980s, conciliation was also a way of adjusting to new conceptions of marriage (Eekelaar and Dingwall 1988 p 15) and divorce. Changes in social work, education and in the moral environment of social work practice in the 1980s meant that the marriage relationship began to be understood differently; a simple marriage-saving or child-saving agenda was no longer appropriate for the practitioners who provided mediation services. They realised they had to provide a modern service designed for 'pure' relationships:

> 'Marriage [became] defined as a relationship which exists purely for the benefit of the spouses involved. If that benefit ceases, then it is not a matter for public concern. All that should be offered is a service to facilitate dispute resolution by helping the parties to identify the sources of conflict and providing an arena where violent emotions can be restrained in the interests of negotiation' (Eekelaar and Dingwall 1988 p 16).

---

1   On the history of mediation in England and Wales, see also *Newcastle Conciliation Project Report* 1989.

The mediation movement begun at this time became stronger in the 1990s. Its current form is said to have been built on the twin pillars of cost reduction and child welfare (Davis et al 2000 p 53). Proponents of mediation relied most strongly on arguments focusing on the welfare of children and harnessed the enthusiasm of divorce court welfare officers to instil in official policy and in the public the 'common sense' that children are the innocent victims of divorce (Piper 1996a). The White Paper on which FLA 1996 was based made its recommendations in favour of mediation on this assumption (Lord Chancellor's Department 1995 para 5.15 and 5.17). It relied upon research conducted in the UK and USA[2] to conclude that 'conflict is harmful to children and the Government is of the view that reduction of conflict should be high on the list of objectives for a good divorce process' (Lord Chancellor's Department 1995 para 5.16). 'The truth that conflict is harmful to children [was] extended to the idea that the legal process itself is harmful to children' (Piper 1996b p 73), so the consultation document that preceded the White Paper listed several advantages of mediation *in contrast to* litigation and to negotiated settlements concluded between legal representatives: 'Marriage breakdown and divorce are ... intimate processes, and negotiating at arm's length through lawyers can result in misunderstandings and reduction in communication between the spouses' (Lord Chancellor's Department 1995 para 5.18). And so, the pilot research conducted on the information meetings required in Part II of the FLA 1996 (see Chapter 3) was also designed to test their effectiveness in diverting people from solicitors and the formal legal process to mediators and the informal process. By adopting the child welfare rhetoric, the dichotomy between solicitors' legalism and mediators' welfarism was formalised.

The other incentive for government to promote mediation was financial. As the cost of legal aid provision for family matters increased through the 1970s and 1990s, reducing public expenditure became a primary motivator in the movement toward mediation. The government was convinced in 1995 that family mediation was more cost-effective than either negotiating at arm's length between solicitors or litigating through the courts. In reaching this conclusion it relied upon evidence presented primarily by mediation services (Lord Chancellor's Department 1995 para 5.19–5.20; Piper 1996b p 64–65). Since then, it has not fundamentally changed this

---

2   See, for example, Wallerstein and Kelly (1980); Richards (1982); and Cockett and Tripp (1996).

view (Legal Services Commission 2002), even in the light of research results reported in 2000 that concluded:

> 'Mediation may prove to be a cost-effective option in resolving some
> disputes, at a particular point. It can only achieve this where both
> parties commit themselves to the process. In other circumstances
> mediation is likely to prove an additional cost. This will apply where
> there is failure of engagement by one or both parties, or where no
> agreement is reached' (Davis et al 2000 p xvii para 31.3).

These political imperatives, coupled with changes in the law of divorce (see
Chapter 3 and MCA 1973), made it clear that the authority of the divorce
court judge, pronouncing upon the fault and obligations of the marital
partners, was out of touch with modern ideas of relationships as individual,
negotiable and fluid. These relationships required a form of justice that
was efficient, private and personal. Formal law relies upon precedent and
agreed norms; justice is based upon objective assessment of absolute values.
Private ordering, on the other hand, allows for a different kind of justice,
one that can be personalised and individualised to suit the parties and their
subjective disputes. Yet in this modern idea we also see remnants of tradition in the way family matters are set firmly within the private side of the
liberal divide. This positioning of the 'family' renders it particularly suited
for mediation's (non-)regulation.

Mediation's personalised justice strengthens the privacy of the traditional
family and the reflexivity of the modern family in which the individuals
themselves remain free to determine the course their relationships will
take by their continual reflection upon, and negotiation of, its terms. It confirms the idea of personal autonomy and individual and parental responsibility (Piper 1993) in which individuals are deemed to know best what is
in their own interests, and parents to know best what is in the interests of
their children. It is thought to be the best way in which the parties can take
responsibility for the break-up of their marriage and for the arrangements
they make afterwards. Relationship breakdown is thus confirmed as a personal matter, responsibility for which the parties must 'own'. They must
also 'own' decisions about arrangements after separation, as they reflect
upon them and remake them from time to time utilising the communication skills they have learned in their mediation sessions.

Principles and premises of mediation

From a clinical perspective, mediation begins with the assumption that the parties are competent to define the issues facing them, discuss them rationally and ultimately agree them (Roberts 1997 p 8). Mediators are not to regard parties as clients or objects of assistance, but rather as 'subjects of rights' (Roberts 1997 p 12). Any emotional trauma or 'preoccupation with one's own troubles' is deemed to have no effect upon this presumed competence. Mediation thus assumes in separating partners a rights-based rationality even at times of acute stress or distress. In some ways the assumption of rationality is ironic, since it is the presumed irrationality of the familial relationship that is said to demand the extra-legal method of mediation in the first place.

Individual autonomy, competence and rationality are at home within the normative family and thus provide political support for mediation, but these family attributes also provide psychological support for it. Day Sclater's (1999a and b) research suggests that the idealisation of the rational divorce may represent a psychological strategy for survival at both the individual and social levels (also see Chapter 3). For the individual, mediation promises that conflict and the dangerous and destructive emotions at its root can be avoided. The fear of conflict, its association with litigation and the consequent idealisation of mediation over formal law is then justified in terms of the welfare discourse, where dangerous parental emotions can be removed from consideration of children's interests. At the social level, in a social and political context of individual responsibility which 'promotes an ideology of rationality and self-control', emotions 'become recast as "feelings" which are seen as manageable' (Day Sclater 1999b p 179). 'Discourses of co-operation deny the psychological impossibilities of compromise, and the ideal of the harmonious divorce sustains our fantasies both that human emotions are controllable and that all is well with the "family"' (Day Sclater 1999b p 180).

> 'Cooperative dispute resolution procedures cannot deal with the emotions of divorce any more than the old adversarial ones could, but they can be seen as a means, typical in late modernity, of imposing prescriptions for behaviour which foreground our rationality at the expense of our emotions. The welfare discourses serve to sever the chaotic and destructive parts of ourselves from the rational and 'civilised' parts, with the former being driven underground, into the

realm of the pathological (as when conflict [or litigation?] is regarded as dangerous, abnormal and avoidable)' (Day Sclater 1999b p 180).

Related to the parties' rationality and competence is the focus of the mediation exercise itself. Mediation looks to the future rather than the past: parties must be steered by the mediator away from the 'minefield of the past' (Roberts 1997 p 13) toward the rationality of the future. 'The facts of the past cannot be negotiated over, they can only be adjudicated' (Roberts 1997 p 13). In contrast, litigation and judicial decisions are based on past experiences; both the doctrine of precedent and the rules of evidence rely upon the interpretation of past events. We have seen (Chapter 3) that a reconstruction of the past is crucial to a party's sense of self and to making sense of the end of a relationship, and might therefore surmise that this psychological 'work' is important to parties' abilities to construct a vision of their future. The White Paper on which FLA 1996 was based acknowledged the importance of this psychological work by reporting that mediation could encourage couples to 'accept responsibility for the ending of marriage; ... deal with feelings of hurt and anger; [and] address issues which may impede their ability to negotiate settlements amicably' (Lord Chancellor's Department 1995 para 5.4). While it is arguable that neither mediation nor litigation facilitates this process in an entirely satisfactory way, mediation's failed promise to acknowledge the psychological importance of reconstructing the past leaves little, if any, room for law's recognition of fluid, contingent and gendered subjectivities (see Chapter 3).

Mediation professionals agree that to be effective it must be voluntarily undertaken (Roberts 1997 p 7). They assume the rational free will of their subjects and thus legitimise the authority of consensual over normative obligations. Mandatory mediation was agreed by the government as unlikely to be successful and to be potentially counterproductive (Law Commission 1990 para 5.34), but it concluded that mediation ought to be *encouraged* as part of the divorce process (Lord Chancellor's Department 1995 para 5.14) and so designed educational and financial incentives to this end (see below). Like the divorcing individual of FLA 1996, the free-willed mediating individual thus became subject to a form of regulation of his or her responsible choices.

The voluntary and co-operative nature of mediation includes the premise that the parties must be willing and able to communicate openly and honestly, and so unqualified disclosure is important for successful mediation. It follows that friendship, trust and the pursuit of mutual interests are key concepts in mediation (Walker 2001 p 402; Walker, McCarthy and Timms 1994): 'when a partner is not trusted, mediation, which relies on mutual disclosure, will be problematic' (Walker 2001 p 428; Piper 1993 p 126). Trust and the pursuit of mutual interests may seem antithetical to law's traditional expression of rationality, but are constructed by mediators as the solution to conflict and therefore as prerequisites for the successful, co-operative post-separation family that defines both mediation and its results (Walker 2001 p 428; Piper 1993 p 126).

Law as exceptional: choosing mediation

So convinced was the government of the advantages of mediation[3], that encouragement to mediate was a pivotal part of its ill-fated divorce reform. The information meetings required by FLA 1996 included information designed to encourage mediation as an alternative to using solicitors and the legal process. The pilot research on information meetings found that there was no 'hard-sell' of mediation in the information meetings (Stark and Birmingham 2001 p 414), but the number of people diverted from solicitors to mediators was seen as an indicator of the success of the pilot projects and of Part II of the Act in general. That the Lord Chancellor re-garded as 'disappointing' the finding that 39 per cent of people were more likely to go to a solicitor after attending the information meeting, indicates the importance the government placed on diverting divorce matters from the public to the private arena.

Part of the government's commitment to mediation as a 'better way' to resolve family disputes is also demonstrated by its commitment to fund mediation from the public coffers. FLA 1996 included a provision requir-ing all people seeking legal aid funding for family disputes to attend a meeting with a mediator to assess their suitability for mediation. Only if they or their dispute were deemed unsuitable for mediation would they be entitled to legal aid funding. This provision, s 29 of FLA 1996, has now been repealed, and Part II of that Act of which mediation was to form an integral part will not be implemented, but s 29's funding requirements have been incorporated into the Access to Justice Act 1999 (s 11) nonetheless. Before this amendment was implemented, government considered the results of large-scale pilots designed to determine the effectiveness of mediation in

3   Mediation's claims have not always been borne out by empirical research. See Beck et al (2003), who review the research in detail.

terms of cost effectiveness, identification of contracting arrangements, levels of legal advice required in addition to mediation, and comparison of the costs and benefits of mediation with traditional lawyering (Davis et al 2000 p 2), and it is in the light of this research that I now turn to the current requirements for public funding of legal services in family matters, for mediation forms an integral part of the scheme.

Separating partners may choose to mediate or litigate outstanding issues between them, or they may choose to avail themselves of both or neither. If they have the resources, they will pay for the services of their lawyer or their mediator or both, as they see fit. If, however, they require public funding for legal assistance, they must engage with mediation as an option before legal services will be funded. The Legal Services Commission Funding Code requires all who apply for funding for legal representation or general family help (Code 11.3 and 11.11–11.12) to attend a meeting with a mediator who will determine if mediation is suitable to the dispute. This requirement was formerly embodied in s 29 of FLA 1996 which was the focus of the intake assessments studied in Davis et al's 2000 pilot research. The researchers found that s 29 clients – that is, those who were required as a condition of receiving (then) legal aid funding to attend an intake assessment (now called an assessment meeting: Funding Code Procedures C27) – were, from the mediator's perspective, less interested, less knowledgeable, less motivated and less conciliatory than their previous clients had been (Davis et al 2000 p 203). Section 29 clients presented a different kind of dispute and had little idea of their partner's likely attitude toward it (Davis et al 2000 p 203). This finding is significant to the extent that government enthusiasm for mediation was based in large part upon mediators' enthusiasm, which seems now to have been the result of their experience of a self-selecting and unrepresentative clientele. The actual families that they now encounter may represent the less than ideal altruistic, rational and free-willed individuals of government expectations.

While the Code places the responsibility upon mediators to determine suitability for mediation, it also requires solicitors to refer all clients who apply for legal representation or general family help certificates for this assessment meeting, unless they determine that one of the exemptions applies (Funding Code Guidance 20.8 para 6). The exemptions relate to, among other things, the urgency of the matter and to a fear of domestic violence (C 29 Funding Code Procedures). The s 29 requirements were similar, and the researchers found that while solicitors displayed a wide variety of attitudes toward their role in this respect (Davis et al 2000 p 205), many resented having to refer those clients they felt were obviously unsuitable. They regarded the obligation to refer as an obstacle that had to be overcome before they could get on with the effective management of their client's case (Davis et al 2000 p 204). They saw the requirement as causing delays that were potentially prejudicial to their client (Davis et al 2000 p 205), and often resented its disregard of their own ability to judge suitability in terms of factors outside the statutory exemptions.

In particular, many solicitors took into account their client's attitude and emotional capacity to engage in face-to-face negotiation, and felt that many were not, *at that time*, in a state to attempt it (Davis et al 2000 p 204). In this respect, solicitors seemed to have a realistic and pragmatic understanding of the families and individuals they encountered. They did not see their clients as rational actors comprising the harmonious, ideal families underpinning this law, but rather recognised that their clients often were distressed individuals whose capacity and competence to negotiate may have been compromised at this difficult moment in their lives. In other words, solicitors recognised the messy families we live with, and were unhappy about the law which appeared only to see ideal families.

The mediator's role during the assessment meeting is to 'assess whether mediation is suitable to the dispute and the parties and all the circumstances'. If he or she determines it is not, then funding for legal representation or general family help is available; if the determination is positive, then funding for full mediation is available (Criterion 11.4.2 and Code Procedures D4.3). Other than the exemptions listed in the Funding Code Procedures and a consideration of the cost benefit potentially provided by the mediation (Guidance 20.10.3), there is no guidance as to what suitability means. The government felt that trained mediators rather than administrators or lawyers were best placed to determine suitability (Lord Chancellor's Department 1995 para 5.30), but Davis et al (2000) found that mediators themselves were initially more apprehensive about this role. Their training and philosophy may previously have led them to see willingness and motivation as the primary criteria for suitability, but their duty to assess seems now to require more than that. The researchers found that many mediators adopted the use of checklists to accommodate their new role (Davis et al 2000 p 215), and while they focused upon factors such as domestic violence and child protection, they did not explore the outstanding legal issues or the client's emotional state, intellectual capacity or articulacy (Davis et al 2000 p 216). In fact, most cases were deemed to be 'suitable' if both parties were prepared to participate (Davis et al 2000 p 216). Mediators in this way seemed to accept law's view of its ideal families and the enduring reasonableness of its members. Further, although mediation is to be presented at these meetings as one possible option only, the researchers found that mediators sometimes presented mediation not in a neutral, factual way, but in a way so as to stress its supposed benefits. Given that clients are in what the researchers call 'advice-seeking mode' (Davis et al 2000 p 214) at the assessment meeting, they may demonstrate what appears to be a willingness to mediate at that time because the, often indirect, suggestion to do so was made by a professional person.

Even if assessors indicated no preference for mediation, their process assumed a capacity in clients for rational engagement with factual information that may, in fact, have been diminished by emotion or other unrecognised factors.

'The purpose of intake is to inform prospective clients about mediation … [The Funding Code] assumes that prospective clients will understand that the purpose of an intake meeting is to consider mediation as a process. The idea is that they will obtain, in the course of the meeting, a level of understanding sufficient for them … to decide whether mediation is appropriate' (Davis et al 2000 p 221).

But clients' responses to researchers' queries after the intake meetings indicated a highly variable level of understanding that often did not relate to the quality of information given to them (Davis et al 2000 p 218). The researchers speculate that people in the throes of separation, emotional distress and often fear, primarily take in information about outcome rather than process. They are, in general, compliant, and resigned to going through with a process they felt was advised by the professionals from whom they sought advice. Mediators must not only be cautious, therefore, about sometimes conflating this 'willingness' with suitability, but policy-makers must also be realistic about the degree to which the goal of educating individuals to make a rational choice about process can be met. The researchers suggest, in fact, that there is an inappropriate emphasis by policy upon providing people with information, options and a rational choice about process (Davis et al 2000 p 271–272).

Further, women may be more susceptible than men to the 'seductive appeal' of mediation, which 'speak[s] softly of relatedness' (Bryan 1992 p 523), compromise and self-sacrifice (Piper 1993 p193–194; Diduck and Kaganas 1999 p 355; Weitzman 1992). While rationality is foregrounded in mediation, it is a rationality expressed through discussion and compromise rather than through competition and claims to abstract rights and thus might appeal to men and women differently.

Taken together, these observations illustrate a further potential conflict between the 'rational man' at the heart of the normative family and our lived, gendered, familial experiences.

Practising mediation

Funded mediators are required to subscribe to a code of practice (Funding Code Procedures D.5) and the UK College of Family Mediators Code of Practice (2000) contains its own guidance on mediators' duties to their clients and their responsibilities of impartiality and neutrality. They are broad guidelines, however, as each mediator will have his or her own personal style of practice. Indeed, the researchers on the Legal Services Commission pilots found that there is a wide variation in practices of mediation and that in comparison with data compiled from earlier mediation services, mediators in their study adopted a brisker, more focused, formal and more professional approach, which they described as either more coherent and businesslike, or alternatively as 'bureaucratized and incorporated into the legal system in a way that compromises the founding ethos of empowerment and client control' (Davis et al 2000 p 232). They found generally that 'mediators have become more sophisticated and subtle than in the 1980s in their management of process and the guidance of clients toward preferred outcomes' (Davis et al 2000 p 232), so that while clients generally felt that mediators were impartial as between parties (Davis et al 2000 p 242), there was evidence that particular outcomes were encouraged over others (see below).

The UK College of Family Mediators' guidelines concerning young people and family mediation state that mediators have a special concern for the welfare of all children of the family and must encourage parents to focus upon the needs of their children, the child's point of view and their children's wishes and feelings. If the mediators and participants consider it appropriate, children may be invited to participate directly in the mediation (UK College 2000 para 4.71–4.73), but all mediators are to encourage parents to 'talk with and listen to their children so that the decisions parents make about arrangements for their children are reached in the light of an understanding of each child's perspective', and 'to consider the different ways in which children may be involved or consulted' (UK College 2000).

No mediators in the LSC research saw the children who were the subjects of the disputes, but the children's perspectives were discussed in virtually all the sessions (Davis et al 2000 p 248). The degree to which mediators focused on the children's wishes and feelings seemed to depend upon the nature of the dispute and the age of the child, and one mediator went so far as to encourage the parents to disregard entirely their eleven-year-old child's opposition to moving house, suggesting that, by their concern, they were giving him too much power (Davis et al 2000 p 249). These findings are in line with mediation's principles of party control and concern for children, but leave open the question of whether children should be considered as parties to the dispute. Law does not routinely define them as such (see Chapter 4), but one could argue that mediation's extra-legal framework could more easily accommodate this view. That it, like law, only extraordinarily does so, fits with the ambiguous view of the ideal child and his or her place in the ideal family. The concern to consult and engage in discussions with children evidences some sense of the child as legitimate participant in the democratic family – the child as being – but the overriding concern for their welfare, and the exclusive parental responsibility to promote it, reflect the traditional 'child as becoming' paradigm (see Chapter 4).

One concluding view of where we are now with family mediation is presented by Davis et al:

> 'Recent government support for family mediation reflects professional enthusiasm, with little regard to the very low client base. This has come about because the "story" of mediation – its association with reasonableness and compromise – is appealing, and secondly because government has accepted the mediators' argument that spiraling legal costs can be cut through diverting cases to mediation' (Davis et al 2000 p 273).

The evidence from their project is that that argument is untrue, yet mediation is still encouraged by law and government policy. Many solicitors believe they see the writing on the wall and are training as mediators, particularly where family legal services are to be publicly funded, and the aims and objectives of the pilot Family Advice and Information Networks (FAINs) include facilitating the dissolution of broken relationships in ways which minimise distress to parents and children and which promote ongoing family relationships and co-operative parenting (LSC 2002). Having learned from the pilot projects that mediation is not always the best way to do this, though, the commission is also 'anxious' that the FAINs project test 'flexible access to both mediation and a wider range of what may termed "family alternative dispute resolution"' (LSC 2002). The government appears to be unwavering in its determination to divert family matters from public to private, whatever form that privacy may take (see Roberts 2001).

Another story: informal justice, privatisation and normative families

Alternative, feminist histories, such as Bottomley's (1985), provide a different perspective from which to understand law's embrace of the mediation ideal. Rather than viewing individualism and changes in the nature of intimate commitment as law's motivation for promoting mediation, Bottomley sees welfarism and social control at its root (see also Rodger 1996). She notes that the liberal ideal of a private family residing outside the public realm of politics and civil society was a lived reality (if at all) only for the middle and landed classes at the beginning of the twentieth century; there was (and is) no liberal apprehension about interference in the private lives of working-class families whose health, welfare and morals were increasingly seen as legitimate concerns for the state. Because welfare and the child-saving which is an integral part of welfarism were, and are, viewed as unproblematic projects for the state, when children became defined as potentially 'at risk' because of the *fact* of their parents' divorce, the distinction between the middle classes divorcing and the working classes utilising the services of social workers and probation officers in Magistrates' Courts became blurred (Bottomley 1985 p 170) and 'child saving, welfare agencies and informality become crucially linked' (Bottomley 1985 p 171). The task of child-saving in the first third of the twentieth century thus became 'transformed from dealing with those families who were clearly "at risk" (in the minds of interventionists), to a concern with the welfare of children of the divorcing population' (Bottomley 1985 p 172). It became a concern to be met by social workers rather than by formal law. On this view, mediation represents only a chimera of individual agency, reflexivity of self and flexible relationships and is more concerned to promote a vision of acceptable family living.

Child-saving

Thus far I have been treating mediation in an almost generic way, which encompasses mediation of child-related, property and financial issues.

Where I have intended to differentiate between these, I hope has been made clear. Davis (1988), Walker et al (1994), the pilot studies on information meetings (Walker et al 2001) and Davis et al (2000) all concerned this comprehensive mediation. There is no doubt, however, that child-saving or the welfare discourse has been a primary motivator (and selling point) of the 'official' position in favour of mediation. It is at this point, then, that I shall divide my discussion. The balance of this chapter shall focus primarily on mediation of child-related issues and I shall deal with the financial consequences of separation in the next chapter.

Again, it may be nothing more than an expression of the 'normal chaos of family law' (Dewar 1998) that welfarism and individualism together can underpin the mediation ideal. But such 'happenstance' is happily exploited by government policy that also embraces those two imperatives. For example, the 'official' view of children's welfare is that children's best interests are served by their living with cohabiting (preferably married) heterosexual parents who manage conflict in constructive or productive, as opposed to destructive, ways (Advisory Group 2002 para 2.3–2.7). Constructive conflict occurs where parties effectively manage and resolve disagreements, and in productive conflict problems are openly discussed, even if not necessarily resolved (Advisory Group 2002 para 2.5). In both cases, the conflict and its management remain private and are confined within the dynamics of individual family relationships. The government intends to provide marriage and relationship support to couples and their children in order to educate them, presumably about these forms of conflict and its management, but also to foster a culture more generally in which relationships are valued and early, accessible help for individuals to save troubled ones is available and acceptable (Advisory Group 2002 s 7; and also see Chapter 2). In this light, the focus on children in mediation policy is not surprising. Mediation clearly represents constructive or productive conflict management, which means that it is uniquely placed to promote the welfare of the child by approximating the privacy and dynamics of the ideal family as closely as possible where parental separation is unavoidable.

Mediation's focus upon 'children's welfare' raises a number of concerns. In particular, because it is private, mediation has the effect of removing from scrutiny the issue of what welfare means (Diduck and Kaganas 1999 p 361 and Chapter 4). One 'truth' about the welfare of children is allowed to prevail at the expense not only of contested views about how children cope after their parents' separation, but also of any individual child's needs, interests or wishes. The individual child's concerns are eclipsed by the presumed concerns of the normative child, and the absence of a forum in which those truths can be tested, and of any mechanism for testing them against 'real' children, means that the orthodoxies of joint, conflict-free parenting and the child 'victim' of divorce both survive unscathed.

As we have seen (also see Chapter 4), mediators rarely involve children in the mediation; the whole process is parent-focused, following the philosophy of parent control as the ultimate decision-makers (Roberts 1997; Piper 1999). Instead, parents are urged to consult their children, but in cases where that consultation produces responses which appear to contravene the truth of welfare, they are disregarded. In this way, the law upholds a 'children as becoming' paradigm. Further, the 'truth' that some form of post-divorce joint parenting promotes a child's welfare defines as deviant not only parents who do not agree to it, it defines children in this way as well. Children, like parents, must therefore be educated to recognise their best interests, and their acquiescence to that result converts them from troubled, unreasonable, or otherwise deviant, to the ideal child of law. According to the Advisory Group on Marriage and Relationship Support (2002) and *Making Contact Work* (Lord Chancellor's Department 2002) (also see Chapter 4; Diduck and Kaganas 2002), the role of the state is to 'help' children as well as their parents to achieve the desirable outcome.

Mediation's focus on children also means that their needs override the needs of the parties (Reece 1996). The good parent denies his or her own interests in favour of the interests of the child, and unless parents express their interests in this, the 'right' way, they are assumed to oppose the child's interests. In other words, there seems to be no room for the possibility that the interests of parents and children may otherwise correspond. This means, for example, that a woman's need, on separation from her partner, to reconstitute herself with a fresh start and some measure of independence (see below and Chapter 3) cannot be seen as also in her child's welfare, rather it is rephrased as the selfish attitude of a bad mother.

Welfarism

Mediators are the new divorce professionals, they are the new 'experts' in family disputes. They speak the language of care, compromise and communication rather than the language of law, rights and adversarialism. Containing divorce matters within a welfare as opposed to a legal discourse serves as a method of reinforcing a particular image of the liberal society, the family and familial relations. Mediation as a process 'emphasises social solidarity and continuing relations rather than discontinuity and conflict', the socially therapeutic effect of which is attractive (Bottomley 1985 p 180; Day Sclater 1999a and b). The symbolism is of a system rooted in harmony and continuity, 'a caring, liberal and egalitarian society which only intervenes in the private domain of the family with good cause and with great sensitivity' (Bottomley 1985 p 185). The normative family is promoted by the combined emphasis upon consensus (Bottomley 1985 p 185) and the presumed equality and autonomy of the parties which masks any conflict or power imbalances. Finally, confining familial matters within the welfare discourse reinforces the idea that family disputes are not the stuff of 'real' law; it implies that relations between children and parents or between intimates do not have to be considered as matters of civil rights, as politically legitimate sites of grievance or as deserving of the authority and protection of the rule of law.

The belief in the profound 'good' of mediation avoids questions about the degree to which welfarism is as much a form of social and normative control as is legalism (Rodger 1996). Donzelot's (1980) work argued compellingly that through a form of tutelage the normative impact of social workers upon families and family behaviours could be great. Bottomley equates this idea with the promotion of mediation:

'a massive increase in the power and legitimacy of social workers and mediators has been rendered benevolent by the twin rhetorics of science and concern (for children)' (Bottomley 1985 p 170).

We are left with the appearance of 'an agreement reached under the benevolent eye of an expert rather than fought out between lawyers. We are, in effect, exchanging one form of regulation for another, and "once adjudicatory forms are abandoned, consideration of individual rights and of justice between the parties can be subverted with notions of treatment and therapy"' (Bottomley 1985 p 175) and also by non-welfare notions of neutrality which take no account of structural inequalities[4]. 'Government sponsorship' (Davis et al 2000 p 272) of this form of regulation simply increases its normative power.

Mediation promotes the general ideal of family harmony and consensus both in process and in its aim to achieve the continuing but separated family. The UK College of Family Mediators Standards and Codes of Practice (2000) require mediators to be neutral as to the outcome of mediation, but

---

4   I am grateful to Christine Piper for this point.

research in the UK and the US demonstrates that mediators use various methods to get parties to transform their view of the issues, to 'come round' to the mediator's view of an 'acceptable' problem and resolution (Diduck and Kaganas 1999 p 352–353; Davis et al 2000; Walker et al 1994; Piper 1996b; Piper 1993; Beck et al 2003).

Davis et al (2000) adopted the phrase 'parameters of the permissible' to explain this process:

'Within these parameters, mediators generally hold back and allow clients to work out their own deals. Mediators are not bothered whether contact is one weekend in three or one in four, for example. However, the residential parent who declares that s/he will not agree to contact at all has breached these parameters and may come under direct pressure to yield' (Davis et al 2000 p 242).

Piper's (1993) study of child-focused mediation demonstrated that at virtually all stages of the mediation, mediators used a variety of techniques to reframe parents' expectations, motives, desires, conflicts, problems and potential solutions to those which emphasised harmony, settlement and continued contact with children. Through 'querying and endorsing of parental problems, and in the manufacturing of parental motivations to agree' (Piper 1993 p 189) mediators may, in fact, have constructed the ideal responsible parent of the Children Act 1989 and of family policy. Her findings shed a light upon the paradoxical autonomy and responsibility promised to parents by government and mediators, all of whom assert that parents know best what is in the interests of their children and must be left, with the help of skilled mediators, to determine this for themselves.

These criticisms of the welfare discourse and observations of mediators' practice also point to issues of how gender is implicated in welfarism. The dominant norms that are purveyed through the welfare discourse may have damaging implications for women. First of all:

'the focus on children is seen as a denial of women's identities distinct from motherhood. It also leads to a preference for a particular model of joint parenting and a presumption in favour of contact, an approach that helps to perpetuate the power of fathers. The emphasis on jointness ignores the unequal contributions of fathers and mothers to parenting prior to separation. It also places the burden of absorbing any strain and inconvenience caused by contact on mothers' (Diduck and Kaganas 1999 p 354–355).

Further, gender differences may also exist in the level of acceptance of norms about welfare (Piper 1996b; Day Sclater 1999a). Mothers may operate within a different value system than many fathers (Weitzman 1992 p 405). They may, for example, enter mediation with existing experience of putting children first on a day-to-day basis and be more receptive to advice about promoting children's welfare and preserving relationships (Piper 1996b; Ribbens McCarthy et al 2000) than fathers whose experience of childcare may be minimal and whose experience of autonomy less relational. Davis et al (2000) found, for example, that mediators often constructed an absent father's claim to see his children in terms of his right to do so and constructed the recalcitrant mother's opposition as 'emotion' (Davis et al 2000 p 243).

The process itself compounds these problems. Piper found, for example, that mediators' rephrasing and normalising of grievances often undermined many mothers' legitimate complaints and devalued their care taking work (Piper 1993 p 193) and the mediation itself may allow men's socialisation and skills acquired through greater access to the public sphere to perpetuate their subtle authority. In these ways, mediation may reproduce gendered power relationships even more effectively than formal legal justice 'because of the very construction and manipulation of images of party control, privacy, neutrality and a "back to the people" grass roots appeal' (Bottomley 1985 p 180).

Informality

The official claim is that parties to mediation benefit from its informality because mediation, more than the legal process, allows for flexible outcomes and flexible processes. As the research has demonstrated, however, neither the range of acceptable outcomes nor party control over process seems to be entirely achieved (Davis et al 2000; Piper 1993). Rather, particular outcomes are often coerced through mediator strategies. Further, the informal and private process that directs these 'responsible' outcomes also follows a pattern. In the result, neither the process nor the norms it promotes are tested in public according to received standards of justice. The 'justice' of the process and its outcome is left to be determined by the individuals concerned. The claim is that 'mediation, since it involves the parties directly, enables their subjective ideas about fairness to be taken into account' (Davis 1988 p 137), but this assumption is problematic for at least two reasons. First, parents are often puzzled by seemingly being left on their own to determine fairness or justice. They find it 'difficult to accept the deliberate removal of a concept of justice from the area of family law when the state continues to uphold the validity of the concept in other areas' (Piper 1993 p 193)[5]. Secondly, mediation assumes that parents possess a shared culture and a similar concept of justice (Piper 1993 p 194; see also Smart 1999; Neale and Smart 1999) notwithstanding evidence to suggest both that that shared culture and that shared concept of justice may be lacking between separating parents (Piper 1993 ch 2 and p 193–194; Smart and Neale 1999 p 171–172) and between parents and children (Smart et al 2001 ch 5).

Justice may be understood in different ways. On the one hand, a subjective fairness would require account to be taken of the particularities of actual relationships, of assumption of past and present responsibilities for the specifics of family life and of the quality of relationships among the family members (Smart and Neale 1999 p 170–172; Smart et al 2001 ch 5; Sevenhuijsen 1998 p 115–121). On the other hand, justice could mean that mediated settlements and the mediation process would take account only of abstract concepts such as equality and the welfare of the paradigm child. It is interesting that despite mediation's removal from the public, formal legal sphere, purportedly precisely to take account of subjective considerations, mediations seem to take place within the latter ethic rather than the former. It is as if mediators 'speak the language' of caring, connection, particularity and nurturing relationships, but beneath that rhetoric operate within the formality and abstraction of generalised principles of rights and justice. The fact that this operation is covert and takes place in the privacy of the mediator's office, means that there is no recourse or appeal for the many parents who feel aggrieved, unhappy or merely uncomfortable with the individualised justice they are told they have achieved, must 'own' and must sustain over the long term.

Many parents do feel unhappy with both the mediation process and its outcome, precisely on the grounds of its perceived lack of 'justice'. Many mothers perceived injustice due to the way in which mediators tended to render invisible the burden and skills of caring they brought with them (Piper 1993 p196), and many fathers perceived injustice because they felt

---

5   Many parents hoped or expected mediators to advise them about a 'fair' outcome and in financial mediation particularly, parents often wished mediators would provide them with some indication of what was fair or normal (see Chapter 6).

mediation lacked the objectivity and formal recognition of rights that law's justice is said to provide. They felt uneasy about mediation's social work rather than legal focus (Smart and Neale 1999 p 168)[6].

Finally, the informality of mediation leaves unchecked any power imbalance that might result from the parties' different moral registers, economic circumstances, negotiating experiences or emotional dependencies (Diduck and Kaganas 1999 p 355–356; Bottomley 1985). Mediators are trained to be conscious of and to ameliorate power imbalances, but the experiences of many parents suggest that they are not always successful in recognising the power dynamics in relationships, or of being capable of dealing with them (Piper 1993). The problem of power and exploitation of power is particularly acute in relationships where there has been a history of domestic violence (Diduck and Kaganas 1999 p 357–361; Kaganas and Piper 1999), and Davis and his colleagues found that 57 per cent of parents who indicated a fear of violence were nonetheless deemed suitable for mediation at intake assessments with mediators (Davis et al 2000 p 58).

Mediators are concerned at all times with safety and with maintaining an equality of bargaining power (Roberts 1997), but it seems to be the case that spousal abuse is still considered to be exceptional; it is not a part of the official story of mediation just as it is not a part of the official family for whom mediation was designed. The ideal separating partners who mediate their points of contention are simply an extension of the ideal cohabiting family before the conflict arose: they are presumed to be able to co-operate, to negotiate decisions about the welfare of children and of the family as a whole on an equal, and equally respectful, footing. To introduce the issue of domestic violence into this apparently coherent story about mediation is to disrupt its coherence and to challenge the ideal of the consensual and conflict-free divorce (Kaganas and Piper 1999 p 183), just as it challenges the normative family.

The final point to be made about the privacy and informality of mediation is to question its very opposition to law and formal decision-making. It is arguable that the current spin about mediation sets up a false contrast between law and mediation and between lawyers and mediators. Recent research on family solicitors (see Davis et al 2000; Eekelaar et al 2000; Piper 1999) agrees that the actual practice of family lawyers often belies

---

6   Also see the research discussed in Beck et al (2003) where gender differences were found in levels of satisfaction with the justice of mediation experiences.

their adversarial and antagonistic reputation. Indeed, a conciliatory and settlement orientation is said to define the 'good' family lawyer (Piper 1999). Yet the reputation persists. Respondents in Davis et al's study (see also Walker et al 1994) believed that lawyers fuel conflict and it is difficult to speculate about whether the official spin sanctioning this view was its cause or effect.

In concluding their report about outcomes of mediation, Davis et al (2000) suggest that defining 'success' as settlement or reaching agreement makes potentially inappropriate demands of mediation. Judging it by reference to this legal yardstick alone places insufficient value upon the supposed 'transformative effect' of mediation in which its aim is to 'improve relationships between the parties and not be concerned with whether the "dispute" is resolved in the course of mediation' (Davis et al 2000 p 136). Yet the government measuring mediation's success or failure in this way makes sense if one of its goals is to make 'good' post-divorce families who are able, through a process of negotiation and co-operation, to designate clear roles for themselves.

Mothers', fathers' and children's stories: introduction

The Legal Services Commission estimated in January 2001 that there are about 10,000 mediations per year (Fisher and Hodson 2001 p 272). No doubt, a significant number of the parties involved in those mediations were satisfied with their mediation experience and reached fair and practicable agreements as a result of them. Of those in the Davis et al study (2000) who reached agreement in child-related mediations, 50 per cent thought the agreement was completely reasonable (Davis et al 2000 p 79) and 73 per cent were at least fairly happy with it (Davis et al 2000 p 80). Conversely, it is also likely that many involved in the 10,000 annual mediations were dissatisfied with both the process and its outcome. In Davis et al's study 55 per cent of mediating couples did not reach agreement and 54 per cent of women and 30 per cent of men found the mediation experience upsetting (Davis et al 2000 p 71). The purpose of this section is not to revisit these experiences in an effort to challenge individual perceptions of them. It is, rather, to shed some light upon the expectations people had upon entering into mediation, and the degree to which those expectations were, or could be, fulfilled.

Mediation's discourses of self-sacrifice, welfare and the enduring family reproduce the dominant discourses of the 'traditional', obligation-based, romantic family and the individual at its heart. They interact, however, with discourses of individual autonomy, voluntarism, negotiation and flexibility, signifiers of the modern, reflexive relationship and the individual also at its heart, to constitute ideal families and ideal family members, protection of which is arguably mediation's most pressing, yet opaque, goal. We have seen that to a great extent mediation is successful in this enterprise. It holds out to consumers that it is they who control both the process and its outcome through the exercise of their autonomy and communication skills in the light of their subjective experiences, while at the same time it exerts subtle pressure upon them to exercise this autonomy in preconceived, 'acceptable' ways so as to ensure maintenance of the harmonious, enduring, status-based family in which sex and generation roles remain within the 'traditional' ideal.

That the discourses of welfare, duty, individualism and harmony are also invoked by people telling their divorce stories (Day Sclater 1999a p 177) demonstrates their importance in the imagination of the divorcing public. They are, according to Day Sclater, 'a variation on the theme of the "happy ever after" of fairy tales', and the power accorded them may be the result of individual and collective psychological needs to manage personal and social ambivalences (Day Sclater 1999a p 176) as much as of political ideology.

Expectations and ideals

Day Sclater found that among many of her respondents mediation was idealised; it was seen to promise an amicable divorce which would be best for the children because it would avoid conflict (Day Sclater 1999a p 165). Similarly, respondents in the information meeting pilot project indicated a number of reasons for choosing mediation, including the belief that it fostered the potential for a more amicable divorce, that the presence of a neutral third party would allow them to talk to and be listened to by their spouse, and would help them to achieve results that were fair (Stark and Birmingham 2001). Many respondents would recommend mediation for others, if not for themselves, and thought it was a good idea in principle (see also Davis et al 2000 p 72). It seems that while many felt their own situations were not appropriate for mediation, the divorcing/separating public seems to have internalised mediation's ideals of harmony and welfare, at least to the extent of believing in its advantages in principle, or for others.

Piper, on the other hand, found that 13 of her 30 parents 'had no reason for attending mediation other than believing that it was expected of them or that it could help to establish their personal good faith' (Piper 1993 p 58). The rest of them provided explanations that fell into one of two categories: either they believed that mediation was a type of advice agency, or they believed it was an arena in which to talk, and possibly resolve disputes (Piper 1993 p 58). The mediators, however, did not acknowledge these divergent motives or expectations. They used the *fact* of attending as evidence of parental concern for children and desire to co-operate and communicate, and conveyed these assumptions to parents (Piper 1993 p 55–56), constituting them as 'good' parents by doing so. Parental expectations of mediation were thus recast early on in the process in an effort almost to manufacture acceptance of the dominant discourses of welfare and harmony.

Davis et al (2000) also found that parties explained in a number of ways their initial decision to attend a mediation service. Importantly, 25 per cent went under compulsion of s 29, and a further 19 per cent went because they were referred by their solicitors. Thirty-one per cent preferred the process (eg talking with third party help) and 18 per cent believed it would be better for the children (Davis et al 2000 p 64). When asked about their expectations of mediation, 76 per cent hoped for a compromise/agreement, and 30 per cent expressed hopes that mediation would in some way allow for communication with their partner (expressed as hope for 'a dialogue', or to 'express my view' or for an 'explanation from partner' (Davis et al 2000 p 65)). Women were more likely to say they attended mediation because they sought dialogue or wanted a chance to express their views; men were more likely to think in terms of reaching a specific agreement (Davis et al 2000 p 65). While these responses seem also to indicate some idealisation of mediation, we must remember, in the context of Piper's research, that 'the fact that clients do as they are told in these circumstances does not mean that they fully comprehend the purpose of the exercise. ... Faced with the unknown, most people will do as they are told' (Davis et al 2000 p 222).

In general, people seem to attend mediation because they feel they should, either because they may be harming their children if they do not, or because they have been told to do so. If they did not hold an idealised image of mediation before, the process ensures that they are 'taught' it at an early stage. Given these understandings and expectations, it is interesting to measure respondents' experiences of mediation. Rather than ask, however, if mediation met separating partners' expectations, I am interested in whether separating partners were able to meet the expectations mediation had of them.

Mediation as a family practice

The possibility that conflict and anger are rational responses to divorce disputes is submerged or reframed in mediation's ideal of co-operative rationality and the psychological or emotional need to preserve or reconstitute one's self is submerged within the welfare discourse. Day Sclater found, however, that some respondents found it difficult to remain focused exclusively within the welfare discourse, and that in contrast to their early idealisation of mediation, they were not always able to be rational, amicable and harmonious (Day Sclater 1999a p 165). One respondent said:

'He wants to be a major part of the children's life without being a major part of the children's life. So, I don't know, in many ways I just, I wish I could be sort of a lot less in contact with him and a bit nasty to him when I do see him' (Day Sclater 1999a p 165).

The same respondent later says:

'And I suppose I just need something that is more for me, rather than constantly thinking of the children all the time [and] ... I don't want to have to consider his needs' (Day Sclater 1999a p 166).

This woman's levels of anxiety[7] increased as the mediation continued until she finally stopped attending. The welfare discourse continued to exert some control over her, however, and asserting her own needs continued to be a source of anxiety and guilt (Day Sclater 1999a p 167). Day Sclater postulates that her respondent's increased anxiety may reflect 'at least in part, the inner turmoil occasioned by the increasing lack-of-fit between the co-operative values which [she] espoused so strongly and the hostile and destructive impulses of her inner world' (Day Sclater 1999a p 167).

Analysis of the information meeting pilots suggests that where relations between the parties were too strained, where there was bitterness and hostility, ill-feeling or blame, the parties did not feel able to mediate and chose instead to rely upon solicitors. This choice does not mean that they abandoned the conciliatory ideal, however, and many felt that they could

---

7   As measured by her GHQ (General Health Questionnaire) scores (see Day Sclater 1999a).

achieve the harmonious divorce either with the solicitors or on their own and at the same time ensure that their interests or selves were protected by the solicitor's partisanship (Stark 2001 p 490). While the message of harmony and welfare extols mediation to the exclusion of formal law, those who choose formal law remain in some way 'exceptional', as do their expectations of legal fairness and formal justice. Indeed, respondents occasionally felt that this was a failing on their or their partner's part, and they wished that they had been able to meet the standard of co-operativeness that would have characterised them and their disputes as reasonable or mediatable.

Mediation is concerned not only with producing responsible post-separation families, it is also concerned with producing responsible family members. Piper's research illustrates the variety of techniques mediators use to alter client's images of themselves, the other parent and the children, many of which involved either trivialising or disregarding family practices or re-characterising them as individualised *normative* difficulties. In defining the problem, mediators attempted to mutualise responsibility for problems relating to marriage breakdown and contact (Piper 1993 p 85). Where setting up contact arrangements was difficult, due, for example, to transport or accommodation problems, parents were encouraged not to find 'external' reasons, characterised as excuses, for these difficulties (Piper 1993 p 88). The common response to past responsibilities for parenting was to neutralise them or to make them irrelevant (Piper 1993 p 91). Mediators tended to equalise the childcare burdens by putting into the balance the father's pain at not seeing his children every day (Piper 1993 p 93; also see Smart 1991). According to Piper:

'Within mediation the concept of a responsible parent, used to rationalise various solutions, to guide problem and motivation construction and to control arguing parents, is of one who wishes and is able to uphold harmonious co-parenting after separation, who is able to understand the child's needs (but is willing to put the child's need for agreeing parents above any specific needs of the child), who is able to agree and communicate with the other parent and can resolve conflict without recourse to courts, who wishes to share the child with the other parent, who wishes to restrict individual responsibility and principles for the sake of this post-separation parenting and who believes that people may act very differently in their parental and spousal roles' (Piper 1993 p 188–189).

Day Sclater's research illustrates the damaging effects this image can have upon parents and Piper's research also found high levels of guilt and senses of injustice particularly among women, who felt they failed to meet the 'good mother' standard (Piper 1993 p 173).

Mediators' 'images of children nearly all concerned children in the abstract, so a premium was placed upon parents being able to accept that their children were "normal"' in order that the grounded images offered by parents and the mediator's abstract images could be merged (Piper 1993 p 138). The resulting imagined child was very 'parent-centred' as it was linked with parental behaviour rather than with children as distinct beings apart from parents' engagement with them (Piper 1993 p 140).

Parents' images of families were also recast by mediators: parents talked about new families, mediators of original ones. The message was clear that the separated family must continue for the sake of the child's welfare; harmony, support and sharing of emotions must continue (Piper 1993 p 144) despite parents' needs to work on new relationships or construct a new sense of family in their singleness. The 'good' parent is one who could run both families and not replace the old with the new (Piper 1993 p 143).

These constructions of the responsible parent, child and family in mediation are crucial to the way it is practised and yet may lead to feelings of resentment and injustice which may only make agreement more unlikely (Piper 1993 p 181). Even where agreement is reached, it may feel to many participants as coercive as a court order because mediation assumes a 'typical' model of family decision-making that may be foreign, inappropriate or simply unjust (Piper 1993 p 182; Beck et al 2003) in particular circumstances.

Conclusions

Mediation may be just what many separating parents and children want or need. We must question, however, whether mediation is *normal* both socially and psychologically given the paradoxical messages it radiates about the currently normative family. It celebrates individuality, individual choice and individual rights and the rationality that underlies these. It insists, however, that these remain within the non-legal realm of emotions and enduring obligation. It takes little or no account of structural or personal factors that direct separating couples' family practices that often reveal styles of decision-making, conflict management and assumption and allocation of family responsibilities at odds with its purported normalcy. It demands compliance at every stage of the separation process. First, good parents must choose to mediate their difficulties rather than litigate them or negotiate them with partisan solicitors. Then, they must successfully mediate them by arriving at an agreed settlement. Finally, they must use the skills they have learned in mediation to continue their relationship for the sake of their children. Deviation at any stage marks them as unreasonable, pathological or extraordinary and recourse to law in particular signifies that they are 'exceptional' if not irrational and unreasonable.

Emotional intimacy is one of the defining features of the ideal family, and the ability to deal with emotions is said to be one of mediation's advantages over formal law. Yet the families for whom mediation's 'rules' were formulated often do not represent the real, distressed people who may feel guilty, betrayed, furious, wounded or confused. They represent the 'rational man' who is able to deny these emotions, or the 'reasonable person' whose separation was amicable in the first place, or simply those people who have conciliatory personalities (Walker et al 2001; Davis et al 2000 p 218). Mediation's rules also do not represent the children who are supposed to be its focus. Yet many of those who experience normal rather than normative emotions blame themselves for their 'lack of fit'.

Smart, Neale and Wade express the need to expand the body of 'cultural capital' on which we and our children can draw to understand our experiences of divorce and separation (Smart, Neale and Wade 2001 p 168). It is a need almost for a collective consciousness-raising exercise to disrupt the ideal image of the families we live by. Day Sclater makes a similar point. She argues that we require a new cultural narrative around divorce and separation which recognises both gender differences and the emotional messiness that divorce entails (Day Sclater 1999a p 177). For women, alternative narratives are hindered by the double bind created by the normative family: 'the discourses of harmony and independence pull in opposite directions' (Day Sclater 1999a p 178). Men face a similar conflict: while many do have a greater stake in their children's lives, these 'have not been accompanied by the necessary practical, cultural and psychic changes for parenting to become a truly gender neutral activity' (Day Sclater 1999a p 178) and so the sex war rages on, on this new frontier (Collier 1999). Children are the focus of much mediation and their welfare was a driving force behind its inception, yet they are abstracted by a procedure that accords them little individual voice or agency.

Perhaps the most damaging effect of mediation's normative family, then, is its suppression of the *experiences* of separation and divorce and thus the potential these experiences offer to create this new cultural capital or cultural narrative. As long as the only separation/divorce narrative on which we can draw is expressed either in expectations of harmony, denial of emotions and enforced reasonableness, or in adversarial litigation, our ill-fitting family practices will always define us as unreasonable and foster (feelings of) injustice.

Chapter 6

Family finances: owning and sharing

The culture of dejuridification and self-sacrifice embraces issues of family finances and property as resolutely as it does issues of divorce and the upbringing of children. It is expressed through encouraging subjective determinations of fairness by the mediation of financial disputes and through procedural innovations designed to discourage litigation and adversarialism once matters have proceeded to court. At the same time, values of individual self-interest and formal equality are apparent in the substantive law by which family finances are organised on separation or divorce. While this law remains largely untouched by legislative reform, it has undergone judicial reform that has engendered a subtle change to the interpretive framework of the governing legislation.

Family financial provision thus remains an area in which the procedural law has undergone radical innovation but in which the substantive law remains much as it was in the 1980s and 1990s. It expresses liberal, market values of individual private property interests and a clean break between partners, but leaves room for paternalism and considerations of welfare in the discretion made available to judges to meet the needs of vulnerable family members. This chapter will examine both the reforms and the continuity in the regulation of family economics, for the messages radiated by legislative absences are as important in constituting a normative family as those conveyed by doctrinal change.

Ancillary relief: maintaining the status quo?

As we have seen, of all the exhortations within current family law policy, perhaps the strongest is the plea for the responsible, two-parent family, where necessary facilitated by the co-operative or 'civilised' (Walker et al 1994) divorce (also see Chapter 3 and Chapter 5). While this objective dominated the discourse around FLA 1996, little of that debate focused upon the procedure for or necessity of the parties arriving at a co-operative or 'civilised' post-divorce financial arrangement. Although a pilot scheme incorporating case management for a quick resolution of litigated disputes was welcomed in the 1995 White Paper on divorce reform (Lord Chancellor's Department 1995 para 9.7), promoting private ordering of post-divorce financial arrangements became subsumed within the procedural changes of FLA 1996, which were made primarily to attempt marriage-saving, to protect children and to reduce cost. If private ordering – notably mediation – worked for those concerns, the assumption was that it would also work for financial matters.

The Act itself made little reference to financial matters. The parties were to receive information about finances and property at the information meeting, they were to use the period of reflection and consideration to consider their arrangements for the future, and presumably the court could have directed them to mediation to focus this consideration, but decisions about finances and property were then left to be decided in the light of, or the shadow of, MCA 1973. Where these matters of ancillary relief were to be litigated, diversion from the adversarial process to a Financial Dispute Resolution (FDR) scheme (to be treated as a meeting for conciliation, Family Proceedings Rules 1997 r 2.75) was presented as the answer. The lack of debate on this scheme was striking; it seems to have been promoted primarily in order to deal with rising costs in family litigation (Thorpe LJ 1998).

The pilot FDR schemes, unlike the information meetings and Part II of FLA 1996, were deemed a success (KPMG 1998 'Executive Summary' p 3), and the Family Proceedings Rules have since been amended (the Family Proceedings (Amendment No 2) Rules 1999, SI 1999/3491) to extend nationally a revised version of the piloted procedure where an application for ancillary relief is presented to the court. This part of the general reform of divorce law has been retained, therefore, without the more dramatic reforms to the grounds and process of divorce that originally were intended to complement it. Significantly, the new rules go further than those originally proposed; they also incorporate a pre-application protocol outlining the steps the parties and their solicitors must take *prior to* the commencement of any application to the court (see below).

These rules are a part of a legal trend generally to encourage the diversion of all civil disputes from court-based adjudication and one that links this diversion with public funding. The Family Proceedings Rules, along with changes to the public funding of family matters generally (see Chapter 5), thus represent important parts of a more widespread shift in the role of the court from adjudicatory body to settlement manager (Roberts 2001), but in the context of private family law, they further the privatisation agenda almost to completion. Indeed, it seems now that only a minority of divorces lead to financial relief orders (Douglas and Perry 2001).

While the procedural context in which financial ancillary matters are determined on divorce may now be clear, the doctrinal one remains murky. On the one hand, the law concerning ancillary financial matters seemed, by the mid-1990s, and after the initial upheaval created by the Child Support Acts 1991 and 1995 (CSA), to have become relatively clear. Solicitors could advise their clients of general trends in the substantive law, which seemed to indicate that courts would be concerned to meet the residential parent's, usually the wife's (and children's), housing needs first, usually in the light of the husband's means (Family Law Committee 1998 para 8.5(a); Solicitors' Family Law Association (SFLA) 1998 para 23; Association of District Judges 1998 p 2). But on the other hand, they also had to advise that property and financial provision were always at the court's discretion and were not about legal entitlements *per se*.

This meant that for most middle-income families the law had settled into a situation whereby the wife would usually remain in occupation of the marital home (because she had care of the children), and she often would receive a larger share of the equity, sometimes to be realised at a later date, in exchange for any claim she may have had for ongoing support from the husband[1]. Any liability or potential liability under the CSA would be taken into consideration in making such a property adjustment. For these families, as for lower income families, the court also considered the availability to the wife and children of state benefits. For high-income families, any support and property distribution would also be based on the court's assessment of the non-earning party's, again usually the wife's, needs or 'reasonable requirements' (for example, *Dart v Dart* [1996] 2 FLR 286) and

---

1   See generally cases and discussion in Cretney et al 2002.

the 'clean break' principle. The dominant discourse in the discretion-based ancillary relief scheme tended to eschew spouse support in favour of property adjustments (Eekelaar 1991), and the values of the adjustments were calculated primarily according to needs criteria[2]. The parties were in this way thought best to be able to get on with their separate lives (for example, *Mawson v Mawson* [1994] 2 FLR 985).

However, the particulars of how the court's discretion would be exercised in a given case were difficult for solicitors to predict. Eekelaar (1998) demonstrated the difficulty solicitors faced in assessing the likely outcomes of individual cases, highlighting that the discretionary nature of MCA 1973 s 25 allowed for more than one 'correct' outcome in any given case (Eekelaar 1998 p 470). So, while solicitors were able to see a broad trend in the law toward meeting needs, details of the way in which needs or reasonable requirements would be assessed and met were variable and indeterminate (see also Ancillary Relief Advisory Group 1998).

The weight attached to meeting the dependant's 'needs' was curious, yet settled law. It was not successfully challenged until the House of Lords in *White v White*[3] found it to be disproportionate[4] given that MCA 1973 s 25 lists eight factors for the court to consider in making support and property allocation decisions (nine, if the welfare of the child is included)[5] and no one factor is given legislative weight over the others. Instead, the Lords stated that the overriding objective for any ancillary relief order ought to be a generally accepted standard of 'fairness' and that the discretionary powers given to the courts ought always to be exercised with this objective in view. It stated further that while 'fairness, like beauty, lies in the eyes of the beholder', one

---

2   Eekelaar (1991) found that if one 'teases out' a common approach taken by the registrars in his study to apportion property and finances on divorce, it would be an individualistic model based upon compensation principles. 'It would be possible to generalise their goal as the common one that the parties should take out of the marriage what they put in or at least some equivalent' (Eekelaar 1991 p 76). Two difficulties remain with this conclusion, however. The first is the valuation made of 'what they put in'. Only some of the registrars were prepared to value domestic contributions equally with financial ones, and many were prepared to do so only in longer marriages. The second difficulty is the registrars' apparent desire to qualify their compensation approach with the overriding influence of the 'circumstances of the case' and the needs of the parties (Eekelaar 1991 p 75-76)

3   [2001] 1 AC 596; [2000] 2 FLR 981 – references hereafter are to FLR.

4   See also *Dart v Dart* [1996] 2 FLR 286 per Butler-Sloss LJ.

5   See *Conran v Conran* (below) and George (1997).

'principle of universal application' is that 'there is no place for discrimination between husband and wife and their respective roles' (p 989):

'[W]hatever the division of labour chosen by the husband and wife, or forced upon them by the circumstances, fairness requires that this should not prejudice or advantage either party when considering para (f), relating to the parties' contributions. ... If, in their different spheres, each contributed equally to the family, then in principle it matters not which of them earned the money and built up the assets. There should be no bias in favour of the money-earner and against the homemaker and the child-carer' (p 989).

Lord Nicholls of Birkenhead then articulated a principle that has a chequered history in ancillary relief law (see Diduck and Kaganas 1999 ch 6): that of equality. He was careful not to create a presumption of equal sharing, but commented:

'a judge would always be well advised to check his tentative views against the yardstick of equality of division. As a general guide, equality should be departed from only if, and to the extent that, there is good reason for doing so' (p 989).

On the one hand, these principles appear to move 'the basis of the award firmly away from a subjective evaluation of desert to a more objective assessment of entitlement', and 'away from the language of welfare and dependence to one of entitlement' (Eekelaar 2001 p 32). Indeed, legal legitimation of the equal value of the marital roles has enormous potential to influence not only constructions of the value of different familial contributions, but also constructions of marriage, husband and wife (Diduck 1999b; Diduck and Orton 1994). It appears to inject a further economic and civil individualism into the romantic complementarity of the formerly legitimated marriage roles, where the value of caring, for example, was assumed to be unquantifiable because it was performed out of love. In the context of cases where assets exceed the needs of the parties, then, the so-called 'big money' cases, some new certainty, in the form of principled formal equality, may have been achieved by the *White* decision. But given that Lord Nicholls saw the basis for equality as lying in equal contributions, he left the way open for lawyers and courts to dispute the *quality* of contributions and 'search for reasons why division should be unequal' (Eekelaar 2001 p 33), and for the courts, in their discretion, to retain 'subjective evaluations of desert' often based in the 'language of welfare and dependence'.

This was, in fact, the short-term result. In cases reaching the courts in the immediate aftermath of *White*, arguments focused upon whether equality should be departed from[6], spawning what was described as a new 'litigation industry' in applications (usually by husbands) to depart from equality[7].

Many of those early applications were successful on the basis that '[t]he first spouse's special skill and effort is special to him or her, the individual's rights to the fruits of an inherent quality of this nature survives as a material consideration despite the partnership or pooling aspect of the marriage' (*Cowan v Cowan* [2001] 2 FLR 192 per Mance LJ p 242). Whether the principles established in the *White* decision clarified or further muddied the relative priority to be attributed to each of the statutory criteria, or the place of non-discrimination and equality in the meaning of 'fairness', thus became a matter of debate.

The debate may now be settled, at least to some degree, by the Court of Appeal in *Lambert v Lambert* [2003] 1 FLR 139. In that case, the court reviewed the 'forensic Pandora's box' (per Thorpe LJ p 157) opened by (particularly Mance LJ's comments in) *Cowan*, and concluded that a detailed examination and assessment of the value of contributions to a marriage was a distasteful exercise. It went back to the principled basics of *White's* approach to fairness and marginalised the 'special contribution' category to exceptional cases only (p 158). In *Lambert* the parties were married for 23 years, during which the company the husband founded nine months before he met the wife became extremely successful. The company was subsequently sold, yielding assets of £20.2m. The couple had adopted a traditional division of labour, with the husband working hard and long hours in the business, and the wife maintaining responsibility for the home and children. At the trial of the ancillary relief issues, the wife claimed an equal division of the family wealth and the husband argued that his 'special contribution' to its accumulation – his long hours in building the business and his skills of negotiating a good share price on its sale – entitled him to a departure from equality. The Court of Appeal said:

---

6   See the cases cited in *Lambert v Lambert* (below) decided by the Court of Appeal in November 2002. See also *S v S (Financial Provision: Departing from Equality)* [2001] 2 FLR 246 (FD), in which the court justified the departure on the basis that the 'shoe pinched' the husband more than the wife; *Cowan v Cowan* [2002] EWCA Civ 679, [2001] 2 FLR 192 where a departure from equality was justified on the basis of the husband's 'genius' or innovation in his business; and *L v L* [2002] 1 FLR 642 (FD) where justification was on the basis of the husband's 'special' if not exceptional business skills.

7   See *Lambert v Lambert* [2002] EWCA Civ 1685, [2003] 1 FLR 139.

'Having now heard submissions, both full and reasoned, against the concept of special contribution save in the most exceptional and limited circumstances, the danger of gender discrimination resulting from a finding of special financial contributions is plain. If all that is regarded is the scale of the breadwinner's success then discrimination is almost bound to follow since there is no equal opportunity for the homemaker to demonstrate the scale of her comparable success' (p 157–158).

The court allowed the wife's appeal and awarded her 50 per cent of the value of the assets, partly on the basis that 'the only justification for a departure from equality ... cannot be upheld without discrimination' (p 161).

The doctrinal context in which the 'civilised' divorce is to be achieved, then, is one which promotes both objective/abstract and subjective/individualised ideas of fairness. This chapter will focus upon this ambivalence and also that inherent in and arising from a law that promotes informal, private determinations of financial and property disputes in a discretion-based ancillary relief system. Mediating or negotiating ancillary agreements on divorce when the legal 'rules' of distribution lack a principled foundation or clear objectives means that neither party can enter or leave negotiations with a clear idea of entitlement, but rather must have recourse only to competing legislative factors for consideration (MCA 1973 s 25), some idea of 'fairness' and their own, often conflicting, senses of justice (see Douglas and Perry 2001). Not only do these considerations often weigh differently depending upon the wealth of the parties, but the procedural law with which all must engage appears to demand a reconciliation of the ambivalence and to insist that individuals themselves take responsibility for achieving it.

Alimony and separate property – history

The way in which MCA 1973 is framed and has been interpreted over the years cannot be separated from its legislative and social history, or indeed from the legislative and social history of relations between the sexes and relations of individuals to private property. The liberal individual at the foundation of English law, particularly property law, is an acquisitive individual whose right to acquire and hold property is fundamental to his legal subjectivity. Indeed, the historical basis for claims to citizenship was ownership of property and in the context of families and family property, this philosophical and political 'truth' corresponded to the common law doctrine of coverture by which the legal personality of women became, on marriage, subsumed under that of their husbands. The wife's 'civil death' made sense in the light of the common law, which decreed that on marriage her personal property, including her earnings from paid work or leaseholds, became her husband's, and he became entitled to a life estate in and sole management of her freeholds (see Finer and McGregor 1974; Holcombe 1983; Blackstone 1778) in return for the obligation to support her for life. While lawyers for the propertied classes developed a sophisticated system in equity to protect a woman's holdings from potential abuses by her husband, the majority of women were subject to the inequity and moralistic paternalism of the common law.

Social conditions and prevailing familial ideology also contributed to the civil and personal identity constructed for and by a 'husband' or 'wife'. In the 1880s, for example, 'many [working-class] men subscribed to a code of masculinity which stressed the responsible and kindly husband and father' (Davidoff et al 1999 p 18), and this view was confirmed by social and legal policy premised on the belief that this version of English manliness was also 'the surest way to lock men, particularly young men, into steady work' (Davidoff et al 1999 p 18). Among the wealthier middle classes, wifely femininity became associated with being the mistress of a household, and masculinity with elevating the *need* to work to a moral and respectable *duty* to do so (Davidoff et al 1999 p 124; see also Chapter 2).

It was as a result of intellectual and political movements toward equality in the nineteenth century, particularly after decades of lobbying on the part of women (Holcombe 1983), that a series of reforming statutes was passed, first in 1870 and then in 1882, which entitled married women to keep first their property and then their wages. It was not, however, until 1935[8] that a married woman was finally enabled to acquire, hold and dispose of any property 'in every respect as though she were single'. These reforms captured the liberal spirit of the times, and meant that men and women, in marriage as in some of the 'public' spheres of life, were to be treated equally in terms of property acquisition and allocation: whoever acquired the property owned it and benefited from all rights accruing with ownership.

The more recent history of support and matrimonial property law is reviewed by Smart (1984). Like in the 1880s, in the 1950s the scheme of

8   The Law Reform (Married Women and Tortfeasors) Act 1935.

separate property existed in a context where there was no reciprocal obligation to support. Wives had to earn any maintenance they received from separated husbands by being 'good wives'. Maintenance was a moral issue, and husbands and courts were concerned to enforce this morality, even to the extent of ensuring that a wife remained 'chaste', often for years after separation, in order to justify her continued maintenance. The separate property regime created in the name of liberation and equality in the nineteenth century, but which operated as a severe hardship to wives who had little or no means of accumulating property, continued to do so in the 1950s. The further tradition of conveying the family home into the husband's sole name meant that often wives had no property interests to protect, and relied purely upon their husband's or the court's goodwill or determination of desert. The only incursion the law was prepared to make into the sacrosanct area of an individual's property rights was to create some rights of occupancy of the marital home for wives (Matrimonial Causes Act 1958; Smart 1984 p 46–49).

Morality continued to preoccupy courts in the 'swinging' 1960s with regard to awards of maintenance, and the incomparable value of a man's work to the accumulation of his property was confirmed at the same time as the value of women's work, to the same end, was disregarded. Smart (1984 ch 4) recounts how the Court of Appeal attempted in some cases to ameliorate the worst excesses of patriarchal authority in the family (Smart 1984 p 96; see also *Gissing v Gissing* [1969] 2 Ch 85) by extending the scope of equitable principles to create trusts in marital property in favour of non-owning women, but how it and House of Lords in other cases were equally adamant to affirm the principle that domestic work and childcare had no relation to the monetary value of a house or business. Only if a wife's or female partner's labour was more than that expected of a wife, or 'if she engaged in waged labour and put her wages explicitly towards the mortgage repayments or original deposit would she earn a share' in the property (Smart 1984 p 86; see *Gissing v Gissing* [1971] AC 886). Similarly, only innocent and deserving wives were entitled to maintenance on divorce (Smart 1984 p 96; see *M v M* [1962] 1 WLR 845), reinforcing the idea that 'married women did not have legal rights but only benevolent concessions made to them when they conformed to the ideal of wife and mother' (Smart 1984 p 96). By treating the parties as economic equals for the purposes of property acquisition and allocation, and reinforcing the norm of the good wife on maintenance questions, courts in the1960s were able to reconcile, after a fashion, traditional sources of obligation with newly emerging discourses of equality and fairness (Smart 1984 p 77).

The Matrimonial Proceedings and Property Act 1970, later consolidated with the Divorce Reform Act 1969 (see Chapter 3) into MCA 1973, brought some change, but this change simply rendered old certainties uncertain. The Act included a new objective and statutory list of factors for courts to consider in exercising their discretion. The objective was to place the parties, as far as was practicable and just, and having regard to their conduct, in the financial position in which they would have been if the marriage had not broken down. Under this principle of 'minimal loss' maintenance awards reflected the idea that marriage responsibilities were undertaken for life, implicitly denying that they were negotiable. In 1984, however, this objective was removed from the legislation, and two new duties were placed upon the court instead. First, courts were to consider the welfare of any children of the marriage (s 25(1)), and secondly, they were bound to consider whether a clean break between the parties was reasonable (s 25A).

Statutory conflict?

Unlike the previous statutory principles, these two duties are immediately at odds, both in terms of their ideological messages and their practical application. First, the clean break ideal, capitalising on the second wave women's movement's achievements of formal equality in the form of the Sex Discrimination Act 1975 and the Equal Pay Act 1970, reflects modern ideas of marriage as a relationship through which separate, equal individuals move freely, while the welfare principle is a part of the more traditional view of the marriage and family as a unity in which bonds are not severable and duties and responsibilities are not negotiable. By placing upon courts a duty to consider giving effect to both of these principles, the legislation promoted more explicitly two competing images of marriage and family (see further Chapter 7). Secondly, a clean break between the husband and wife seems to violate the legal 'truth' that the welfare of the children is promoted, at least in part, by the continuing relationship of their parents. Yet the law apparently easily accommodated parties maintaining their relationship *as parents* while making a clean break between them *as spouses*, even though parties often found this spurious split of their identities more difficult to understand and effect (see further Chapter 4 and Chapter 7).

It was in this ambivalent context that the case law, including the reasonable requirements principle discussed above, 'settled' the law, on the one hand by ensuring that spouses' (usually wives') interests could not be determined separately from the welfare of their children, and on the other, by treating them (usually husbands) as autonomous individuals moving freely in and out of relationships. Before the widespread procedural reforms and *White*'s judicial 'gloss' on the legislation, the reasonable requirements principle, judicial discretion to protect dependants and, arguably, dependencies, and the imperative of preserving individual proprietary interests combined to produce a body of case law that systematically reinforced traditional identities for husbands and wives (Diduck and Kaganas 1999 ch 6), while also reinforcing the message that these were freely chosen identities. It presumed, in other words, a version of the ambiguous normative family.

For example, s 25 was interpreted so as to minimise the value of domestic labour to the overall wealth of the family (*Page v Page* (1981) 2 FLR 198) and it required maintenance to terminate upon the wife's remarriage (MCA 1973 s 28(1)(a)–(b)) or to be reduced or reviewed upon her cohabitation with another man (*Suter v Suter and Jones* [1987] 2 FLR 232; *Atkinson v Atkinson* [1988] FLR 356; *Clutton v Clutton* [1991] 1 FLR 242). Focus on the welfare of the child meant that spouse support became eschewed in favour of child support or property awards and legitimated combining the wife's interests with the children's so that her entitlement as spouse was either replaced by or subsumed within her role as mother.

The Matrimonial·Causes Act, s 25 was not the only source of financial family law to convey these messages. Judicial interpretations of statutes and common law principles alike affirm the gender disadvantage in Law's protection of both property interests and welfare. First, the Pensions Act 1995 allowed courts to include the value of an occupational pension in the assessment of parties' assets and allowed them to 'earmark' a share of it for the benefit of a non-pensioned spouse when it accrued to the pensioner, and then the Welfare Reform and Pensions Act 1999 allowed the court to make an order splitting the pension entitlements at source. Justification for pension splitting and sharing comes from principles of compensation in which the non-pensioned spouse is deemed to have 'earned' a share in her spouse's pension by virtue of her 'work' as his spouse (Diduck 1999b). Research shows, however, that divorced women continue to suffer poverty in later life disproportionately compared to divorced men, and while this has much to do with their familial responsibilities limiting women's ability to accrue pensions entitlements of their own, it also is a result of the courts' reluctance to award them a share in their husband's pensions (see Ginn and Price 2002 and sources cited therein). Divorced women's poverty in later life may also be related to how these norms are incorporated into the dominant culture of settlement. Douglas and Perry found, for example, that both husbands and wives regarded pension assets (and other investments) as the property of the person who had paid for them and so were reluctant to include them in settlements. They observed 'a clear view among the men that "their" pension belonged to them and they did not recognise the wife as having earned a share in it' (Douglas and Perry 2001 p 78 reference omitted) and found it 'striking how the mothers traded their long-term financial position in favour of short-term security in the shape of the home' (Douglas and Perry 2001 p 78).

Secondly, in equity, *Lloyds Bank plc v Rosset* ([1991] 1 AC 107; [1990] 1 All ER 1111) remains the leading authority on recognising equitable interests in the marital home. In this case, the wife's actions of assisting with the building work, painting, decorating and renovating the marital home were described by Lord Bridge of Harwich as 'the most natural thing in the world for any wife' to do and, as such, were insufficient to evidence the required 'common intention' that she obtain an interest in the property. The court concluded that 'it is at least extremely doubtful whether anything less [than direct contributions to the purchase price by the partner who is not the legal owner] will do' (p 1119). By valuing financial contributions to the acquisition of property over non-financial ones, law legitimates a systemic disadvantage for the 'traditional wife'[9].

The system of separate property combined with judicial and social sympathy for traditional roles remains the foundation of the law today (see Diduck and Kaganas 1999 ch 5). Together they bear the Enlightenment legacies of formal equality, economic rationality and disconnected autonomy, as well as separate spheres of family and market and the gendered economic consequences that follow that separation. They also bear, in the discretion provided to courts in both common law and equity to adjust legal property interests, remnants of law's paternalistic concern to protect a man's family from his unfettered self-interest (Smart 1984). The legislation allows and encourages marriage partners to maintain their individuality through the pursuit of their individual self-interests, while tempering the potentially

---

9   As yet, the non-discrimination principle articulated by *White* and *Lambert* has not been extended to this area of equity, but there seems to be no reason why it might not (Diduck 2001b).

severe effects of this pursuit by investing the court with a discretion to re-allocate an individual's legitimately earned property to his dependants on divorce. The way in which the courts order this (re)allocation, however, always remains subject to ideas of the inviolability of property interests even when it is coupled with the promotion of children's welfare and subjective fairness in family relations.

'The scheme of [MCA 1973] must also be set in the wider perspective of history and of the general civil law. In this jurisdiction rights of property are not invaded or reduced by statutory powers save for specific and confined purposes. The purpose of this statute was to make fair financial arrangements on or after divorce in the absence of agreement between the former spouses. Beyond that power was not introduced to reorganise proprietary rights within families' (*Dart v Dart* per Thorpe LJ at p 294).

Ancillary relief, gendered subjectivities and the property rhetoric

It is important to identify how the gendered subjects 'husband' and 'wife' fit into the ambivalent rhetoric of property rights and family altruism beneath ancillary relief law. The property rhetoric is evidenced first of all in Thorpe LJ's comments above. He makes it clear that even family relationships must be comprehended through law's 'supporting ideologies of property, liberty, the minimal state, and the rule of law' (Cotterrell 1988; Ingleby 1992 p 146), which privilege the preservation of individual possessive property interests at the expense of ideas of community or shared interests. Even on a romantic view of family and family obligations in which the interests of the unit take precedence over individual interests, these 'supporting ideologies' affect how we and law forge individual subjectivities and understand and enforce obligations to share in marriage and on divorce. They create a form of 'property rhetoric' (Regan 1999 p 162) that relates to our conceptions of both intimate commitment and self/autonomy and therefore to conceptions both of marriage/family and family identities.

Regan (1999) distinguishes between that which he sees as two irreducible orientations toward marriage: the external orientation and the internal one. The external view emphasises the discrete individual whose entry into, and maintenance of, commitments is by consent and is subject to continual reflection. It sees marriage partners as having their own unique interests.

It is, in these ways, similar to Giddens' modern, pure relationship. By contrast, the internal view takes the relationship as 'a given without reference to individual costs and benefits' (Regan 1999 p 11). It is a commitment to a 'shared purpose that transcends the self' (Regan 1999 p 30), and in this way resembles a romantic idea of love and marriage. Regan suggests that each stance represents an important moment of marriage and that 'in the course of everyday life, spouses move back and forth between these two stances, seeking to balance their status as separate individuals and their roles as members of a marital community' (Regan 1999 p 29). He also suggests that law seeks to reconcile these competing visions of marriage, but that it does so implicitly rather than by frankly asserting the need to attach a particular stance to a particular set of circumstances (Regan 1999 p 30).

Regan thus identifies many of the antinomies between competing visions of marriage I have discussed in Chapter 2, and while he agrees that both visions are important to law and to individuals, he ascribes less mutual influence to law's norms and individual behaviour to affect each other, and does not politicise that process in the way that I do. Further, in suggesting that both individuals and law are engaged in ongoing shifts between the two visions, he also seems to downplay the possibility that individuals often seek to achieve a normative balance in achieving their *simultaneity*, the difficulty of meeting this demand, and its ideological power.

Regan does, however, go on to develop his thesis into an analysis of the economic consequences of marriage and divorce and isolates the self as an important component in the analysis. I have reviewed how different ideas of the self create different connections and commitments in intimate relationships and different abilities to disengage from those connections. Regan places these differences in the context of marriage and divorce finances. He starts from the proposition that related to, or indeed, prior to, these competing visions of marriage, is the normative self. Beginning with the essential authenticity of self-ownership, the rhetoric of property infuses notions of autonomy with notions of independence and the 'absolute control over the disposition of a thing or set of resources' (Regan 1999 p 163), including the self. In this version of autonomy, obligations to another, including obligations to share or otherwise dispose of property, are only legitimate if they are voluntarily undertaken. Interference with this sovereignty of self, ownership and free will becomes a form of interference with the individual autonomy, liberty and rights that constitute the liberal subject and therefore must be politically and philosophically, as well as legally, justified. This model of the autonomous self sees social interaction as economic or market interaction, where obligation becomes justified according to principles of compensation. It is held by both law and individuals within Regan's external view of marriage, or in a model of the modern, pure relationship in which partners remain independent, and stay together only for as long as they continue to 'get' something from the relationship. It is one half of the normative family.

This model of the self and the family it creates fundamentally reshapes family relationships. While they remain within the sphere of the private, they adopt the lexicon and culture of the public. Normally, 'the [public] is the realm in which all conduct conforms to the model of consent, [and] all things that do not or cannot fit this framework – that is non-consensual obligations – are consigned to the private realm' (Regan 1999 p 166), but in this model, at least for wealthy families, principles of marketisation and compensation replace predetermined and non-consensual obligations. These emergent conceptions also have a distinct gender dimension.

'The ideas of autonomy as independence and obligation as consensual rests upon the valorization of a realm in which men traditionally have been the primary agents, and the marginalization of a realm in which women traditionally have been the primary actors. Relationships marked by personal dependence, vulnerability, care and affection are taken as irrelevant in conceptualising the fundamental terms of human interaction' (Regan 1999 p 166).

Such relationships are therefore left to a realm in which that interaction is not traditionally measured in economic terms. If the basis for even intimate human interaction is now a marketised type of exchange of benefits, it follows that those family members who are able to operate easily within this rhetoric will receive the primary benefit of the law, and it illuminates the reasons why housewives who are able to reframe their care and home work into this rhetoric may also benefit.

Perhaps the 'principal normative theory of property' (Regan 1999 p 169) is 'market labour desert' theory (Regan 1999 ch 8) in which 'property rights are justified as a reward for the expenditure of one's labor' (Regan 1999 p 169), and its logical consequence, the inevitability of inequality in property holdings because talent and the willingness to expend effort are unevenly distributed among individuals (Regan 1999 p 187). These precepts are affirmed by Mance LJ in the *Cowan* decision and by the House of Lords' principled valorisation of market labour over domestic labour in the *Rosset* decision. They operate, however, unequally across the social spectrum.

White's prohibition of a discriminatory valuation of non-financial contributions to family wealth in the context of MCA 1973 means that support or property redistribution on divorce becomes justified on the market principle of exchange or compensation for services provided, yet the application of the principle only to 'big money' cases reinforces traditional ideas that rights to equality and the form of familial 'citizenship' they bring come only with sufficient wealth and significant property ownership. Only a minority of women will receive this benefit of recognition of their domestic labour (Boyd 1994) and in this way the principle may be the new millennium's version of the nineteenth-century marriage settlements favoured by propertied women.

Further, the principle supports the continued privacy of the family and its obligations:

'The valuing of women's domestic labour in the family law context is achieved only for a woman who did that work for another person with whom she no longer lives, specifically a male partner. The arguments that her male partner would otherwise be unjustly enriched. ... a single mother doing much the same work for herself and her children ... would not have ... recourse to anyone's property to compensate her. The benefit that society as a whole receives from women's (usually unpaid) domestic labour, particularly in the context of raising children is thus not recognized' (Boyd 1994 p 67).

The public dimension of familial lives and identities is thus denied while ideological support is provided for equality in the private marketising of those lives.

An alternative vision of subjectivity, autonomy and commitment lies in Regan's internal view of marriage, in which the self becomes a part of the other and of the relationship. Autonomy itself is conceived of differently and so, consequently, is its affiliation with property and obligation.

'Rather than take isolated independence as a given and obligation as problematic, we might well take obligation as our point of departure, and isolation as the condition that must be justified' (Regan 1999 p 167).

This inversion of liberal orthodoxy (see Chapter 1, particularly Sevenhuijsen 1999; Hirschmann 1992) is the philosophical expression of women's traditional experiences with private, non-consensual, *familial* obligations. In legal discourse, a form of it is expressed by community of property regimes, or by financial rewards for those who cast themselves and their behaviour in caring or interdependent roles. Its power, however, is attenuated in both legal and common-sense discourse in which it is usually expressed either as an unattainable ideal or as a vague source of dissatisfaction on the part of (usually) women who sought fairness in and at the end of relationships on its terms. Further, while individuals may feel an idealistic commitment both to the submission of self that characterises falling in love (see Chapter 1; Regan 1999 p 70) *and* to the need to maintain their unique identity while in love (see Chapter 1 and Chapter 2), they, like law, tend to base obligations, particularly financial obligations, that arise from these relationships in the marketised model of autonomy and obligation, rather than in one which recognises the *fact* of the relationship as giving rise to them. Where an individual or the law does take an internal stance to obligations, it adopts a half-way approach that locates obligation in the legal status of 'spouse' and determines it according to traditional gender roles, while proclaiming that that status and the roles and dependencies it engenders are voluntarily assumed and rationally negotiated. Indeed, it is *marriage* that the law protects and that Regan wishes to protect when he advocates legal ordering based upon this stance (Cohen 2002).

Family practices

Individual husbands and wives construct their familial identities within this same ideological context that reveres both market principles and institutional obligation. Often the families that individuals live by can accommodate both equally acquisitive individuals and co- or mutually dependent husbands and wives, but their family lives are practised in a social and economic context that makes the accommodation less successful.

We have seen, for example, that women's role in families is perceived to be primarily as carer (Chapter 4), and this means that even when they are engaged in paid employment outside the home, that employment tends to be part-time or work which can accommodate domestic responsibilities (Family Policy Studies Centre 1995; Lewis 2002 especially at p 53; Neale and Smart 2002 below; Hatten et al 2002). It tends, therefore, to be lower paying than men's work and to have fewer benefits attached to it (Morris and Nott 1995; Lewis 2002; Irwin 1999; Hatten et al 2002). Women, even employed women, still bear primary responsibility for housework and care work (Brannen et al 1994; Neale and Smart 2002; Silva 1999; Hatten et al 2002), or housework *as* care work (Silva 1999), and women's paid work is still viewed as secondary or marginal to the household income (Pahl 1989; Irwin 1999).

Men, on the other hand, find their familial roles constrained differently. Men still tend to be viewed as breadwinner rather than carer: they participate in housework to a lesser extent than their female partners (Brannen et al 1994; Hatten et al 2002) and their role as husband or father tends to be secondary to their role as worker, despite idealisation of a dual-earner, dual-carer model of family (Lewis 2002; Neale and Smart 2002; Sevenhuijsen 2002; Chapter 4; Hatten et al 2002) because the work world assumes a worker with little or no familial responsibility. Finally, law, while professing a disinterest in the sex of its subjects, serves to perpetuate these gender differences by discouraging workers from having identities also as family members. There is little state-subsidised childcare (Fox-Harding 1996) and no legal requirement for employers to provide it. While providing only moderately generous maternity leave and no paid parental leave, law, only from 2003, provides for only two weeks' paid paternity leave[10]. Law and state policy thus create an economic advantage for men and childless single women to the disadvantage of wives and mothers by directing the economically rational choices individuals must make (Hatten et al 2002). Importantly, 'these arrangements have been incorporated into modern identities of masculinity and femininity' (Neale and Smart 2002 p 185).

Whilst the marriage subsists, economic imbalance may or may not be problematic to the spouses[11]. The material implications of a wife's lower income or earning capacity may be masked by her interrelationship with her husband's wealth, and both may be content with settling their roles and identities in this way. Pahl's (1989) interviews with married couples, for example, revealed unproblematic gender differences in the organisation of family economics.

> 'A woman may contribute a higher proportion of her earnings to housekeeping than her husband but her income is still likely to be regarded as marginal; a man may contribute a lower proportion of his earnings but he still feels justified in spending more than his wife on leisure *because both define him as the breadwinner*' (Pahl 1989 p 170 emphasis added and references omitted).

10   The Employment Act 2002.
11   Backett (1982), for example, provides interesting research on how women 'explain' inequities while their marriages persist.

Her research, however, also enabled Pahl to confirm the existence of 'his' marriage and 'her' marriage (Pahl 1989 p 4–6 and 169; see also Backett 1982) where adherence to the gendered norm did sometimes cause difficulty. The following passage illustrates this difference in the context of household incomes:

> 'Husbands typically earned more than wives and had more fringe benefits from their employment. They usually saw themselves as breadwinners for the family, even when they retained substantial sums for their own use; wives' earnings were seen as more marginal to the budget, even though most women spent their wages on the family. Husbands were less likely to have to justify the money they spent and they tended to spend more on their own leisure. In general, husbands were likely to perceive a greater degree of sharing in marriage than wives, who were more aware of conflicts of opinion and of interest' (Pahl 1989 p 171).

Further, even those who wished their relationship to be based upon equality often found that they 'slipped into' a traditional division of labour (Neale and Smart 2002 p 187; Hatten et al 2002; Chapter 4). Pahl (1989), for example, found that the husband's greater earning power was associated with greater decision-making power. More importantly, the classically patriarchal ideology of husband as breadwinner/decision-maker and wife as dependant legitimated his power even where wives earned more than their husbands.

Since Pahl's important work, there may now be evidence that individualisation is affecting the traditional ideal: men and women may be working harder to achieve idealised, equal, dual-carer, dual-earner relationships (Neale and Smart 2002; Hatten et al 2002). This work is difficult, however, and its success variable in an economic and social policy context that assumes the 'rational economic man' as its actor (Barlow and Duncan 2000a and b; Barlow et al 2002) promotes individualism, individual responsibility and 'paid work for all', but at the same time relies upon (partial) wife dependency (Barlow et al 2002; Lewis 2002) and preserves women's economic disadvantage in employment (Irwin 1999). It is an example of the difficulty Beck and Beck-Gernsheim identify for women to achieve individualised biographies (Chapter 1). So, while Neale and Smart (2002) found that many fathers did take childcare into account in their strategies for paid work and many mothers did take financial considerations into account in their strategies for motherhood (Neale and Smart 2002 p 186), and indeed, usually after divorce but sometimes before, some began to see themselves in these new, non-traditional ways, traditional norms about motherhood, fatherhood and market engagement remained evident in their identity construction (see also Chapter 4).

'The identities of the mothers in our sample appeared to be bound up primarily with their relationship with their children. They were more likely to start with an imperative to care ... They also recognised the economic imperatives of raising children and may have extended their role to accommodate this ... In contrast, the identities of most of the fathers in our study remained bound up primarily with their employment. They were likely to start with an imperative to secure paid work ... They were also likely to recognise the imperative to care for their children, and some extended their role to accommodate this' (Neale and Smart 2002 p 196).

They conclude that 'a strong element of choice is still associated with a mother's decision to enter or stay in the labour market' and the same 'element of choice is still associated with a father's decision to care' (Neale and Smart 2002 p 196). These people were, in other words, unable to see themselves as the equally caring and earning individuals idealised in policy rhetoric as embodying the good (post-divorce) family; the best they could achieve was this unsatisfactory, partial reconciliation (see also Chapter 4; Hatten et al 2002). Perhaps their failure is not surprising, though. The policy rhetoric is ambiguous for mothers who are, ideally, to be at home and in paid employment and for fathers who are to provide financially but must also 'be there' for their children. Lewis (2002) concludes that the reality of the one-and-one-half earner family rather than the myth of the dual-earner family may, in fact, suit social and economic policy best.

Family laws that organise the (re)distribution of familial wealth by defining and enforcing obligations thus depend upon the rhetoric of property, including the 'market labour desert theory', of liberal equality, of choice and free will and of the traditionally gendered subjects who engage with it. These subjects are, in fact, the men and women who are also concerned to meet the degendered, abstract carer/earner of law, but who practise their familial lives less ideally.

Solicitors, procedure and the construction of identities

Parties bring with them to litigation, mediation or negotiation not only their perceptions of their ideal familial selves but also the actuality of their different material circumstances and their different degrees of affiliation with the property rhetoric. Men, for example, who may be used to seeing themselves as the primary decision-makers in the family, may find it difficult to accept a mediation or FDR session which gives voice to their wives' views of the marriage, obligation and finances (see also Chapter 5) and this difficulty may be exacerbated where husbands perceived a degree of sharing in the marriage that their wives did not perceive. Further, the dominance of the property rhetoric in these sessions means that a spouse who locates him or herself within this rhetoric has an advantage over one who does not. Davis et al (1994) note that many men negotiating ancillary matters on divorce felt that it was 'their' money that was being dealt with (Davis et al 1994 p 49) and research from the United States found that in divorce 'men discuss with their attorneys ways to "keep" their property or assets, and women discuss ways to "get" assets' (Gray and Merrick 1996 p 243). Finally, mothers' pragmatic but short-term concern for their children often outweighs concerns for their longer-term, personal financial welfare (Douglas and Perry 2001).

Few people will enter into FDR sessions or attempt to negotiate the separation process without assistance from others, whether it be from family members, friends, mediators or solicitors, and these third parties may play a part in the identity-forging process both prior to and during the mediation or negotiation of family obligations. Solicitors are an important influence for those who rely upon them, not only because they represent to the parties the law and its authority, but also because in the complex process of negotiation between solicitor and client, legal and extra-legal stories are exchanged, 'truths' are confirmed and rejected, and 'meaning' is made not only of a client's case but of her or his identity (Chapter 3; Sarat and Felstiner 1995; Diduck 2000). When clients negotiate with their solicitors the financial positions they will adopt with 'the other side', therefore, we must also be attentive to ways in which these negotiations also affect the ultimate subject positions they adopt.

Eekelaar et al (2000) studied the divorce work of solicitors by observing meetings between solicitor and client and by interviewing solicitors. Their observations confirm that family law solicitors are, by and large, settlement – rather than litigation – oriented but that the process of reaching a position from which to negotiate settlement is often difficult. The process involved seeking 'a convergence' among the client's interests, normative standards, and the client's instructions (Eekelaar et al 2000 p 90–91) and often required the solicitor to work to raise women's perceptions of their 'entitlement' and to lower men's (Eekelaar et al 2000 p 93 and 99). The language they used was particularly salient. Even while solicitors advised husbands and wives that legal ownership of property was not strictly adhered to on divorce, their language both supported and revealed the extent to which the property rhetoric was implicated in the law and in the identities 'husband' and 'wife'.

In advising wives of their interests and 'entitlements', solicitors tended to emphasise more subjective ideas of fairness, sometimes relating this fairness to women's responsibilities for the children who were to remain in their care (Eekelaar et al 2000 p 91–93).

'I ... pointed out the unfairness of the husband's proposals, the likelihood that she would not be able to buy somewhere decent with her share of the equity, the need to provide a secure base for her sons until they were ready to leave home and so on' (Eekelaar et al 2000 p 92).

In advising husbands, on the other hand, the rhetoric of care and responsibility was used infrequently. The rhetoric of property rights dominated and solicitors, perhaps unknowingly, colluded with its gendered assumptions through the language they used. In a case, for example, where the wife sought the entire proceeds of the sale of the home, the solicitor advised his client that her proposal was 'daylight robbery' (Eekelaar et al 2000 p 92). In another, the solicitor advised his client that he was going to have to 'pay [his wife] off' (Eekelaar et al 2000 p 93). Eekelaar et al conclude, in fact, that, in general, 'the lawyer's language did seem to employ a rhetoric which was cast in terms of the client's entitlements rather than their duties ... [E]ven where they were curbing the hopes of the husbands, they did this more on the basis that these hopes were unrealistic rather than by emphasising the legal [or moral?] duties the men owed to their families' (Eekelaar et al 2000 p 99). Eekelaar et al suggest, however, that this is as it should be. To them, lawyers and law should have no place in 'preaching' to clients or in being agents in transmitting a particular government's messages about duties or responsible behaviour (Eekelaar et al 2000 p 101). While this argument has some force, it fails to acknowledge the degree to which lawyers seem already to be doing just this (see also Chapter 3) in the degree to which they participate in the normalisation of identities, responsibilities, and the protection of private property interests. Sarat and Felstiner (1995) conclude also that in the process of meaning-making that occurs between lawyers and clients, lawyers 'reify the boundaries of legal relevance, legitimating some parts of human experiences and denying the relevance of others. … The program lawyers present to their clients appropriates the marriage to the realm of property and defines the connection to their spouses exclusively in those terms' (Sarat and Felstiner 1995 p 147).

Even the most well-intentioned lawyers, then, affect the process of negotiation by affecting the constitution of their clients' identities and responsibilities. These are constituted in both a property discourse of equality and a romantic discourse of dependence, yet it is a process that tends to increase the distance between the two discourses rather than to harmonise them.

Law and informal ordering

We have seen that divorce often acts as a catalyst for change as parties seek new ways to practise family life (Neale and Smart 2002 p 186; Chapter 3) and that parties bring to private ordering their interpretations of justice, both objectively viewed and arising from subjective aspects of their relationship (also see Chapter 5). 'Justice' for different people may demand consideration of power, intimidation or guilt, or of recognition of the history of care, home and paid work in the family, or of understanding the importance of relationships with other loved ones or the community. The location of private ordering within the property rhetoric and the ideal of individual autonomy and responsibility (Regan 1999 p 51–52), however, minimises the roles these considerations can play. Further, while the flexibility inherent in a discretionary substantive law should be able to accommodate these contingencies and particularities, the extraordinary synthesis of liberal equality and gendered familial roles in that law means that the legal rules, while they exist only as 'default rules' in a scheme of private ordering (Regan 1999 p 52), weigh heavily in the process.

The ancillary relief procedure

Whenever a petition includes an application for ancillary relief, the ancillary relief procedure operates to provide rules for both courts and parties, but as is stated in the President's Direction 25 May 2000, 'a key element in the [ancillary relief] procedure is the Financial Dispute Resolution appointment' (President's Direction 2000 para 3.1). The FDR appointment 'is to be treated as a meeting held for the purposes of discussion and negotiation' (President's Direction 2000 para 3.1), and in this respect is more than merely a case management scheme. Parties are expected to provide complete disclosure of financial information, of their offers and their proposals to resolve outstanding issues. Their disclosures are not later admissible in evidence (President's Direction 2000 para 3.2). Similarly, the judge in the FDR is to consider openly the court's reasoning process should the matter proceed to litigation (Bird 2000) and in this way give the parties norms with which to work as well as incentives for settlement. 'The most important part of the [judicial] role seems to be the elimination of unrealistic expectations' (Bird 2000).

Since the procedure came into general application in June 2000, reviews have been favourable, although a few difficulties have been identified with how it has been implemented by individual district judges and solicitors (Bird 2000). In other words, criticisms have not been raised about the procedure itself, but about those few 'bad' solicitors or district judges who have not seemed to have grasped its value and played their parts properly. The solicitors interviewed by Eekelaar et al were similarly impressed by the pilots when they encountered them, notwithstanding that some of these also were disappointed with the few 'bad' district judges they encountered (Eekelaar et al 2000 p 156–162) who did not appear to utilise the scheme effectively.

In the light of the preceding discussion of justice and gender, a number of difficulties can be identified with this scheme and its normative undercurrents. It is a procedure driven by the imperative to narrow the issues and the evidence to relevant ones, and to encourage, if not coerce, settlement. But it is also about free negotiation and the parties' responsibility to reach their own agreements. It means that families therefore appear to remain free of law's direct intervention while law's norms are brought to bear in more subtle ways.

First, the scheme's assumption that all conflict is to be avoided must be questioned (see Chapter 3 and Chapter 5). Conflict in family disputes may be the result of many factors, including gendered perceptions of 'his' and 'her' marriages and the expectations these create. By submerging conflict, the material differences created by those different perceptions are buried as well and the result can easily be a homogenisation of the marriage on the dominant terms (Ingleby 1992).

We have seen, for example, that divorcing parties are more concerned with attributing blame and responsibility for the marriage breakdown than is law (Ingleby 1992; Chapter 3 and Chapter 5) and that a psychodynamic perspective provides an explanation for this 'need'. Clients also tend to believe that 'fairness' or justice dictates recognition of this 'culpability' through financial rewards and punishments. Perhaps the most extreme example of this belief was that felt by the UK Men's Movement (UKMM). The movement interpreted statistics showing that almost 75 per cent of all decrees of divorce are granted to wives (Social Trends 1998) as demonstrating that '80% of divorces' are sought by and granted to women on their 'unilateral demand' so that the husband's 'commitment to the marriage is arbitrarily swept aside' (UKMM 1997 p 2). Its website in 1997 spoke of the 'divorce racket' in which the innocent 'respondent victim is robbed of his home, his money and his children' (UKMM 1997 p 1). Less strident, but echoing similar sentiments, is Barry (1995) who writes of one's 'moral duty' to comply with the expectations of marriage, and the adverse financial consequences which he feels ought to accompany breaches of those expectations (Barry 1995 p 51).

While these views may provide evidence that some men adhere to a romantic or internal view of marriage where obligations ought to be considered in the light of more than merely economic rationalism, they also may be evidence of a desire to return to the more blatant gender expectations of the pre-1973 law and the traditional duties and certainties of that romantic family (see Chapter 1 and Chapter 2), rather than to its ideas of unity and sharing.

Conflict or fault is also relevant in another way. Obstructive or destructive conduct on the part of one or other of the spouses after the separation and/or during financial negotiations often influences the instructions clients give to solicitors. Women, in particular seem prepared to settle for less than their solicitors think they might be entitled to on the basis of meeting immediate as opposed to long-term need, having 'a quiet life', maintaining the relationship for the sake of the children, or extricating themselves from frightening, overbearing or violent relationships (Eekelaar et al 2000; Douglas and Perry 2001; Chapter 7). They make these financial decisions on the basis of moral rationalities as opposed to merely economic ones (Himmelweit 2002; Barlow et al 2002), and while their solicitors do not formally countenance these considerations as legitimate, they seem often to accept them as pragmatic (Eekelaar et al 2000 p 95–96). This may be as it should be, at least in part; it gives some legitimacy to these non-financial considerations and thus disrupts the rational economic man paradigm and the property rhetoric of which he is a part. But husbands invoke these moral rationalities less frequently than wives (Weitzman 1992). They tend to confine their negotiations to their rights to property. Their pragmatism, consonant with law's property rhetoric, thus creates for them an economic advantage in divorce negotiation.

Secondly, a difficulty relates to the procedure where the applicant for ancillary relief, usually the lower-earning or non-earning wife, is obliged to file her application first. Although her 'needs' should no longer determine the outcome of her application, she must still establish some case for them at the outset. As the matter progresses, including at the FDR, the onus remains upon her to justify her claim 'because the underlying assumption is that it is "his money"' (George 1997 p 730). Thus, the process, as well as the underlying property rhetoric places her in the position of supplicant.

Thirdly, both parties are obliged to exchange and file with the court a completed Form E which details not only present and anticipated future income and expenses, but also their standards of living, contributions to the marriage, and personal details. The first thing to note about this detailed financial disclosure is Pahl's observation that of those who refused to take part in her study, it was men who tended to be more reluctant than women to disclose details about their income and finances (1989), and Eekelaar et al's confirmation of (usually) husbands' tendencies to obstruct or avoid disclosure (Eekelaar 2000 p 162–165). The second point is that the onus upon the applicant to establish her reasonable needs in the future places her at a disadvantage relative to the respondent in anticipating the many details required for Form E. Much legal effort is then spent in scrutinising her claims. As one practitioner stated:

> 'with the emphasis on reasonable requirements the scrutiny of the budget has developed an increasingly important role in these cases. ... Are budgets to be tested against "what we used to spend" or "what he can afford" or "what I think I need"? ... Understandably a lot of wives say "why do I have to go through all this and not him?"' (George 1997 p 730).

White's de-emphasis of needs does not de-emphasise the importance of Form E and the questionnaires resulting from it. These exclusively financial concerns limit the bounds of legal 'relevance' to those which concern the rational economic actor and will 'form the basis of the court's interpretation of what is at issue in the case' (Bird 2000).

Finally, the role of the judge in the FDR was unclear during the pilots; it was still 'in a state of development' (Frenkel 1997 p 727). He or she was not to act as a mediator, but rather was there to make findings of fact and to facilitate settlements by canvassing possible outcomes or objectives of any court order (Frenkel 1997). This new judicial role was problematic for parties and remains so. The discretionary nature of s 25 and the indeterminacy with which courts treat the s 25 criteria make any 'narrowing of the issues' or closing down of 'hopeless' arguments (Frenkel 1997 p 728) at the FDR a potentially inconclusive exercise. On the one hand, a particular judge's reasoning process, objectives or assessment of the criteria carry the weight of judicial authority and are thus, as they are intended to be, powerful settlement incentives. On the other hand, if negotiation is unsuccessful, it is too easy to assume that another judge – the ultimate trial judge – can take a completely different view of the strength of an argument or the statutory criteria. The SFLA found that the uncertainty engendered by s 25 meant that some district judges are 'less vigorous' than others in stating a view of a potential final outcome, and that some parties were therefore reluctant to settle (SFLA 1998 p 6) and Eekelaar et al (2000) also found that the judicial role was variably performed.

Guidance from the Court of Appeal on the issue of the judge's role confirms that it can take many forms (*Rose v Rose* [2002] EWCA Civ 208, [2002] 1 FLR 978), including an early neutral evaluation after hearing submissions. That the suggested outcome offered by the judge has become more than an incentive to settle is also confirmed by this case in which the agreement the parties reached as a result of the court's suggestion, but had not yet submitted in the form of an order, was held to be an unperfected order of the court rather than a contractual agreement between the parties and that they were, therefore, bound by it, notwithstanding the informal process by which it was reached.

Further, judicial case management was still controversial in England and Wales in 1997 (Zander 1997), and it therefore made sense to pilot it before implementing it fully. It has since become more widespread and more accepted (Roberts 2001). While I do not adhere to all of Zander's criticisms of judicial case management, I do sympathise with his view of the importance, yet difficulty, of training judges for the role. If 'justice' is to mean more than simply keeping families away from formal adjudication, district judges must have some awareness of gender issues, relationship dynamics and how these interact with family practices in order to achieve it in their directions or decisions. As I observed regarding mediation (Chapter 5), dejuridification can allow subtle forms of coercion and power to remain unchecked.

Pre-application Protocol

Along with the Practice Direction, the President of the Family Division issued a Pre-application Protocol, which 'outlines the steps the parties should take to seek and provide information from and to each other prior to the commencement of any ancillary relief application' (Pre-application Protocol para 2.1). It advises as to best practice for solicitors, encouraging them 'to explore, timeously and efficiently, the scope for early settlement between the parties. Thus, while the new ancillary relief procedure is itself intended to promote settlement, the protocol is designed to prevent, as far as possible, cases reaching the application stage in the first place' (Douglas and Murch 2002 p 59).

The aim of the protocol is to ensure that:

'(a)   Pre-application disclosure and negotiation takes place in appropriate cases.

(b)   Where there is pre-application disclosure and negotiation, it is dealt with

    i.   Cost effectively;

    ii.   In line with the overriding objective[12] of the Family Proceedings (Amendments) Rules 1999

(c)   The parties are in a position to settle the case fairly and early without litigation' (Pre-application Protocol para 1.2).

The standards set in the protocol are more than simply guidance to solicitors and clients, however: '[i]f proceedings are subsequently issued, the court will be entitled to decide whether there has been non-compliance with the protocol and, if so, whether non-compliance merits consequences' (Pre-application Protocol para 1.3). As Douglas and Murch point out, such consequences appear to mean costs sanctions (Douglas and Murch 2002 p 59).

Procedural law seems to be implicated here in shaping more than litigation practice. It is designed to shape solicitor and client practices from the moment they meet to discuss ancillary relief issues. The direction in which

---

12   The overriding objective of the rules is to enable the court to deal with cases justly (SI 1999/3491 para 2.51B).

it moves them is firmly toward private ordering, with its emphasis upon sharing information ('openness in all dealings is essential'), but it remains resolutely within the property framework with its insistence upon 'clarifying the issues' (Pre-application Protocol para 3.4) and limiting disclosure to that which is relevant to them: 'Documents should only be disclosed to the extent that they are required by Form E' (Pre-application Protocol para 3.4). Solicitors and clients are therefore encouraged, at the risk of incurring costs sanctions, to disregard facts, information, perceptions and considerations other than financial ones. Dealing with cases 'justly' in the view of these rules appears to prioritise justice for the rational economic actor, who is then provided with the freedom to negotiate his own post-divorce financial arrangements.

Comprehensive mediation

There is little reason to expect that these difficulties can be surmounted completely where the parties attend mediators' rather than lawyers' offices. Mediation of ancillary relief issues is likely to become more usual, given its encouragement in the Pre-application Protocol (para 2.3) and its importance in the Family Law Protocol issued by the Law Society (2002a). Further, its central place in regulations concerning the public funding of family law matters (Chapter 5) means that it will play a significant role in more divorces, particularly those of the less wealthy, and will thus affect women disproportionately to men (Mossman 1994).

As reviewed in Chapter 5, mediators aim to facilitate personal agreements between the parties, ones that they themselves feel are fair. In this way, it is subject to similar criticisms as those made of informal solicitor negotiations, but because mediations lack the partisanship provided by solicitors, the parties' determinations of their own interests dominate the sessions. Interestingly, when mediating parties in Walker et al's sample referred their agreements to a solicitor, they ran the risk of being told they were settling for too little. 'What might be viewed by the parties as "fair" within mediation may be considered "unfair" by a solicitor acting purely and properly in one client's best interest' (Walker et al 1994 p 134). Solicitors were seen to 'change the focus of mediation towards entitlement rather than focusing on mutual needs and mutual fairness' (Walker et al 1994 p 135).

Mediators, like lawyers, disregard issues of fault or conduct in mediation sessions (Walker et al 1994; also see Chapter 5) and spend a 'great deal' of time establishing the factual financial positions of the parties (Davis et al 2000 p 233). 'Fairness' is comprehended and legitimated in this context only:

> 'The result [of mediators' fact-finding focus] may be to dampen the emotional engagement of the parties and to prepare them to negotiate more coolly on what tend to be more readily divisible and liquidatable assets' (Davis et al 2000 p 233).

Mediation's focus on needs, even though they are said to be 'mutual needs', still places the wife in the position of having to justify her request for 'assistance'. The time spent by mediators going over budgets with their clients, and the detail required, has been identified as a cause for concern, by parties and mediators alike (Walker et al 1994; Davis et al 2000). Further, Walker et al (1994) also found evidence which suggests that men and women have different priorities in household spending (also see Chapter 7). The value placed upon leisure activities, for example, differs between men and women. Mediators had to encourage women to include expenditures for leisure, even though these were not within their actual means. Like 'He put down forty pounds a month entertaining, for going out basically. I put nothing and thought "Oh sod that" so I put forty quid in too ...' and 'He claimed "golf", so I claimed "golf", even though I don't play!' (Walker et al 1994 p 67). Walker et al summarise the difficulty as follows:

> 'For many women the basic problem was having enough money to feed and clothe the children. They were more inclined to focus on necessities than luxuries. On the other hand, men with more time on their hands were more likely to attribute importance to leisure pursuits' (Walker et al 1994 p 67–68).

The point is that mediations focus on mutual needs and personalised fairness may not end up 'balancing' the calculations out (Walker et al 1994 p.68), so long as luxuries are viewed by husbands as 'needs', and by wives as 'wants' (Walker et al 1994 p.67).

Family Advice and Information Networks (FAINs)

Section 8 of FLA 1996 required attendance at an information meeting before making a statement of marriage breakdown and/or application relating to financial and property matters. It will not now be implemented, but policy to educate and inform people before they take steps to end their relationships is preserved by the newly created and piloted FAINs. Attendance at a FAIN will not be mandatory for divorcing or separating couples, but it is envisaged that they will provide a single point of reference to provide information and access to a range of services which would facilitate the dissolution of broken relationships in ways which minimise distress to the parties and their children (Legal Services Commission 2002). Presumably this information will be similar to that imparted at the information meetings, although it will be able to be tailored to the parties' individual circumstances (Legal Services Commission 2002). The content of this information is crucial to determining how husbands and wives will perceive the relative strengths of their positions; it will affect their choice of whether to negotiate, mediate or litigate their financial issues and also how they proceed in their chosen route. Legal information directed at presumptively equal parties, and which appears to be neutral, remains subject to law's 'supporting ideologies', and may have the effect of psychologically empowering the property-owning and earning partner at the expense of the non-earning, non-owning partner, or may create expectations of a fairness rooted in the equality of contributions to wealth. As I have argued, the former tends to advantage men over women and the latter is more aspirational than real for many parties.

Conclusions

The observations and arguments in this chapter suggest that normative values expressed by law and held by individual men and women are reproduced and legitimated by a system of private bargaining where they remain implicit and therefore unchallenged. In this system, parties are encouraged to make their own identities, as worker and/or carer, to organise their families and relationships on the basis of merging, yet maintaining the integrity of these identities, and on divorce, to reach a fair agreement about allocating the wealth they have accumulated as a result of those choices. Both the system and the parties acquire meaning from within the competing frameworks of market equality and romantic obligation. In the market framework, the claim must be framed in terms of compensation, reinforcing the property rhetoric and the privacy of the family at the expense of other moral and public considerations. Awards to wives in this framework often leave husbands feeling that their rights have been violated, that they have been 'robbed' of their money and their house (UKMM 1997). In the alternative framework, legitimated by a discretionary notion of fairness that often rewards sharing based not upon market principles but upon the romanticised marriage and its traditional masculine and feminine familial identities, a successful claimant wife can be left to feel that she succeeded in establishing not a legal entitlement to share family assets, but rather her (or her lawyer's) 'wiles', her moral worthiness as wife/mother or her dependence upon her husband's wealth and goodwill. That the parties or the courts sometimes do view such a settlement as vaguely 'fair' is, therefore, not the point. That which may seem 'fair' to a supplicant and a provider is almost certainly different from that which seems fair either to equal, independent partners in a modern, marketised relationship, or to interdependent partners in a unified one.

There is currently no articulated theoretical basis for support or reallocation of property in English law. Why ex-spouses, as opposed to the state, parents or children should bear any obligation to support each other is nowhere made clear. It remains part of the history and tradition of marriage and is assumed to be a fundamental part of that institution. It indicates that there is something peculiar about the marriage relationship; the *fact* of it gives rise to obligations[13]; duty inheres in status, even if those obligations and duties then can be evaluated in marketised economic terms and can, in appropriate cases, cease with a clean break. On divorce, parties often attempt to sustain this image: they see themselves as distinct individuals with distinct interests, asserting claims and assuming obligations on the basis of these interests, even while the claims they assert and the obligations they assume flow from the fact that in the past they were members of a marital community (Regan 1999 p 140) in which individual interests were indistinguishable from the collective interest of the unit. Ancillary relief law also seeks to preserve the integrity of both the unit and the individual, yet the consequences of gendered imperatives to care and to earn are that it upholds the normative (post-divorce) family in which romantic traditional roles for spouses are reinforced by the privatisation of economic rewards and punishments, while sustaining the myth that those roles and the risks attendant on them were voluntarily assumed, both pre- and post-divorce.

13   The Law Society has recently prepared proposals for reform of the law concerning support and property distribution on the breakdown of same and opposite sex cohabitation. It recommends assumption of the law in this respect into 'Family Law', but while it proposes some financial protection from the economic disadvantages of cohabitation be provided by law to some opposite sex cohabitants, it is clear that these rights should not be made equal to the rights of spouses. Interestingly, it also recommends offering same sex couples an opportunity to register their relationships, take up of which would give them property and support rights similar to those of married couples (Law Society 2002b).

Chapter 7

Child support: the new co-parenting

In the previous chapter I discussed the way in which the rhetorics of property and choice interacted with a form of traditional paternalism in law to promote a normative family able to sustain apparently contradictory images of voluntarily assumed and status-based familial obligation. Legal treatment of the child support obligation also provides evidence of an attempt to inscribe and enforce legally both a status-based, absolute moral obligation and a freely chosen, reflective one. Child support is more than merely another form of family financial obligation, however. While it can be conceived as an aspect of the package of financial matters that must be determined 'ancillary' to divorce (see MCA 1973 s 23(1)(d)–(f)), it can also be understood as an aspect of parental responsibility – one of the 'rights, duties, powers, responsibilities and authority which by law a parent of a child has in relation to the child' (Children Act 1989 s 3(1)). Child support determinations must, therefore, achieve some degree of 'fairness' as between divorcing parents, yet they are increasingly seen also to be an important expression of the welfare principle.

Child support's dual character means that while the welfare of the child remains important, if unarticulated in the legislation, it cannot override the goal of justice between parents. And so, determinations of child support do not subsume parents' individual interests to those of the child. Their interests are important in the interests of justice, but they are located in, and expressed through, the rhetoric of responsibility – social, familial and parental – that is central in family law discourse generally. Here, justice reflects law's altruistic and romantic family in which burdens and benefits are shared in the interests of the unit as a whole *and* the modern individualistic family that prioritises individual choice, individual well-being and financial independence. This chapter will examine the way in which child support law historically has accommodated these two parts of the ideal and will argue that the Child Support, Pensions and Social Security Act 2000 can be seen as an attempt to harmonise the two in an unprecedented way. It will also explore the material consequences of shifting priorities within the ideal for fathers, mothers and children.

Law's assumptions and family practices

When children and parents live in the same household, the law says very little about how they carry out their financial obligations to each other. It is clear, however, that children have no right to share in the overall family wealth, but simply the right to be supported during their dependence (Douglas 2001 p 185). Law thus does not assume democracy or children's economic 'citizenship' within the family, but rather relies upon an idea of children's status to endorse their (economic) dependency (see further, Chapter 4). Apart from a duty on spouses to provide, or make a proper contribution to provide, 'reasonable maintenance' for a child of the family (MCA 1973 s 27(1)(b); see also DPMCA 1978 s 1(b)), the law allows decisions about the financial welfare of members of 'intact' families to remain private. This duty to provide, in any event, is a purely statutory creation. The common law imposed only a moral duty upon married fathers to support their children, and created only 'imperfect' legal mechanisms to enforce that duty (Smart 1987; Maclean and Eekelaar 1997; Barton and Douglas 1995; Finer and McGregor 1974). Children born out of wedlock, who had no legally recognised guardians, had no one against whom they could claim even a moral obligation for support (Maclean and Eekelaar 1997 p 34), although justices of the peace could make orders against mothers or fathers of children who were supported by the parish. Where the mother wished the unmarried father to provide some assistance, she was forced to rely upon quasi-criminal bastardy or affiliation proceedings which often seemed designed to give the father a 'sporting chance' to get away with paying nothing (Barton and Douglas 1995 p 200). It was not until relatively recently that the unconditional moral duty of married parents was extended legally to all parents, first by the Family Law Reform Act 1987, and then by consolidation in the Children Act 1989 (Children Act 1989 Sch 4) and later, the Child Support Act 1991 (CSA 1991).

The law assumes, then, that parents share their financial resources with their children, so that the standard of living of individual family members is usually measured by that of the earning parent(s). The duty to provide reasonable maintenance, however, interacts with law's individualism and the property rhetoric, often with consequences that reflect gendered and generational familial positions that belie this assumption. Despite, for example, trends towards more fathers doing more care 'work', the fact that when parents and children reside in a single household, the primary responsibility for childcare usually falls upon mothers (see Chapter 4) means that just as mothers tend to be more aware of the actual physical, mental and emotional labour involved in caring for children, they also tend to be more sensitive to the daily financial requirements of childcare (Neale and Smart 2002 p 191–195). The actual costs of rearing children can, therefore, be obscured from fathers. Perhaps it is a result of this *experience* of childcare as much as it is an expression of normative motherhood, but mothers also exhibit stronger preferences than fathers for putting the children's financial needs before their own individual needs for leisure (Walker et al 1994 p 67–68; Lister et al 1999) and for spending to benefit children (Pahl 1989; Ringen and Halpin 1997; Lister et al 1999).

Lister et al (1999) studied couples with children in receipt of means-tested social security benefits and found that spending patterns *and* expectations regarding those patterns were highly gendered.

> 'Men prioritized personal spending money more highly than women, who typically took responsibility for vigilant restraint over both their own and their partners' spending, going without themselves to prioritize their children's needs. In practice, the distinction between "individual" and "collective" expenditure was sometimes muddied; men tended to legitimate elements of their "individual" spending as having a collective benefit and to define women's "collective" spending on their children as "individual". The latter reflected a belief, shared by men and women, that responsibility for meeting children's everyday needs was the woman's domain' (Lister et al 1999 p 205–206).

As long as there is sufficient money to meet everyone's needs and priorities, these gender differences need not disrupt the dualistic ideal; mothers' and fathers' family practices can accommodate both acquisitive individualism and altruistic collectivism, both gender equality and gendered roles, both status-based duty and negotiated responsibility. When issues of child support come to be determined at law, however, these actual family practices reveal a challenge to the ideal. Many non-resident fathers, for example, expect to maintain the economic pattern they established within their 'intact' family, but child support law reveals to them the actual costs of rearing a child, ascribes economic value to the 'work' of caring and requires them to share equally in these costs. It is thus not surprising that many of them perceive injustice in what they perceive to be shifting normative goal posts.

Law's idealised assumptions about shared family wealth when parents live together are extended to when they live apart. Just as assumptions of co-parenting cause difficulties when separating parents negotiate residence and contact, however, the ideal of *economic* co-parenting, which may never have been consistent with families' actual behaviour, may cause problems when they negotiate child support because parents' *actual* behaviour tends to remain consistent before and after separation. It should come as no surprise then, that many fathers see child maintenance – payments representing the day-to-day costs of rearing children – as something to 'beat'; to them it is inconsistent with the fatherhood they enjoyed in their 'intact' families in which the care work they did with children consisted mainly of days out or 'fun' times (see Chapter 4) but was re-framed as equal caring. After separation, therefore, many are happy to buy presents for children, pay for treats, and buy large items of clothing for school, all on an informal basis and so at their discretion, but they balk at knowing about or paying for the day-to-day 'maintenance costs' of childcare. That many residential mothers also seem to wish informal financial arrangements to continue as expressions of fatherly care, as much as for the financial benefit they provide, demonstrates that law's assumptions about equal, shared parenting both during cohabitation and after may be out of step with family practices.

The ideal of shared parenting that is evident in child support law appears to be an attempt to reconcile two parts of child support's legacy. The first is its political/economic origins in the 'Poor Law' which has caused it to be seen as a 'liability' of parenthood (Douglas 2001 p 85) and the second is its legacy in the moral obligation that is inherent in the status of parenthood. This attempted reconciliation means that the law must have regard to issues of fairness in the distribution of the financial 'burden' as between parents and also to the child's welfare and to a parent's responsibility to promote that welfare. This law, now contained in the Child Support, Pensions and Social Security Act 2000, is based upon the framework of the revolutionary Child

Support Act 1991, but adapts that law toward a new vision of the 'good' post-separation parent and family that incorporates both the traditional romanticism of moral duty and freely chosen, freely exercised and negotiable responsibilities. Substantively, it 'embraces both a partnership of equals and joint enterprise approach to the family unit' (Douglas 2001 p 185). Before I review the new law and its meaning for parents and children, however, I wish to turn to its provenance, first by reviewing the courts' interpretations of the statutory discretion they enjoyed in child support matters in the 1980s and then by reviewing statutory reform in the 1990s.

The Matrimonial Causes Act 1973: divorcing parents

Under MCA 1973, child maintenance is one of the orders for ancillary relief available on divorce (see further Chapter 6). The statute provides guidance to courts in making these orders and in 1984 that guidance changed from requiring courts to consider the objective of placing the wife and children in the position they would have been in had the marriage not broken down, to requiring them 'to have regard to all the circumstances of the case, first consideration being given to the welfare while a minor of any child of the family who has not attained the age of eighteen' (MCA 1973 s 25(1)). The court also has a duty, when deciding to exercise its discretion to make an order in favour of a party to the marriage, 'to consider whether it would be appropriate so to exercise those powers that the financial obligations of each party towards the other will be terminated as soon after the grant of the decree [of divorce] as the court considers just and reasonable' (MCA 1973 s 25A(1)). In this change we see a shift from the enduring, traditional, pre-1984 family towards a more modern idea of consensual, negotiable and transient commitments. The clean break provision seems to envision adults passing through a series of 'pure relationships', while the 'first consideration' principle appeared to temper the potentially harsh effects these relationships could have upon children (see Chapter 1 and Chapter 6).

Early commentators were unsure of the effect the first consideration principle and the clean break principle would have upon ancillary relief orders (Bromley and Lowe 1992 p 758–760 and sources cited therein), yet their combination was not thought by the Law Commission that recommended them to be a problem. It thought that clean-break orders would be appropriate in 'comparatively few' cases, and 'where there were infant children almost non-existent' (Law Commission 1981 para 24). In practice, clean-break settlements whereby the husband provided no, or only nominal, maintenance for the wife and children in exchange for transferring to the wife 'his share' of the marital home were made frequently (Douglas 2001 p 186), and orders approving these settlements were made 'in the hundreds' (Priest 1997 p 115) by county courts in England and Wales. While the jurisprudence of the courts did not directly endorse this practice, the popularity of these settlements evidenced a form of 'submerged jurisprudence' (Priest 1997 p 115) which said much about how solicitors interpreted the law to their clients (Barton and Douglas 1995).

Even before the House of Lords clarified 'fairness' as the overriding objective for ancillary relief orders (see Chapter 6), the courts saw their aim as achieving fairness, justice and reasonableness between the parties (Ancillary Relief Advisory Group 1998 p 33), and the first consideration principle has never been seen as incompatible with this aim. 'First consideration' was held, early on, not to mean 'paramount consideration'[1] and the Lord Chancellor's Advisory Group on Ancillary Relief reported in 1998 that '[t]he existing provision requiring first consideration has been interpreted judicially as not intended to override the general objective, not express but implied, to attain a financial result which is just as between the parties' (Ancillary Relief Advisory Group 1998 p 15).

Thus, child support law in the context of MCA 1973 sought justice rooted in the separateness of the parties to a marriage, and while their individuality was traditionally gendered rather than abstractly universal (see Chapter 6), it appeared to take precedence over any moral connection with, or legal duty to, their children. Further, as a result of child support being a part of the overall ancillary relief package, the interpretation of 'first consideration' and the overriding objective of fairness and justice, there appeared, in the 1980s, to be an ill-defined relation between child support, spouse support, social security payments (Eekelaar 1991 p 98 and Chapter 6), and property adjustments. This amalgamation of what can arguably be described as provisions designed to meet separate objectives and resting upon divergent theoretical bases also meant that any moral duty a parent owed to his (or her) non-resident children became secondary to issues of justice as between husband and wife.

The first consideration requirement was intended to encourage the courts to make an appropriate order for the children first, and then to consider an order for the spouse from the remaining resources (Bromley and Lowe 1992 p 759), but Eekelaar's (1991) study of registrars revealed that only

1   *Suter v Suter* [1987] 2 All ER 336.

54 per cent of respondent registrars accorded priority to child support
over spousal support (Eekelaar 1991 p 94) and that frequently the two
types of orders were not conceptually distinguished (Eekelaar 1991 p 95).
Moreover, 54 per cent of registrars declined to use any kind of guideline
to determine the amount of child support to order. Instead, they seemed
to rely upon their experience as registrars or their 'common knowledge'
(Eekelaar 1991 p 95). Those who were inclined to use guidelines favoured
the social security scales (Eekelaar 1991 p 95), which were, of course,
based upon a subsistence level of income. Finally, because courts tended
to protect the financial interests of the payer's 'new' family by taking these
new dependencies into account when assessing maintenance levels for 'old'
families[2], many divorced lone mothers and their children were forced to
rely upon means-tested state benefits in order to survive.

Thus, the consequences of the 1984 shift in policy, which tended to
accommodate and possibly encourage apparently confluent relationships,
were often unfortunate for newly single women and the children in their
care. Combined with the effects of the strength of the property rhetoric,
subsuming child support into an overall ancillary relief package meant that
the standard of living of lone mothers and children tended to drop quite
dramatically on divorce (Douglas and Perry 2001), even if they continued
to live in the former marital home. Further, the number of lone parents
dependent on state support more than doubled between 1980 and 1989 from
330,000 to 770,000 (Hoggett and Pearl 1991 p 106).

Support for non-marital children: the Children Act 1989

The situation with respect to support for non-marital children was no better in the 1980s. Although unmarried mothers could, within a three-year
limitation period, take affiliation proceedings in the Magistrates' Court
against putative fathers, before the Family Law Reform Act 1987 'equalised
the private law financial opportunities for marital and non-marital children', the law was 'notoriously reluctant to "punish", as the law would have
seen it' (Barton and Douglas 1995 p 200), a man who had not established
a relationship with the mother. Financial obligations to children ran with
obligations imposed by traditional family membership. Even after 1987,
awards, when made, were low (Barton and Douglas 1995), so that by 1990,

the single largest group of income support recipients was lone mothers who simply were not receiving maintenance from non-resident fathers (Diduck and Kaganas 1999). The law was not substantially changed when it was ultimately consolidated in the Children Act 1989.

Under the Children Act 1989, Sch 4, the court is empowered to make periodical or lump sum payments for the benefit of the child, and the High Court or County Courts can also secure payments and order settlements of property or property transfers for the benefit of the child. In exercising their jurisdiction, courts are directed to consider a statutory list of factors that includes the income and financial resources and needs of the parties (parents) and the children and the manner in which the child was expected to be educated or trained (Children Act 1989 Sch 4 para 4(1)), but excludes the welfare of the child[3]. Even under the Children Act, then, allocation of financial responsibility for children prioritises issues other than the child's welfare.

By 1990, the government felt that the courts were protecting second families unduly by relying too heavily upon the state's provision for first families. Douglas (2001) summarises the results of government research at the end of the 1980s as follows:

'[E]ven where child maintenance was ordered or agreed, the amounts payable were all too often based on little more than "gut feeling" as to what it was appropriate to expect a particular parent to pay, rather than on a rational assessment of what the child needed. To add to the inadequacy of the court regime, the Government found widely differing levels of maintenance being set in similar circumstances. As the final straw, they also found that barely a quarter of those required to pay were making regular payments' (Douglas 2001 p 186).

In the light of these findings, government appeared to construct the problem of child support as its failure to display rationality and achieve consistency as much as its failure to ensure the privacy of family financial provision. The men, women and children who encountered the law, however, often perceived its deficiencies differently.

3   Section 1(1) establishes the paramountcy of welfare when a court determines any question with respect to the upbringing of a child or to the administration of his or her property, but s 105(1) defines upbringing to include the care of the child but not his (or her) maintenance.

Mothers' and fathers' perspectives

Findings of inconsistency and inadequacy in the assessment and enforcement of child maintenance were of obvious financial concern for government. These findings, however, might also have caused concern in a more abstract way by providing evidence of apparent irrationality and inconsistency in a system which purported to be coherent, certain and rational. Further, they may also have provided evidence of an apparent lack of respect, either for the system or, worse, for a traditional morality in which duty and responsibility are absolute and predetermined (see Chapter 2). It is possible, however, to see these findings as evidence not of *disorder* but of a negotiated and personal ordering of individual family practices. Findings of apparent inconsistency and inadequacy may reflect what decision-makers (Eekelaar 1991), solicitors (Davis et al 1994) and parties alike see to be pragmatic solutions to difficult circumstances (Burgoyne and Millar 1994; Clarke et al 1994 and 1996a). What some may see as low or inadequate assessments may in fact be realistic ones intended to encourage consistency in payments, to recognise payers' responsibilities for new dependants, and to allow recipients to maintain the benefits they receive from social security. Apparent inconsistency in assessments, despite similar income levels, can be similarly reframed from violations of a principle of certainty into the promotion of the value of discretion and the flexibility to take into account factors, conditions and concerns apart from merely financial ones. Irregularity of payments may not reflect merely irresponsibility or selfishness, but rather one-off large purchases or other informal, often non-financial, assistance that is critically important to parents and children.

This exercise in re-evaluation allows us to view parents' dissatisfaction with the court-based system in a different light from that shed by government. While many lone mothers echoed the government's frustration with the court's assessment and collection of child maintenance (Clarke et al 1996a p 16–17), for example, they also appreciated the control it gave them over the process and the way in which it linked child support to other issues, both financial and non-financial (Clarke et al 1996a p 17–18).

Clarke et al (1994; 1995; 1996a) interviewed lone mothers about their experiences of and attitudes toward the obligation to support, both under the court-based system and after implementation of the Child Support Act 1991. They found among their respondents 'considerable dissatisfaction' (Clarke et al 1995 p 29) with the discretionary court-based system both in terms of levels of maintenance assessed and enforcement of it. They also found, however, that many mothers were happy with informal, extra-judicial arrangements for support agreed with their ex-partners, usually because they conferred greater financial benefit on the children than formal payments would have done. Some of these informal arrangements took the form of money payments and many were help in kind or occasional contributions toward the cost of holidays, presents or toys for the children (Clarke et al 1995 p 30). Sometimes mothers were content with informal arrangements because it helped to maintain an amicable relationship with their former partner (Clarke et al 1994 p 140) and did not encourage direct attempts to control them in the way that formal arrangements did.

'Their experience of receiving maintenance was that it conferred power on their former partner ... "he sent me a letter, 'I want a list of everything you buy, baby foods, don't put any extra pennies on ... ', he wanted a list of everything I bought for her, nappies and things like that"' (Clarke et al 1994 p 139).

Further, many mothers thought that receiving maintenance conferred rights upon fathers (Clarke et al 1996a p 34), particularly of contact (Clarke et al 1994 p 138; 1996a p 32), or created a dependency the mothers wished to avoid for any number of reasons. For example, many women had chosen to rear their child independently and wished this choice to be respected (Clarke et al 1996a p 32). Many felt that fatherhood was more than biological and so, in the context of their histories with the man, they attributed to him no obligation to support their children: 'he wasn't that interested in me, just used me, so why should he be interested in Kelly?' or 'he's never bothered the years I was with him, so why should he bother now?' (Clarke et al 1996a p 33). In general, these mothers were keen to preserve their sense of control over their lives and their relationships, and therefore valued the voluntary nature of informal agreements and court proceedings in which their *choice* to utilise them was respected.

Non-resident fathers paying maintenance pursuant to court orders in 1989 also expressed general agreement with the principle that both parents should contribute to the support of children, but, like their former partners, they qualified this belief in a number of ways (Burgoyne and Millar 1994). They did not want to pay too much, they did not want any of their payments to represent support for their ex-partner, and probably most importantly, their willingness to pay child support depended upon their acceptance that the payments were a legitimate and fair demand on their resources; they did not consider child support to be an unconditional obligation (Burgoyne and Millar 1994 p 103; Bradshaw et al 1999).

Similar to Finch and Mason's (1993) findings concerning adult kinship responsibilities (see Chapter 2), Burgoyne and Millar (1994) found that fathers believed that financial obligations for children 'reflect a history of social exchange within the relationship itself and are negotiated in ways that allow for considerable variation' (Burgoyne and Millar 1994 p 103). Other factors that were important for separated fathers were obligations to second families, reasons for the separation, the other parent's circumstances, and a desire to keep control (Burgoyne and Millar 1994 p 99–101). Fathers attempted to keep control by 'paying in kind rather than cash': 'I try to keep it as low as possible and pay for the children's clothing out of my own pocket' or else 'she would probably just spend it on something I would not think necessary' (Burgoyne and Millar 1994 p 101), or by offering to put money into a trust fund for the children where it would be out of the resident parent's reach (Davis et al 1994 p 59).

While control was important for many fathers, Bradshaw et al (1999) found that informal support sometimes represented more than this; for some fathers it was an expression of care:

'Spending money on informal support was an important aspect of non-resident fathers' social relations with children. ... It was primarily a medium through which fathers could express their feelings to their children directly. Therefore, strictly speaking, informal support was not a form of payment ... but was mainly an integral part of active relationships. Thus it was distinguished from maintenance' (Bradshaw et al 1999 p 221).

Fathers' conceptual distinction between maintenance and informal payments is important. Maintenance payments were viewed by most fathers, in Bradshaw et al's study, as an obligation to the child, but because they were paid to the mother, they were seen as open to negotiation based upon either their history with her, upon her willingness to enable contact with the children, or upon her ensuring, usually by her spending patterns, that the payments were visibly from the father. Fathers viewed the mothers as 'trustees' of their relationships with their children – 'and trustees of both the maintenance monies and the expressions of care attached to them' (Bradshaw et al 1999 p 222). The fairness or justice of the claim for child support was thus perceived by fathers as legitimate based upon more than the level at which it was assessed; it was bound up with past and present relationship exchanges and negotiations.

Parents thus appear to recognise factors other than economic ones as being important to the support obligation. Neither mothers nor fathers appear to operate on the assumption that support should be provided unconditionally by all biological parents in all circumstances, although, as we have seen, there were gender differences in the types of circumstances deemed important. Maclean and Eekelaar (1997) also found evidence of the perceived conditionality of the support obligation, and they also found gender differences in how it was expressed. For parents in their study, however, these differences related to gender differences in opportunities for parenthood by choice. Parents responded to a hypothetical fact scenario in which they were asked whether a non-resident father's obligation to his 'natural' children ought to change in various circumstances.

> 'Our attitudinal data reveals that fathers adjust the extent of the obligation which they feel they owe towards their natural children by reference to their subsequent social parenthood whereas mothers do not think they should do this' (Maclean and Eekelaar 1997 p 142).

Attention to these gender differences is important. While relationships, negotiability and social circumstances are important for both mothers and fathers, their meaning to each is subtly different. Fathers seem to be able more easily to position themselves as morally responsible or not based upon their relationship with the mother. She is the focus and the father's duty to his children is mediated through, and is even sometimes dependent upon, her. Mothers, on the other hand, tend to consider the quality of their relationship with the father more in terms of the potential it, or he, has either to disrupt or enhance the interests of the children. The children are their focus. This difference may be another manifestation of women's tendencies to, and men's expectations that they will, assume responsibility for maintaining relationships (Bradshaw et al 1999) and may also illustrate differences in men's and women's relative abilities to move freely in and out of relationships of choice and their consequent linking of moral and legal obligations to those choices.

Finally, gender differences are also evident in the discourses within which parents conceptualise the support obligation. Mothers may more frequently and more clearly articulate it within the welfare discourse, while fathers appear more at ease within the individualised rights and property rhetoric. In a study of custody bargaining in the United States, Weitzman (1992) concluded:

> 'when women think about child support, they are likely to focus on how the financial transaction will affect their relationship with their former husband [either by maintaining his goodwill or by extricating themselves from him] ... Men, in contrast are more likely to see child support as a purely economic matter or a purely legal matter; they think about how much it will cost, what a judge is likely to order, and how much money they will have left' (Weitzman 1992 p 399).

In general, the court-based system appeared to offer, to judges, a flexibility to use their discretion to take into account any number of factors in awarding child support and, to parents, some agency in determining fairness according to their individual circumstances. Law's normative assumptions about the source of family obligation and about motherhood, fatherhood and property, however, meant that in practice, that discretion was limited to a search for fairness as between the parties that resulted in mothers and children becoming dependent upon the state (or new paternal providers), while fathers assumed responsibility for 'new' dependants. As we have seen, for different reasons, neither payers nor recipients were entirely satisfied with the results.

Professionals' and children's perspectives

Solicitors, for their part, felt that the system worked well and that the broad statutory discretion was necessary to take welfare into account properly in court orders (Ancillary Relief Advisory Group 1998). They and family court judges were cautious about any proposed abridging of that discretion, yet, ironically, solicitors frequently found themselves in the position of denying to mothers and fathers any connection between child support and the history of the relationship, or between child support and contact (Eekelaar et al 2000), limiting for themselves the breadth of the discretion they extolled.

Mediators' views were more equivocal. Mediation had a much lower profile and take-up rate before 1993, particularly for financial matters, and comprehensive mediation was only in its infancy in the 1980s. Mediators were only just coming to terms with the lack of financial 'norms' to follow in mediation sessions and with the detailed financial information required to mediate property and maintenance issues (Walker et al 1994) when it was announced that CSA 1991 would take child support decisions out of their hands entirely. The process of all-issues mediation was similar to that used in child-focused mediation sessions, however, with mediators encouraging clients to achieve their own ideals of fairness (see Chapter 5 and Chapter 6). Where mediators found men placing more weight on leisure and personal spending and women placing more weight on spending for the children, they responded simply by encouraging the women to include more in the budget for themselves (Walker et al 1994 p 68; Chapter 6), further endorsing the rhetoric of economic justice as formal equality.

Children's views of child support generally reflected the adult debates (Smart, Neale and Wade 2001 p 91–92). The (limited) research done with children shows that most believe that parents share equal moral responsibility for their (the children's) financial support. Also, like their parents, most children see fairness in accommodating within this moral responsibility factors such as the quality of the relationships between the parents and the child, or the actual financial circumstances of the parents. Children in Clarke et al's (1996b) study, for example, saw the support obligation as rooted in biological paternity (Clarke et al 1996b p 27), but thought that parents should sort out the detailed arrangements themselves (Clarke et al 1996b p 30). Finally, for many children, the length of time required to resolve maintenance issues through the courts was the cause of some distress (Gillespie 2002).

Thus, it seems that all people (except perhaps solicitors and judges) potentially touched by the court-based system of child support had concerns about it. British families and government were not alone in thinking that the system 'needed' changing: low levels of child maintenance and inadequate enforcement of it led many countries in the 1980s to review their child support law and procedures (see Maclean and Eekelaar 1993; Garrison 2001; Canada Department of Justice 2002). The schemes adopted in other countries included producing guidelines for the court, creating stricter enforcement mechanisms, creating a purely administrative regime, and providing further state support for lone-parent families. The way in which individual countries constructed the 'problem' influenced their chosen solution.

I have suggested that in the UK, the 'problem' was perceived as arising on two levels. The first was on a purely economic level while the second was symbolic. The court-based system of child support failed to meet law's objectives of fairness as measured by rationality, consistency and certainty and, importantly, it may also have appeared to promote an image of negotiable and flexible families and negotiable and flexible family responsibilities. The law seemed to allow parents – fathers most clearly – to pass through a series of relationships leaving the state to deal with the financial and moral consequences. In the context of 1980s moral conservatism and official 'back to basics' policy, this behaviour seemed to represent a dereliction of familial duty and a further retreat from the traditional family values that were said to promote the 'good' society. Further, while the old law purported to keep family financial responsibilities private and regulatable through the courts, the increasing numbers of lone-parent families receiving state support provided evidence that it was failing to achieve that which it claimed. Thus, measures were introduced to recover some public funds from absent parents (Social Security Act 1990), but the most radical solution came when the government took the opportunity to 'hitch its own financial worries to the interests of children' (Maclean and Eekelaar 1993 p 213). The imperative to restore 'traditional family values' became established as part of the welfare discourse through the creation of a natural and non-negotiable support obligation based purely upon the biological status of parenthood.

The Child Support Acts 1991 and 1995

The statutory response to the 'problem' of child support has attracted the attention of academics, legal practitioners, journalists and grass-roots parents' and fathers' groups. The 1991 Act has been said to be principally concerned with the Treasury (Child Poverty Action Group 1994; Keating 1995), with the concept of fatherhood (Collier 1994; Wallbank 1997), with the image of the 'family' (Diduck 1995), with the negotiation of the public/private divide (Boden and Childs 1996), with the dejuridification of family matters (Maclean and Eekelaar 1993; Rodger 1996) and with the creation of a new sense of family and individual responsibility generally. All of these descriptions of the Act may be valid. The White Paper on which it was based, however, suggests that it was also concerned with the welfare of the child. The document was entitled 'Children Come First' (DSS 1990) and its commitment to the welfare principle is stated immediately: 'The measures set out in this White Paper will secure many advantages. Most important of all they will serve to advance the welfare of children' (DSS 1990 'Foreword'). Welfare was clearly linked, however, to a particular view of responsible parental behaviour. The CSA 1991 did not go so far as to proclaim that the welfare of children was to be paramount or even a consideration at all in determining maintenance assessments, but the rhetoric pervading the White Paper was of a parent's responsibility to promote his or her children's welfare by exercising *financial* responsibility for them: 'The payment of child maintenance is one way in which parents fulfil their responsibilities towards their children' (DSS 1990 'Foreword').

Romantic/traditional, status-based responsibility was thus confirmed, yet its expression as an element of fairness between parents as equal market actors was also confirmed in the way that the maintenance assessment was to be carried out and in the assumption of parental equality in both financial and caring responsibilities.

The CSA 1991 thus harnessed the new (at the time) concept of parental responsibility in order to coerce a type of 'traditional' family responsibility upon apparently non-traditional families. In the Act's family, duty was neither negotiable nor flexible. First, it was the *fact* of biological parenthood that created the responsibility, which then persisted whether or not the parents ever lived together, formed any relationship with the child or indeed any other relationships with new partners or children. Secondly, unmarried fathers had this responsibility whether or not they had parental responsibility pursuant to an agreement or court order under the Children Act 1989. Parenting for them meant paying (Keating 1995). Thirdly, the amount they were to pay was determined by a rigid formula that allowed for little variation regardless of either party's circumstances. It, like the obligation itself, was externally predetermined and non-negotiable.

The Act thus endorsed the ideal two-parent family by connecting or re-connecting (usually) fathers to lone-mother families (Clarke et al 1994; Diduck 1995). Further, because the responsibility that it created was purely a financial one, it endorsed the father as distant provider and mother as carer (see Chapter 4). Despite its rhetoric of welfare, there was no reference in the White Paper or the Act to the other incidents of parental responsibility, to the importance of caring for children or of maintaining contact with them.

Endorsing traditional gender roles and reasserting the primacy of the family that relied upon them may have been one of the (perhaps unintended) consequences of the Act, but it conveyed an important normative message. It also prioritised biological over social relationships, imposed duties on the sole basis of those relationships and coerced the privatisation of financial support in families by reinforcing those relationships and traditional generational roles. It meant a very important change: it shifted a man's 'responsibility' – his child support obligations – from his 'second' family back to his 'first' family, reversing the pragmatic policy adopted by courts in the years before which was seen as 'permitting men to move from family to family, having more children, and then moving on again' (Smart and Neale 1999 p 178).

Adopting the language of children's welfare, the Act was intended to make men more responsible by attaching a legal duty to a moral one which was said to inhere in their biological status as parent: 'The former ideology that marriage sets up obligations which cannot be removed by later commitments to another person [was] strikingly replaced [CSA 1991] by an ideology that the obligations incurred by parenthood cannot be cast aside or reduced by taking responsibility for another person's children' (Eekelaar 1991 p 120).

Economic incentives were adopted to encourage compliance with this moral obligation. 'It was assumed that if he had to pay for his first family, he would think hard before starting a second family he could ill afford to support' (Smart and Neale 1999 p 178). Women's behaviour was also deemed amenable to economic inducements. New partners were to understand that they took their men 'encumbered' and lone mothers were no longer able to choose the nature of their financial relationship with their former partners, unless they were sufficiently wealthy. Those on income support were required to provide the names of biological fathers of their children, or risk the 'punishment' of having their income support reduced. Further, the fact that a CSA 1991 assessment reduced pound for pound her income support meant that a lone mother and her children would not see any financial benefit from child support unless she moved into employment. The CSA 1991 for these families had merely a symbolic effect which could be converted to a material one only if the mother acted economically responsibly. The government thought that to allow a mother to keep any of her child support on top of income support would constitute a 'work disincentive' (Maclean and Eekelaar 1993 p 227). The actor assumed to respond to these economic rewards and punishments is clearly the rational economic man for whom factors other than financial are deemed irrelevant to voluntarily chosen intimate and reproductive behaviour.

There is the beginning of a paradox here. On the one hand, CSA 1991 attempted to establish or re-establish a form of the traditional family, albeit one spread across households, but on the other, it appealed to an individual's economic rationality to do so. It looked to the idea of the individual's responsibility, not only to his or her family members but also to society, to sustain this family form. Thus the legislation appealed to a non-traditional morality rooted in the responsible exercise of choices:

> 'It is right that other taxpayers should help to maintain children when the children's own parents, despite their own best efforts, do not have sufficient resources to do so themselves. That will continue to be the case. But it is not right that taxpayers, who include other families, should shoulder that responsibility instead of parents who are able to do it themselves' (DSS 1990 para 2.1).

The CSA 1991 was thus a profoundly but paradoxically moral document; it was concerned with imposing a *traditional* moral imperative upon an apparently increasingly non-traditional public, but as in the ill-fated divorce reform (see Chapter 3), the means of achieving this aim was by identifying a *new* morality: one's personal responsibility to exercise one's choices for the well-being of children and society. Unlike in divorce reform proposals, however, in which information and education was designed to shape moral rationalities, in the case of child support these were not thought to be sufficiently persuasive, and incentives were designed to appeal also to an individual's economic rationality.

Implementation of the Act

The essence of the UK scheme (see also Maclean and Eekelaar 1993) was to create a formula, based upon income support levels of both the 'absent parent' and the 'person with care', by which child maintenance was to be assessed. It created an agency (The Child Support Agency (CSA)) with officers to administer the assessment, and gave this new authority exclusive jurisdiction over child support where the 'person with care' of the child received state support or approached the agency for an assessment. It thus dramatically reduced the range of cases over which courts would have jurisdiction to exercise their wide discretion. One of the remarkable features of the Act was the speed with which this procedure was developed and implemented. The first public announcement of the government's intentions came in January 1990 and the legislative process was completed in July 1991 (Maclean and Eekelaar 1993 p 205). This short time-frame allowed for little consultation and research (Maclean and Eekelaar 1993 p 205)[4], and it was therefore not surprising that many of the difficulties with the scheme were not identified until after it was implemented. The Act came into effect in 1993 and problems became apparent almost immediately. The government itself identified deficiencies in implementation and administration of the scheme. Not only did the scheme lack public confidence, it 'was the subject of angry, sometimes violent public reaction, when (mostly) absent fathers and their "new families" objected to the increased levels of maintenance they were ordered to pay and to the formula's disregard for "clean break" property settlements effected in the past' (Diduck and Kaganas 1999 p 398).

As a result of criticism from many sources, government made a number of changes to the calculation of the maintenance assessment and the administration of the Act, including raising absent parents' 'protected income' levels to take into account responsibilities for their new families and for taking into account, in certain circumstances, previous clean-break settlements. The Child Support Act 1995 (CSA 1995) allowed for discretionary departure directions to be issued by child support officers and for persons with care to build up credits which could be 'cashed in' up to a maximum of £1000 on obtaining employment over 16 hours per week. These changes represented a marginal shift from the extreme position the 1991 Act adopted towards new relationships and carers' decisions to earn, but reports from mothers, fathers and children may indicate that it did not go far enough to reflect their needs and actual family practices (see below).

Clearly the 1991 Act was intended to change people's behaviour (Keating 1995; Smart and Neale 1999). It was designed to motivate individuals to think before procreating and/or separating, and it wanted to effect a cultural shift in which child support was no longer seen as 'optional' (Keating 1995 p 30). Equally clearly, it was about recovering for the state as much of its expenditure on single parent families as possible (Maclean and Eekelaar 1993 p 216). Finally, another goal of the legislation may have been to relieve

---

4   This process can be contrasted with the process undertaken in other jurisdictions where the issue of child support was also of concern. In Canada, for example, government ministers directed a Family Law Committee to study the issue of child support in 1990, a series of reports was produced from 1991 to 1995, in 1996 the federal government announced a new child support package including child support guidelines, new enforcement measures and increases in public spending and public information, the relevant legislation came into effect in 1997, and in 2002 a report evaluating the first five years of the scheme's operation was published (Canada: Department of Justice 2002, appendix 1).

expenditure and costs related to the litigation of child support disputes. This sideways shift from the litigation to the administration of disputes may be a part of the larger project of the dejuridification of family matters, but unlike other dejuridification measures which provided incentives to encourage families to order their own affairs and 'messages' about how to order them, this was a shift *towards* interventionism, albeit in an unusual form. It meant that for the first time, about ten million new people became subject to a social security formula that would affect their behaviour and their finances, and introduced a more explicitly political form of control over their family matters (Rodger 1995 p 66).

Consequences

Implicitly, and perhaps in a way not envisaged by government, the CSA 1991 and 1995 seemed to effect a shift in concepts of fatherhood, motherhood and family. By constructing the child support obligation as a 'parental responsibility', the government was able to work within a discourse of children's welfare to justify its radical legislation. Perhaps outside of its vision, though, was the result that many families would take seriously the idea of parental responsibility as a part of a shift in the meaning of fatherhood (see Chapter 4) by expecting fathers to become more than merely distant providers. In this way, limiting a non-resident father's parental responsibility to financial responsibility failed to capture the spirit of change in the families Britons lived by. Wallbank (1997) suggests that absent fathers were able successfully to construct themselves as 'victims' of the 1991 Act by harnessing both this discourse and the Act's failure to actualise it:

> '[D]ue to the increased burden of child support fathers are able to argue that their capacity for fulfilling their parental responsibilities is undermined due to economic hardship. In so doing, they are able to demonstrate that the allegations of fecklessness are false by stating that their priorities lie with the sustenance of mutually beneficial father/child relationships' (Wallbank 1997 p 212).

Collier, too, argues that while the 1991 Act may have attempted to reassess father absence, it was its failure to reassess father presence that was more problematic (Collier 1994 p 386). It is important to note, however, that motives beyond that of merely establishing the 'new' fatherhood in law may have played a part in campaigns against the CSA. Collier, for example, notes how the CSA was portrayed by segments of the media and campaigning fathers' groups as a part of a feminist conspiracy to 'sack fathers' from families (Collier 1994 p 386) – it appeared to undermine not just traditional fatherhood but ultimately the traditional family and the social order (Collier 1994 p 387). What was really at issue in the campaigns against the CSA, he says, was 'the confused nature of the concept of fatherhood in law, and the uncertain nature of men's (of all classes) "responsibility" and "commitment" to women and children' (Collier 1994 p 386). Wallbank notes how the CSA presented a challenge to the gains made by men in the bargaining and settlement of financial matters on divorce (Wallbank 1997 p 211), and generally to the perceived gains women made in achieving power in families (Wallbank 1997 p 212) to parent autonomously (see also Diduck 1995).

The CSA was thus profoundly *about* fathers and fatherhood. It attempted, without apparent success, to reconcile two competing images of fathers and fatherhood: that of the distant provider and the new, responsible father. The image of mothers and motherhood invoked by the CSA, were also less than coherent. Mother was constituted as dependant and carer who was required, in the (financial) interests of her children, to (re)attach them to their biological father (Diduck 1995). The Act did allow mothers some responsibility to head their man-absent families, but it ascribed little agency to them to manifest this responsibility by determining for themselves and their children the best means of supporting that family (Diduck 1995). Finally, the CSA's vision of the children who were its stated focus was also conflicted. The White Paper made a gesture toward some recognition of children's personhood by suggesting that they had a right to financial support, but it gave them no means to enforce this right.

Most importantly, the CSA disregarded the moral and social factors guiding people's family practices. Conceiving of welfare and responsible behaviour in purely economic terms, it disregarded the conditional and nuanced view of obligation held not only by 'persons with care', overwhelmingly lone mothers, but also by fathers and children. In fact, the majority of persons with care experienced frustrating administrative difficulties with the agency and overall felt that 'the new system had few advantages, and many disadvantages, over the former maintenance system' (Clarke et al 1996a p 18). Further, despite the fact that many of the assessments made by the agency resulted in higher levels of maintenance, none of the mothers in Clarke et al's (1996a) study felt better off as a result (Clarke et al 1996a p 20). Some suffered direct loss of income, some indirect losses of benefits such as gifts of cash and kind to children (Clarke et al 1996a p 21), and, crucially, many felt let down by the scheme's lack of other measures to support their other family practices such as helping them to obtain employment, or provide assistance with childcare or training.

Despite its language of welfare and parental responsibility, and uniquely out of line with other aims to promote harmonious co-parenting, the scheme did not aim to improve relations between parents or between parents and children. But the 'complex set of material and emotional relationships' (Clarke et al 1996a p 25), important to parents and children, were indeed affected. Clarke et al's research found that the effect of the agency's intervention on the relationship between former partners 'differed according to the prior state of the relationship and the extent and quality of contact between the parents' (Clarke et al 1996a p 28).

'Where there was little or no contact and a poor relationship, the Agency's intervention had had little long-term impact on the relationship. The greatest impact was where parents were in relatively frequent contact because of the father's contact with the children. These fathers were likely to be paying reasonable levels of maintenance already; both they and the lone mothers felt the Agency's involvement was an invasion of a set of relationships worked out, often painfully, over some time. For these former partners, the Act had in some cases made relationships more difficult still' (Clark et al 1996a p 28).

The Act also sometimes *adversely* affected relationships between parents and children. Clarke et al found damaging effects in one quarter of the lone-mother families they interviewed (Clark et al 1996a p 29) where there was some contact between non-resident fathers and children. These effects ranged from the financial impact of the assessment reducing frequency of contact, curtailing activities or altering children's day-to-day living arrangements, to the new assessment generating new conflict between the parents (Clarke et al 1996a p 29). Finally, there was some evidence that agency involvement might act as a deterrent to fathers or mothers establishing stable second families (Clarke et al 1996a p 41).

Despite these adverse consequences for mothers and children, it was fathers' responses to the Act that captured the public imagination. Wallbank (1997) observes how the press colluded with 'absent fathers'' attempts to construct themselves as victims of the Act[5]. At its extreme, we see the views

5   A (highly selective) list of press accounts of men's often tragic reactions to the CSA involvement appears on the Child Support Analysis website (see note 6 below).

of fathers' groups on websites such as the Child Support Action Group, which entitled its web page in 1997 'The Child Support Agency – The Enemy of Parents and Children Everywhere', and then proceeded, in highly inflammatory language, to provide information about 'how to beat the CSA' (1997)[6]. Burgoyne and Millar's (1994) research may suggest that much of this hostility may be accounted for by the 1991 Act's refusal to recognise the importance of the father's relationship with his children, former partner and new partners and children, but also that many were unhappy with the coercive measures the Act adopted that undermined their sense of control over their actions and commitments. Fatherhood has traditionally been more a matter of intention and choice than has motherhood (see above and Douglas 1994; Diduck 1995), and Maclean and Eekelaar predicted in 1993 that as a result of the CSA '[t]he creation of children is now more likely to have lasting effect on the lives of men, as it always has for women' (Maclean and Eekelaar 1993 p 226). It seems that many men were unhappy with the extent to which this prediction came true in the 1990s.

Many were also unhappy with the way in which it came true. Fathers in the 1990s were attempting to negotiate new roles and meanings of fatherhood; 'being there' for their children became a part of a normative fatherhood with which they had previously had little experience (see Chapter 4). The CSA obstructed their delicate negotiations by its apparently contradictory messages that, on the one hand, financial support was a part of parental responsibility, but on the other, creating no space for other expressions of care or responsibility (see Bradshaw et al 1999).

The Department for Work and Pensions (Wikeley et al 2001) completed a survey of the characteristics, experiences and attitudes of 2,500 CSA clients to provide a baseline against which to assess forthcoming reforms to the scheme. They found generally that non-resident parents (92 per cent of whom were men) earned more than persons with care (94 per cent of whom were women), that non-resident parents had contact with their children in about half of the cases (Wikeley et al 2001 p 3) and that perceptions of fairness of the CSA assessments were associated with contact with children (Wikeley et al 2001 p 4). Compliance with CSA assessments was, in turn, associated with contact and thus with perceptions of fairness (Wikeley et al 2001 p 5). Forty per cent of non-resident parents reported that involvement of the CSA had caused upset in their relationship with their former partner, but fewer claimed it had affected relationships with children or with subsequent partners (Wikeley et al 2001 p 6).

Davis and Wikeley (2002) assess the implications of these results, particularly the connection between perceptions of fairness and compliance. They highlight the results that show a clear relationship between first, perceptions of fairness and frequency of contact and quality of the relationship (Davis and Wikeley 2002 p 524), and secondly, between strength of the parent-child relationships and compliance with the maintenance obligation (Davis and Wikeley 2002 p 526).

'This survey has confirmed the extent to which perceptions of fairness, and compliance, reflect the degree to which the lives of non-resident parents remain intertwined with those of their children. It is not just that they take account of other commitments (as is often asserted), but that they respond emotionally and intuitively to the maintenance requirement, this in turn reflecting the strength of the ties that bind them to the parent with care and to the children of the relationship. This demonstrates what seems to be a fairly fundamental characteristic of family life, which is that it involves the negotiation of responsibilities and commitments rather than an adherence to fixed norms' (Davis and Wikeley 2002 p 526).

Children's views of the CSA have been canvassed on only small scales but the evidence suggests that they, like their parents, value some negotiation of commitment. Gillespie's interviews with children (2002) reveal that most do not want to be involved in decisions about monetary issues, but Clarke et al's (1996b) research with 12 children revealed that some did think children should be consulted about these decisions (Clarke et al 1996b p 27). Some children felt uncomfortable seeing their parents make such a close connection between contact and finances (Gillespie 2002 p 531) and many saw contact as an important responsibility deriving from children's needs rather than as rights deriving from paying child support (Clarke et al 1996b p 27). While the children in Clarke et al's study took a more unconditional view of parental support obligations (Clarke et al 1996b p 27) many had experienced the involvement of the CSA in negative terms and were worried about its impact upon their families, their father in particular (Clarke et al 1996b p 30).

Most empirical work with parents and children thus confirms Finch and Mason's (1993) insights about the fluidity and negotiability of modern familial responsibilities (see Chapter 2). Adults work out the support they will give to family members on the basis of negotiated commitments developed over time, rather than through fixed rules. So, while mothers, fathers and children interviewed about the CSA believed, in principle, that parents had an obligation to support their children, parents' actual commitment to acting on that principle remained the result of their histories, of their perceptions of the moral principle of fairness, of their experiences of reciprocity and of their negotiations with *each other* (Bradshaw et al 1999). Policy or law that creates or defines duties without taking these negotiations into account runs the risk of being perceived as unfair, and therefore of failing. It is this message, a message that validates family practices rather than a mythical family, that law-makers might have taken from the failure of CSA 1991 and 1995.

In sum, CSA 1991 (and CSA 1995) seemed to be designed for only half of the families individuals lived by: that half that accounted for their belief in principle in the moral duty to support children and in the moral certainty of traditional gender roles. Where it did take account of the other part of the ideal, the part that allows for personal choice, negotiability and individual subjectivity in making and remaking commitments, it did so only so far as these choices are conceived in economic terms. It revealed the difference between the ideal of family responsibilities and the way in which parents practise those responsibilities.

It also failed to acknowledge adequately the fluidity of concepts of motherhood and fatherhood and the social and economic conditions in which motherhood and fatherhood are lived, both in the home and outside it. Importantly, this failure came at a time in which new norms about both, but particularly about fatherhood, were being worked out. Burgess (1998) captures the difficulty of working through this process in the context of current child support law. She argues that until the co-parenting ideal becomes a reality, that is when the father's breadwinner role is equalised in practice with his caring role, the support obligation will be seen as a 'punishment for the feckless and an imposition on the virtuous' (Burgess 1998 p 4). She argues that the state must do its part to change this view so that paying child support becomes seen as a privilege: 'no father should be seen as of such little value, that his personal contribution – however small – can be waived, or substituted for' (Burgess 1998 p 4). Burgess argues that the current child support scheme creates a context in which these emergent possibilities are discouraged rather than encouraged. She says the legislation and policy should eschew the language of responsibility/irresponsibility and appeal to a father's sense of pride in and commitment to his children as a carer, rather than merely as a provider. While CSA 1991 and 1995 may have made some attempt to do this by adopting the language of welfare and parental responsibility, major amendments brought in by the Child Support, Pensions and Social Security Act 2000 appear to attempt it with more vigour.

Child support in the new millennium

The Child Support, Pensions and Social Security Act 2000 (CSPSSA 2000) retains 'traditional' ideas of connections and the duties that arise from those connections, but it seeks also to recognise, to a degree the current law does not, an emergent model of responsibility based upon modern, negotiated, freely chosen commitments. It has also incorporated some aspects of the 'new' fatherhood and motherhood that may exist still only as ideals. It thus continues New Labour's trend toward creating a normative family that accommodates conflicting dualities. Given the research upon experiences of the 1991 scheme I shall assess the Act's potential for achieving a form of justice for parents and children.

The detail of the mechanics of CSPSSA 2000 are reviewed elsewhere (Pirrie 2002a; 2002b; Wikeley 2000a)[7] and commentary upon it and upon the White Paper reveal mixed levels of support for its principles and practicalities (Pirrie 2002c; Barton 1999; Douglas 2001; Davis and Wikeley 2001). The new legislation does not repeal the old; the government has shown its support for the basic framework of the 1991 model, even though the scheme itself has 'altered beyond recognition' (Pirrie 2002a p 196) and family economic policy seems to have shifted somewhat from a needs model toward a 'symbolic joint enterprise' one (Douglas 2001 p 189). It continues, however, to express the assumption of economic co-parenting:

> 'Fair maintenance needs to recognise these real costs [of supporting a child from day to day] – and find a proper balance between the responsibilities of both parents. The best starting point is to look at what the non-resident parent would pay if the family were still

7   The new scheme was supposed to come into effect in April 2002, but the Secretary of State announced in Parliament on 20 March 2002 that difficulties with the computer software have meant that implementation has been delayed.

together. When parents live together, they normally share family expenses' (DSS 1999 ch 2 para 2)

and to assume that this 'normal' model applies after separation as well as before:

'parents who live together expect to meet their children's needs first – and this applies equally when parents have separated. This means that non-resident parents should plan their lives on the basis of the income that they have after meeting their responsibilities to their children' (DSS 1999 ch 2 para 3).

As we have seen, this assumption does not always reflect family experiences, yet it grounds the legislation either on the basis that it does, or as an attempt to change behaviour to conform to its ideal. The formula for calculating a non-resident parent's maintenance obligation has thus been dramatically simplified to take into account research that shows that the average, intact, two-parent family spends roughly 30 per cent of its income on a child (DSS 1999 ch 2 para 5). The non-resident parent's contribution for one child is therefore set at 15 per cent of his net income (20 per cent for two children and 25 per cent for three or more), regardless of the income or actual expenses of members of the qualifying child's household. Further, calculation of the non-resident parent's net income will now take into account an allowance for any children in his new household whom he is in fact supporting.

These changes to the formula represent a slight shift back toward 'official' recognition of 'modern' familial behaviour in which parental equality of provision is assumed, and in which an individual may have more than one 'family' and set of responsibilities at any given time. At the same time, however, it attempts to protect an idealised image of the first family which standardises the romantic altruism of that provision.

The CSPSSA 2000 makes, however, only a small concession to fathers' concerns about the financial context in which their obligation rests. It recognises any responsibility he has taken on for new dependants, but fails to take any account of the financial circumstances of his former partner. Gillespie's (2002) small-scale study of parents with care and non-resident parents anticipating the new scheme reveals that feelings of unfairness or inequity are likely to continue on the part of non-resident parents as a result of this disregard (Gillespie 2002 p 531), and that many non-resident parents said they would try to avoid any new assessment by the CSA (Gillespie 2002 p 532).

Under the new scheme the courts will retain their jurisdiction to make orders by consent, where maintenance is sought from a step-parent (under MCA 1973), where payments are sought for school fees or other training or for payments of lump sums or transfers of property (under the Children Act 1989). Unlike the old scheme, the new one will allow a parent with a consent order to apply to the CSA after the order has been in effect for at least one year. Parents with care who apply for state assistance will continue to come under the jurisdiction of the agency, but now 'the maintenance process will flow automatically from a benefits claim' (DSS 1999 ch 4 para 21). 'We need to make it clear that applying for child support is not a matter of choice for parents on Income Support' (DSS 1999 ch 4 para 21).

Policy here seems to be mixed as well. Like CSA 1991, the new Act removes choice entirely from some parents, but unlike the 1991 Act it encourages others to order their financial circumstances privately, by negotiation, while retaining the shadow of the CSA over those negotiations. By allowing an application to be made to the agency after a consent order has been in effect for one year, it adapts the dejuridification model by allowing recourse to an administrative rather than judicial overseer of agreements. Perhaps unsurprisingly, parents with care in Gillespie's (2002) study indicated they would be likely to apply for a CSA assessment under this new provision, as the income of non-resident parents is likely to rise far more quickly than their own (Gillespie 2002 p 530) and non-resident parents felt this potential to overturn negotiated settlements to be a source of unfairness (Gillespie 2002 p 530; also see Pirrie 2002c).

As in other recent proposals for law reform, the White Paper on which CSPSSA 2000 Act is based adopts the language of responsibility throughout. It takes up where CSA 1991 left off, appealing to an individual's sense of personal responsibility to the taxpayer as well as to her or his children. Importantly, it constructs as irresponsible not only non-resident parents who avoid the agency's involvement, but also persons with care who '*choose to* rely upon the benefit system rather than applying for a child support assessment' (DSS 1999 ch 4 para 2 emphasis added). It is her presumedly exclusively economic choice that renders her irresponsible and thus the Act retains the punitive elements of its predecessor to coerce responsible choices to benefit both children and 'society'. It is concerned both to remove choice and to foster it.

Further, the Act merges welfare and responsibility, more directly than does the previous legislation. It therefore aims 'to protect children – and responsible parents – from … irresponsible parents' (DSS 1999 ch 4 para 2). It aims to focus on 'the needs of children and good, responsible parents' (DSS 1999 ch 1 para 9), but does not explicitly make welfare a factor in support determinations. It is clear in its aim to foster responsible behaviour, to put into a place a system which will succeed where the old one failed: 'to help responsible parents' and force irresponsible ones to act responsibly (DSS 1999 ch 1 para 2).

The White Paper describes the new child support scheme as a service that encourages parental responsibility (Chapter 4), and while it highlights paying as an exercise of that responsibility, as did the old scheme, it also makes an 'official' connection between contact and support as important parts of exercising parental responsibility and promoting welfare. While the Act does not link contact directly with maintenance liability, it provides for variation of the standard rates where exceptional contact costs are incurred by the non-resident parent, and also where parents 'share' care of the child. 'Shared care' is defined as the child spending at least one night per week with the non-resident parent. In such a case, their maintenance liability will be reduced by one seventh for every night that the children spend with them. This change again appears as a concession to non-resident parents and disregards the concerns of parents with care for whom the cost of keeping a child is not greatly reduced if he or she spends one or two nights away from home. Yet, the economic advantage to be gained by increasing contact is used as a 'carrot' to encourage fathers to remain (or to become) involved with their children. Limited evidence to date suggests that it may be successful in this enterprise. All the non-resident parents in Gillespie's (2002) study stated that 'they would consider re-examining the link between financial support and the level of staying contact, including the possibility of returning to court to vary orders currently in effect' (Gillespie 2002 p 530) in the light of the change. The effects, financial and otherwise, on the mother and children of this kind of trade-off are unknown.

Finally, the legal context in which these changes have been made is important. They occur at the same time as the Adoption and Children Act 2002 gives, for the first time, automatic parental responsibility to unmarried fathers who register their child's birth jointly with the mother. As Wallbank (2002) points out, this reform is promoted in the name of fairness to unmarried fathers (interestingly as compared with unmarried mothers rather than with married fathers) and to recognise their 'commitment' (as evidenced by joint registration) to their child (Wallbank 2002 p 276). It may also be a normative statement designed to instil commitment, but whether it will affect a father's parenting behaviour and not remain only of symbolic importance is questionable.

Its symbolism is important, however, and is consistent with messages radiated from CSPSSA 2000. Together, these legislative statements provide support for the 'new' fatherhood in which commitment to children is presumed to be natural and to be desired by fathers. The legislative statements thus proclaim a co-parenting norm that has yet to become normal, and may have onerous consequences for women as well as for men. They mean that women must work harder to facilitate positive relationships between non-resident fathers and children, they must either earn sufficient income to avoid income support or lose their autonomy over support decisions and, in effect, over their non-marital families. Finally, the government's lack of concern over the fact that 'the new rates [will] produce a slightly lower average weekly liability' (DSS 1999 ch 1 para 21) raises questions as to its commitment to the actual well-being of women and the children in their care in cases where women do want support from fathers.

Conclusions

One of the primary effects of the CSPSSA 2000 will be the streamlined administration of child support decision-making and this result is of more than passing interest. The regulation of family practices in this way, entrenched in the discourses of welfare and personal responsibility, successfully brings together the moral imperatives of individual free will and traditional obligation, and rejects the apparent moral authoritarianism of judicial decision-making. It is another example of 'law as inducement' (Roberts 2001) or of a form of governmentality (Vaughan 2000) that appears to be central to much legal reform generally.

From its inception the CSA was an example of the dejuridification of family law, displaying and resulting in ideological and practical ambivalence (Diduck 1995), but CSPSSA 2000 provides for policy and procedures that attempt to strike a more palatable balance between two apparently competing imperatives. It, like FDRs (see Chapter 6), mediation (see Chapter 5) and Marriage Support services (see Chapter 2), is a part of the law/government (Cotterrell 1993) that attempts to influence not only the relative legal positions of subjects, but also the shape their identities take. It provides support for both the 'new' family in which obligations and duties flow from the choices and negotiation that create social status, and for the traditional family in which those responsibilities flow from biological and legal status. Both of these messages express support for an ideal that is held by families and by law alike. It is an ideal, however, that empirical research demonstrates few families to be able to achieve without concurrent structural change and recognition of their complicated, often sophisticated, moral and emotional negotiations.

Chapter 8

Justice: old certainties and new beginnings

For many of us family living is an ongoing search for ways to satisfy personal needs for emotional fulfilment and commitment to self and to others. Like the society in which we live, it demands both stability and dynamic change. Negotiating the delicate interaction between continuity and change means that the way forward often seems to lie in different directions. At some moments it appears to compel a retreat to the certainty thought to be provided by 'tradition', while in others the allure of new understandings of love and stability tempt a flirtation with 'modern' uncertainty and its non-traditional forms of attachment. At other moments, individuals find ways to tread both paths simultaneously, but at all times they exercise choice and agency in constructing familial identities throughout the life-course in a normative context that both encourages and inhibits that choice.

Law, as an important part of the overall context in which family lives are made, is concerned with regulating both norms and behaviour; it is 'at *every* bloody level' of social life, as Edward Thompson famously observed (Thompson 1978 p 96), even in relationships rooted in passion rather than reason. Those relationships, characterised by ambivalence and irrationality, as much as by predictability and rationality, are subject to laws that have also been described as 'chaotic' or ambivalent. Family law aims to reconcile people's desires and actions as they try to make commitments while pursuing the project of individualism (Lewis 2001), and it must reconcile these two apparently conflicting imperatives. I have suggested throughout this book that, to the extent that it has not achieved this reconciliation, it is because it has not found a way to harmonise the two simultaneous narratives through which family is constituted: a 'traditional' narrative of romantic love embodying an altruism and moral absolutism that tends to obscure and exploit gender and generational inequalities, and a 'modern' narrative of confluent love with its individualism, democracy and demands for reflexive autonomy and the rational negotiation of self-interest. This normative family then sets the standard by which less-than-ideal family practices are judged and too often are found wanting.

I have also observed, however, that the two narratives need not be dichotomous, but in fact may be brought together in different ways that could provide something additional to the range of discourses or 'cultural capital' from which people draw in order to make sense of their family lives and of the justice achieved in those lives. I have also suggested that it is how people *do* family, the families we live with, that provide much of the fabric from which this new capital can be woven. These families are the ones in which complicated and chaotic behaviour belies dichotomous categorisation. In them, responsibilities and obligations are negotiated in their particularities with attention paid both to self and to others, and rights, welfare and moral and economic rationalities blend together with social and economic conditions in new ways.

It is both the politics and the justice of the attempted reconciliation of a legal dichotomy with an experiential pluralism that has concerned me in this book. In this concluding chapter I shall consider this issue by revisiting the broader themes of dejuridification and individualisation I identified in Chapter 1, but I will do so in a more direct way by exploring their manifestation through two different and apparently divergent trends that have come to family law from the broader political context. The first is an increasing legal commitment to appraising behaviour by reference to human rights principles, and the second is a simultaneous commitment to less formal means of appraisal. Both illustrate law's potential to incorporate the experienced realities of family lives, but also its failure to capitalise on that potential.

In remarking upon the differences between these two trends, I shall not disregard what I also see to be their similarities. They are different in that increasing legal deference to rights evidences an apparent increase in the importance of universal and abstract legal principles to the formal law governing intimate relationships, while the second legitimates alternative strategies of legal regulation: those, like mediation or mandatory marriage preparation classes, which remain at the level of the social, are more subjective and are promoted through less formal, apparently 'non-legal' means. Their similarities lie in the fact that they both increase, rather than decrease, the scope for regulation of family life and they both expand the range of factors that are considered relevant in making them law. By taking into account family experiences as much as externally prescribed norms, both forms of family regulation can include relationships previously excluded from the normal, while maintaining, if not strengthening, the source of their legitimacy as law. As constituents of family law, both are profoundly political. They belie the division between the public and the private: they implicate private behaviour in public/legal norms and public/legal norms in private behaviour.

Neither of these trends is novel. Adopting a role for rights in families, for example, has a long pedigree. Rights have always been a part of liberal law's project of constituting its subjects and of regulating relationships between them. In the family law context, consider, for example, the way in which rights underlie the property rhetoric and shape personal and legal attitudes about the legitimate ownership and allocation of property in families. What appears to be new in the more recent engagement with rights in the family context, is the value accorded to principles of *human rights*, rights premised upon ideas of the inherent dignity of the individual and of respect for his or her choice of *who* and *how* to be as a family member[1]. These principles of respect for choices and for human dignity, including principles of non-discrimination, have become a part of family discourse at the formal legal level (see, for example, *White v White*, discussed in Chapter 6) often *because* they were first expressed at the level of experience.

At the same time, the socio-legal project has for some time maintained that law is more than that proclaimed by law-makers. In questioning the very nature of law, it has adopted a legal pluralist approach that locates the source of law in the social as much as in the state (Cotterrell 2002). It sees law as more than a response to disputes, 'as a part of social pathology' (Cotterrell 2002 p 639), but also as contributing to the mundane, to the 'routine structuring of social relations' (Cotterrell 2002 p 639) and

---

1   Indeed, there has been a recent call for the regulation of intimacy along these lines. Cohen (2002) suggests that it is through a new reflexive paradigm of law that state regulation can foster constructed, relational autonomy and recognise plurality and an individual's ethical competence. She advocates a constitutional right to privacy that would serve as a 'protective shield' for a person's concrete identity and decisional autonomy while ensuring that the demands of justice are not violated. While such a right is universalistic, what it would protect is our particularity (Cohen 2002 p 57).

individual lives. On this view, the experience of *living* as a family member is as important a source of law as is 'the state' through the practices of judges, lawyers, legislators and policy-makers. Like regulation through rights, the informal, social or disciplinary regulation of families is not a new phenomenon, but it seems to me that a critical analysis of this form of regulation is particularly apposite in the context of recent government initiatives. Consider, for example, proposals designed to regulate marriage, divorce and childcare responsibilities through education and the provision of information about what is deemed to be socially desirable change in the culture of responsibility. Law here is about proclaiming social norms and about 'doing' them; it shapes and is shaped by formal objective principles and by informal, individual family practices, and in this way, it, like importing human rights principles into family life, blurs the distinction between the public and the private.

One may view these trends as evidence of the enlargement of law's cultural capital, and therefore as evidence that in both its formal, positivist, and its informal, pluralistic, senses it has been more successful in reconciling its conflicting ideals than I implied above. But, as I will argue, there is a long way to go before 'new' families and family identities become accepted and acceptable in law. In part, this is because family behaviour itself reflects both the traditional and the modern; it is unpredictable, is often spontaneous rather than purposive and is the result of moral, cognitive, emotional and physical demands as much as of legal ones. In part, it is also because law remains resistant at a fundamental level to such perceived breaches of its objectivity and integrity, and it may also be because the chaotic family practices that inform these trends are so potentially destabilising of the social, economic and gender order.

Politics, families and rights

Family laws have begun to legitimise families and family identities that would have been unrecognisable even a decade earlier. Indeed, even during the gestation of this book, longstanding legal principles have been revisited by both the courts and Parliament, often with remarkable results. Without a doubt, much of this change has been a direct result of an emergent political culture of individual rights and the ensuing deployment of rights discourse in law; this aspect of individualism now seems to have found a place in the private, irrational, affective sphere of familial attachments. Rights, seen for so long as important only in the 'public' sphere, now resonate in the 'private'; the line between the two is blurred as the personal has now, in this way, legitimately become political.

Of course, feminist and other critical commentators for some time have declared a public/private divide to be specious and have recognised the political nature of family relationships. We have highlighted issues of power within families and between families and the state, and while not all of us would concede the efficacy of claims to individual rights as a *politics* to remedy structural domination either within or outside of families, many would concede a place for human rights principles such as non-discrimination in the realm of the private. As law engages with and shapes individual behaviour in families, it must also be concerned with such political matters and with how they are mediated by changing norms about family lives and changing family practices. So, while it is true that our family identities are constituted at a normative level, they do not float free from, and cannot be made apart from, what we *do* in the social world, including in the home. In this way, the personal has always been political – and legal.

This book has been about *this* politics of family law: it has explored the link between the normative and the experienced and has examined the way in which family laws and family policies manage this link to regulate, stabilise and achieve justice in and for families. At the normative level, then, the politics of rights has been important in matters of property accumulation and allocation and in matters concerning the care of children. The 'justice' of decisions concerning money or children is perceived by separating partners or parents in terms of rights, although law has not always accounted for gender differences in this perception. The expression of *human rights* as meaningful for family justice is a more recent phenomenon that could add something new to the link between the normative and the experienced.

Three recently decided cases illustrate this point. They are about the legal legitimation of a chosen familial identity and the way in which rights as well as family practices are implicated in that legitimation. More importantly, however, they also illustrate the way in which continuity and old certainties endure in the process. While the cases I discuss below may result in 'justice' for an increased population, they have not resulted in a new vocabulary or new categories for intimate lives as much as they have simply expanded the meaning of family (Smart and Silva 1999 p 10 and also Diduck 2001a). They are an example of change being both embraced and spurned by law, of continuity both maintained and disrupted.

Human rights, family experiences and the courts: *Mendoza, Goodwin* and *Bellinger*

The experiences of same-sex 'families of choice', located within modern and traditional narratives of choice and romanticism, influenced their legal legitimation in the *Fitzpatrick* decision in 2000 that so radically expanded the category 'family'. In that case, while integrated narratives of care, sacrifice, choice, reflexivity and love were drawn upon by both the House of Lords and Mr Fitzpatrick, the House of Lords declined to see rights and issues of discrimination as relevant to the arrangement of familial lives. Two years later, the Court of Appeal in *Mendoza v Ghaidan* [2002] EWCA Civ 1533, [2003] 1 FLR 468 held that human rights *were* relevant to the legal and social construction of familial identities and while it, like the House of Lords before it, did not expand the meaning of the word 'spouse', it accepted that in some familial arrangements, principles of human rights may play a part in determining social and legal justice for intimate partners.

Mendoza raised again the issues of statutory protected tenancies for family members and spouses, but unlike the House of Lords in *Fitzpatrick*, which faced the same questions, the court in *Mendoza* believed that human rights were fundamental to a just construction of a statute designed to protect families and spouses. Further, and crucially, it held that the Human Rights Act 1998 imposed a duty upon courts to interpret the word 'spouse' in the Rent Act 1977 in a non-discriminatory way that included same sex partners:

'That duty can properly be discharged by reading the words "as his or her wife or husband" to mean "as if they were his or her wife or husband". ... Parliament having swallowed the camel of including unmarried partners within the protection given to married couples, it is not for the court to strain at the gnat of including such partners who are of the same sex as each other' (*Mendoza v Ghaidan* per Buxton LJ at p 480–481).

By locating family firmly within the discourse of human rights, the Court of Appeal politicised family relationships in a way that the House of Lords declined to do in *Fitzpatrick*. It admitted human rights into the range of narratives used to construct justice, family and justice *for* families and means that along with subjective ideas of fairness, traditional ideas of altruism and modern ideas of individualism, universal values such as non-discrimination that stem from the *politics* of human rights are now meaningful in the intimate relationships individuals forge with each other (see also *White v White* and discussion in Chapter 6).

Both the Court of Appeal and the House of Lords acknowledged the politics of family life in a different way. The decisions in *Fitzpatrick* and *Mendoza* implicitly accept that actual family behaviour is important in constructing legal norms. In addition to universal norms of human rights, both courts added individual and social *experience* to the otherwise traditional legal tools they deployed in reaching their decisions, in effect expanding both the range of the legally relevant and the range of cultural capital from which to define the familial.

In July 2002, the European Court of Human Rights decided the second two cases that illustrate the significance of both the universal and the particular in family justice. In the case of *I v UK* [2002] 2 FLR 518, decided together with *Goodwin v UK* [2002] 2 FLR 487, the court held that the UK's refusal to recognise legally the new gender of a post-operative transsexual person violated the individual's right to respect for private and family life under art 8 of the European Convention on Human Rights and his or her right to marry and to found a family under art 12. These cases are probably the clearest examples of law taking individual choice and action seriously. Whereas English law has always refused to acknowledge an individual's gender as changeable, this unanimous court said in the clearest terms that gender identity is as much a matter of individual choice, action and life as it is of biology or law:

'[T]he very essence of the Convention is respect for human dignity and human freedom. Under Art 8 of the Convention in particular, where the notion of personal autonomy is an important principle underlying the interpretation of its guarantees, protection is given to the personal sphere of each individual, including the right to establish details of their identity as individual human beings ...' (*I v UK* para 70 at p 536).

The court's words regarding art 12 were no less clear:

'The Court is not persuaded that at the date of this case it can still be assumed that these terms [ie a man and a woman] must refer to a determination of gender by purely biological criteria. ... There are other important factors ... [including] the provision of treatment including surgery to assimilate the individual as closely as possible to the gender in which they perceive that they properly belong and the assumption by the transsexual of the social role of the assigned gender' (*I v UK* para 80 at p 538–539).

Thus, it seems that in the sphere of family life in particular, gender is, at least partly, a matter of lifestyle and choice. Other courts have agreed. In Australia, to determine a person's sex for the purposes of marriage, the relevant matters include:

> 'the person's life experiences, including the sex in which he or she was brought up and the person's attitude to it; the person's self-perception as a man or a woman; [and] the extent to which the person has functioned in society as a man or a woman' (*Re Kevin* [2001] Fam CA 1074, quoted in *I v UK* para 39 at p 528; affirmed by Federal Family Court 23 February 2003, unreported and cited in *Bellinger v Bellinger* [2003] UKHL 21 para 16).

The experiences of transsexual persons have thus informed law at the level of human rights and in the light of these decisions the Lord Chancellor's Department has accepted that MCA 1973 s 11(c), restricting valid marriage to male and female persons only, is incompatible with the European Convention on Human Rights and has announced its intention to revise the law accordingly. Unsurprisingly, therefore, the House of Lords in the third example to which I refer, the case of *Bellinger v Bellinger* [2003] UKHL 21, agreed unanimously to make such a declaration of incompatibility.

The *Bellinger* decision, however, also illustrates the intransigence of law, of the normative family, and of normative familial identities. Notwithstanding its declaration of marriage law's incompatibility with human rights principles, the court was not prepared to make the further requested declaration that the 1981 marriage between Mr and Mrs Bellinger (a male-to-female transsexual person) was valid. It specifically rejected the idea that sex/gender was a matter of individual choice and experience:

> 'Individuals cannot choose for themselves whether they wish to be known or treated as male or female. Self-definition is not acceptable. That would make a nonsense of the underlying biological basis of the distinction' (*Bellinger v Bellinger* per Lord Nicholls para 28).

It held that to allow self-perceived gender to be recognised in marriage law would 'involve a fundamental change in the traditional concept of marriage' (*Bellinger v Bellinger* per Lord Nicholls para 48) that must, if it were to be made, be effected by Parliament rather than the courts.

Read together, these cases illustrate law's potential to re-interpret justice for an increased population who might now be able to receive the social and legal benefits conferred by familial or marriage status. They also illustrate, however, law's reluctance to embrace fully the potential to re-imagine what family or marriage *means*. The *Bellinger* case does this most strikingly, in a way which would probably perplex most non-lawyers. The court was able to legitimise, in the same case, two distinct legal conceptions of gender, marriage and family and find formally for both change and continuity. In the legal discourse of rights, fluidity was countenanced but in the discourse of the common law it was rejected. This decision is a clear illustration of law's ambivalence and reveals a questionable distinction that may lie at the heart of that ambivalence: the distinction between law at the level of the universal and at the level of the particular.

But even the *Mendoza, I* and *Goodwin* cases can be said to have engaged with family practices simply by adopting the rhetoric of diversity while at the same time shoring up a vision of the 'traditional' family (Crow 2002)[2]. The *Mendoza* case regulates as much as it defines by requiring even non-traditional partnerships to look 'as if they were' traditional marriages before they achieve the privileges that come with recognition. In *I* and *Goodwin* while the European Court of Human Rights allowed that sex/gender was changeable, rather than accept a fluid definition of marriage to account for that changeability, it required a choice to be made to fix identity so that intimate partners could make an orthodox, heterosexual marriage. Further, the basis for choice of gender identity remained rooted in a medical or psychiatric dysfunction. It was seen to be an abnormality that could be remedied by law for the purpose of encouraging 'normal' traditional marriage. Therefore, what we see in these cases is an incorporation, albeit a safe one, of the politics of family practices and human rights into a law in which old family certainties and meanings are sustained.

In the parliamentary process as well, we can see the way in which law accommodates family practices and narratives of rights in achieving both continuity and change.

The Adoption and Children Act 2002

Transformation and continuity in ideas of public and private, and appropriate interventions in each, are apparent in normative expression of Giddens'

---

2   See also the discussion in Chapter 6 of traditionalism and modernism – continuity and change – in the context of importing principles of non-discrimination into post-divorce financial arrangements.

and Beck's family democratisation, which they say applies to children as much as to adults. We can see this tension at work in the Adoption and Children Act 2002. It provides that the welfare of the child is to be paramount in determination of adoption issues. This prioritisation represents a change from the current law, which constitutes adoption as a remedy for childless families as much as for family-less children and therefore does not give children's welfare statutory priority (Adoption Act 1976). Now, however, the message is that potential adoptees are vulnerable in the same way as are children of divorce: both are family-less, a status that renders them potentially dangerous or at risk. On either view, their welfare lies in their being placed in a family. From the romantic developmentalist perspective, these children defy childhood, they are virtually un-childlike in their imperfect, un-familial independence, and the law therefore looks to remedy this imperfection by placing them in a family. Significantly, 'family' in this context is to be broadly construed; it includes even unmarried opposite or same-sex parents, testifying to the importance of containing children and childhood within the familial, even if it means expanding ideas of the familial and of welfare to accommodate them.

Merging welfare with non-traditional families in this way is a good example of law's attempt to incorporate both traditional and non-traditional narratives into its normative family. This is a case, however, where rights were also considered, broadening even further the range of acceptable narratives about children. At the same time as it proclaimed the importance of welfare in adoption matters, Parliament also reviewed that proclamation in the light of its human rights implications. It is bound by the Human Rights Act 1998 (HRA 1998) to review proposed legislation for compatibility with it, and in the case of adoption the Parliamentary Joint Committee (House of Lords, House of Commons 2002) reviewed the effect of the legislation not only upon the rights of the adults affected by it, but, importantly, also upon the rights of the children. While the 2002 Act was primarily directed toward their welfare, and any breaches of the HRA 1998 probably could have been justified on this ground, Parliament felt it important to consider children's rights, even though they were rights to protection, to a family life and to promotion of their welfare.

This example of the formal legal legitimation of children's rights, along with accommodation of non-traditional parenthood within the welfare discourse, provides further evidence of how formal law engages with the imperatives of continuity and change. Change is seen in the way human rights are engaged and non-standard families are valued, while continuity is maintained by framing these considerations within the newly prioritised discourse of welfare.

Informal regulation

Legal regulation comes in the form of adjudicatory and legislative statements, as in the examples above, but it also has a more pluralistic meaning. We might, in other words, see legal regulation not only as something that is 'imposed on the rest of social life', but also as something that 'might grow out of social life and provide a part of the cement which gives moral meaning to social existence' (Cotterrell 1993 p 11–12). This socio-legal perspective, in part, characterises my suggestion that family practices have begun to shape formal laws, but also captures the idea that they are a part of a type of legal regulation that derives from social or cultural disciplinary practices that take the form of guidance rather than prescription. As I have observed throughout this book, this cultural capital, expressed from the ground up, increasingly shapes legal 'inducements' (Roberts 2001).

I have observed that recent legislation and policy about families and individuals in families is framed in terms of social and personal responsibility. These terms reflect more than political rhetoric, however, as legal reforms *as well as* community expectations and social norms based upon them create new economic, criminal and disciplinary consequences for those who fail to carry out their responsibilities appropriately.

The discourse of responsibility is a particularly suitable regulatory technique in the family context; it works on the level of conscience and thus engages morality, emotion and sentiment (Vaughan 2000), rather than merely intellectualised, abstract rights or formally prescribed duties. It, more easily than formal prescription, relies upon and exploits emotions as much as it does cognitive processes and it legalises the truism unacknowledged by formal law that what we do has as much to do with what we feel as it does with what we think (see Lange 2002). It engages a modern, active form of subjectivity while establishing limits upon complete freedom to act. To refuse to take responsibility is to cast one's self from the moral community and justifies either punishment or discipline (Vaughan 2000).

Vaughan (2000) develops the literature on governmentality[3] to explore these ideas in the context of family lives. He looks specifically at the messages about young people in the Crime and Disorder Act 1998 and finds

---

3　There is a growing literature on governmentality that explores the many levels and strategies of the regulation and discipline of contemporary social life. See, for example, the sources cited in Cotterrell (2002), particularly Rose and Valverde (1998) and Van Krieken (2001), for the way in which the work of Michel Foucault has been developed in this theorisation of the nature of law.

a continuing paradox: children still seem to be defined as both a source of risk to others and as at continual risk from others. Unlike in previous generations, however, they are now expected to extricate themselves from this state of dangerousness. Active, responsible citizenship applies in this statute to children as well as to their parents. In part, this requirement evidences a modern view of childhood that accords children with some autonomy and agency in affecting their lives and environment. It remains a flawed modern view, however, because it appears in policy statements more as a means to achieve an end in which the responsible child subject remains ensconced in the familiar rather than as an agent for the new. This responsible familial citizenship is also demanded by other policy initiatives as a strategy to remedy other social, familial 'crises' (Day Sclater and Piper 2001), rather than as a statement about the inherent value of a form of family democracy.

In the context, for example, of post-divorce residence and contact with children, recent policy to 'make contact work' (Lord Chancellor's Department 2002) makes education, training or counselling of both parents and children key, both before contact arrangements are made and to enforce them once they are agreed. Whether people attend these education sessions on their own initiative (but see Chapter 5 on voluntarism in attending divorce mediation) or pursuant to proposals increasing courts' powers to 'refer' them to these resources, the message is that they ought to *choose* contact on the 'premise that more contact is better for children' (Eekelaar 2002 p 272). As Eekelaar notes, notwithstanding its language of choice and negotiation, 'the recommendations of the report signal a significant increase in legal coercion over family arrangements' (Eekelaar 2002 p 272).

Other parallels can be drawn between the perceived crisis of childhood that pervades the Crime and Disorder Act 1998 and the broader crisis of the family implicit in the policy on contact. Like children, families are identified both as sources of danger and as at risk from danger and so are implicated more generally in their own regulation through the discourse of responsibility. In this discourse education and counselling are normalised and provide a source of authority for the newly active citizen/subject to revise expectations and assumptions in the hope that behaviour will follow (Vaughan 2000). Behaviour and experience in turn become relevant in creating new authoritative knowledge[4]. This pluralistic vision of law is

4   There is a vast literature on this idea of 'regulation', some of which adopts a socio-legal perspective of legal pluralism, and some of which provides new theoretical tools to analyse the decline of central planning and central authority. See Picciotto and Campbell (eds) (2002) for a good review and critical analysis of much of this material.

most evident in the active citizenship envisioned and encouraged in family and marriage rhetoric (Home Office 1998; FLA 1996; Advisory Group on Marriage and Relationship Support 2002) in which individuals are to be trained by experts in preparation for marriage and counselled to maintain the health of their relationship throughout its course. While the state will not become directly involved in regulating the terms or nature of marriage or family, it will encourage responsible individual decision-making concerning them. Therefore, by governing marriage indirectly, law belies the legal privacy it attaches to marriage behaviour while supporting the emotional, psychological and social privacy it requires to legitimise its focus upon the exercise of personal responsibility. On divorce as well, counsellors and mediators provide messages about achieving that which has become the new 'just' divorce – the 'healthy' divorce. Their messages include admonitions to manage emotions appropriately and thus import these intensely private considerations into the realm of the 'good' legal divorce.

Informal regulation: continuity and change

Informal regulation on the level of conscience, feeling and the exercise of moral responsibility also expresses imperatives of continuity and change. Marriage in a normative context of both tradition and confluence, has both psychological and social meaning and serves both psychological and social needs. It serves as both comfort and discipline for relationships based exclusively upon the insecurity and caprice of emotions. Marriage imposes the rationality of 'rules' upon the irrationality of love (Lewis 2001) without quelling the apparent freedom of, or desire for, love's irrationality. The importance of this link is not lost upon husbands and wives or upon law/policy-makers, as both the psychological and social expressions of marriage are harnessed so as to regulate heterosexual and, increasingly, homosexual intimacy.

Informal regulation of family lives therefore involves the manipulation of social norms and expectations by taking into account actual life experience. It is *about* the mutual incorporation of that experience and family norms and expectations because it requires individual action that can only be manifested by a series of emotional, cognitive and behavioural choices. It is informal because it operates on the level of the personal and the social. It is regulatory because it designates the direction choices ought to take and it is effective because it operates on levels often inaccessible to formal law.

Because it derives from a wide range of human characteristics and disciplines that study them, we could see more potential for informal regulation than for formal law to expand ideas of justice and fairness in families. In other words, informality might be more susceptible than formal law to legitimating changing family practices and resistant behaviour. Instead, however, (even informal) law polarises rather than harmonises the chaos of that behaviour. Mediation of childcare arrangements on divorce is a good example. In accepting that some marriages will end, law encourages parents to exercise flexibility and rational negotiation of the terms of that end so as to achieve an individualised, responsible co-parenting arrangement that expresses the traditional ideal of the enduring two-parent family *and* the modern ideal of the negotiable and fluid family. With its aim of personalised, subjective justice, sought through a therapeutic rather than legalistic discourse, mediation could countenance parents' individual experiences of irrational emotions, reflexivity of self or moral imperatives outside the bounds of the 'responsible', but too often it does not. Their complex experiences are not understood by the dichotomous norm which tends either to suppress them or to render them pathological.

Further, the 'new childhood studies' have revealed the difficulty children themselves have with being heard exclusively within either a discourse of rights or of welfare, and have insisted that adults listen to children differently. They say that if we did, we would hear neither a plea for traditional autonomy and rights claims nor for classic developmentalist welfare ones and would therefore free ourselves from the specious 'rights versus welfare' competition inherent within the dichotomous normative child of law (see also Bainham 2002). Rather, we would hear claims for situated rights: a contextual citizenship that requires a form of democracy that understands human rights *and* children's unique vulnerability and requirements for care and connection. Indeed, the legal formulation of children's welfare is said to have come from non-legal experts who listen to children, attend to their experiences and define their welfare in that light. In the context of contact with a non-resident parent, the Court of Appeal has agreed that 'the assumption that contact benefits the child cannot be derived from legal precedent or principle. It must find its foundation in the theory and practice of the mental health professions' (*Re L, V, M and H (Contact: Domestic Violence)* [2000] 2 FLR 334 per Thorpe LJ at p 365). While these health discourses, relayed in turn to parents and mediators, may thus appear to be able to accommodate children's hybrid subjectivity because they are derived from direct experience with children, they have not, to date, harnessed the possibilities that children's voices and experiences have offered. The court's further characterisation of the focus of clinical practice may explain this missed opportunity:

'assessment[s] of welfare in the individual case are to be derived from the expertise of mental health professionals *whose training and practice has centred on the development, needs and vulnerability of children*' (Thorpe LJ at p 365 my emphasis added).

Another example of the way in which informal law fails family experiences is in the negotiation of family finances. The dual aspects of the family norm are expressed in the link between gendered familial roles and assessments of desert, and the presumed equality and independence of marital partners in choosing those roles and in negotiating a redistribution of family wealth based upon them. That familial choices are often the result of negotiations of social and economic *structural* conditions, moral influences and feelings, and are therefore more nuanced, reflexive or ambiguous, is not comprehended by either part of the normative ideal.

Final thoughts: politics and families

All these observations lead me to say no more than that *something is changing*. This might, therefore, be a particularly active and adventurous time for family law. Indeed, the examples I provide in this chapter are evidence of some legal recognition of this mood. But, my further observations in this chapter, indeed throughout this book, of law's reluctance to capitalise fully on the possibilities that family practices offer to remake the normative family, must be read in the light of an equally strong desire for stability and continuity. People seem to be seeking an alternative to their parents' love and their parents' families and are relying upon both precedents and new ingredients in inventing it (Zeldin 1994). Traditional values of caring and obligation have not been abandoned, but 'people are finding different ways to express those values' (Crow 2002 p 293). What may be most exciting about recent legal activity is that it demonstrates law's potential to take account of these efforts of reinvention, but what is disappointing about this same legal activity is its failure to achieve this potential. The 'talk is about choice' and about respect for the dignity of choices and the freedom to make them (see Cohen 2002). On the one hand, this talk is liberating and transformative, but on the other, it is dangerously misleading.

Throughout, I have described family law as expressing a series of ambivalences and that these ambivalences, or rather the dualistic forms they take, were useful, if not purposeful, as a means of regulating family behaviour so as to sustain a political vision that incorporates both romantic/traditional values of enduring love and family stability and modern values of individualisation and reflective choice in partnering and parenting. In this vision, family living remains an intensely private affair. What I hope I have also demonstrated is that the families we live with also express ambivalence, they reflect both change and continuity, but theirs is a more chaotic or nuanced expression that is both private and public. The test for law must always remain how successfully it does justice for *these* families. They demonstrate individuals' daily efforts to achieve a type of justice or fairness in family living that has yet to permeate the norm.

Where law does take family practices into account, it tends to do so on its own terms, in ways which sustain its claims to autonomy and minimise the resistant and destabilising potential family practices offer. Therefore, we should be cautious in attributing to family practices an ability to transform legal norms or dominant frameworks of meaning without the concurrent *structural* changes they demand that belie that autonomy and form of stability that are necessary to allow family to be practised free from the economic conditions that constrain them. Law's incorporation of choice and respect for individualism, for example, includes sometimes reconceiving family 'work' as work, such as in the context of 'big-money' ancillary relief cases, and sometimes by refusing to do so, such as in the context of attributing social value to childcare. That law assumes that family choices are made rationally and responsibly by an abstracted reasonable subject is clear from its ordering of financial provision for spouses and children, but that it sometimes particularises that subject according to gender and generation is also clear from these examples. Its dual vision of the vulnerable child-victim and the autonomous responsible child also reflects a partial, sometimes particular, subjectivity that often reinforces not only gender discrimination, but often cultural and racial discrimination (Jackson and Pabon 2000). Law both abstracts and particularises its subjects; it reveres the rational economic man but often expects him to make choices determined and normalised by his (or her) place in the gender order. Most paradoxically, family law's rational individual is often required to be self-sacrificing in his choices regardless of his personal or social situation.

It is thus the theme of lack of realisation of the potential offered by family practices that comes through most clearly to me in contemporary family law. The family on which family law and policy are based bears only slight resemblance to the way we do family inside and outside the home on a day-to-day basis, yet it is precisely by valuing the potentially revolutionary 'messiness' of actual family behaviour by seeing the boundaries it blurs, that individuals and law can create new meanings of family and of justice. My claim, therefore, is to assert this – the politics of family living – as an expression of family law and of justice.

Bibliography

Advisory Group on Marriage and Relationship Support (2002) 'Moving Forward Together: A Proposed Strategy for Marriage and Relationship Support for 2002 and Beyond' Lord Chancellor's Department London: The Stationery Office

Ancillary Relief Advisory Group (1998) *Report to the Lord Chancellor by the Ancillary Relief Advisory Group* London

Anderson, S (1984) 'Legislative Divorce – Law for the Aristocracy?' in Rubin, G R, and Sugarman, D (eds) *Law, Economy and Society. Essays in the History of English Law 1750–1914* Abingdon: Professional Books

Archard, D (1993) *Children: Rights and Childhood* London and New York: Routledge

Aries, P (1962) *Centuries of Childhood* London: Cape

Association of District Judges (1998) 'Submission of Association of District Judges' Appendix 8 to the *Report to the Lord Chancellor by the Ancillary Relief Advisory Group* London

Backett, K (1982) *Mothers and Fathers* London: Macmillan

Bailey-Harris, R (1999) 'Settlement Culture and the Use of the "No Order" Principle Under the Children Act' 11(1) *Child and Family Law Quarterly* 53

Bailey-Harris, R, Davis, G, Barron, J, and Pearce, J (1998) 'Monitoring Private Law Applications under the Children Act' *A Research Report to the Nuffield Foundation* Bristol: University of Bristol

Bainham, A (2001) 'Men and Women Behaving Badly: Is Fault Dead in English Family Law?' 21 *Oxford Journal of Legal Studies* 219

Bainham, A (2002) 'Can we protect children and protect their rights?' *Family Law* 279

Baker and Emry (1993) 'When Every Relationship is Above Average. Perceptions and Expectations of Divorce at the Time of Marriage' 17 *Law and Human Behaviour* 439

Barlow, A, and Duncan, S (2000a) 'New Labour's communitarianism, supporting families and the "rationality mistake": Part I' 22(2) *Journal of Social Welfare and Family Law* 23–42

Barlow, A, and Duncan, S (2000b) 'New Labour's communitarianism, supporting families and the "rationality mistake": Part II' 22(2) *Journal of Social Welfare and Family Law* 129–143

Barlow, A, Duncan, S, and James, G (2002) 'New Labour, the rationality mistake and family policy in Britain' ch 5 in Carling, A, Duncan, S, and Edwards, R (eds) *Analysing Families: Morality and Rationality in Policy and Practice* London: Routledge

Barrett, M, and MacIntosh, M (1991) *The Anti-Social Family* (2nd edn) London: Verso

Barry, N (1995) 'Justice and Liberty in Marriage and Divorce' in Whelan, R (ed) *Just a Piece of Paper?* London: Institute of Economic Affairs Health and Welfare Unit

Barton, C (1999) 'Child Support – Tony's Turn' *Family Law* 704

Barton, C, and Douglas, G (1995) *Law and Parenthood* London: Butterworths

Bauman, Z (1993) *Postmodern Ethics* Oxford UK and Cambridge USA: Blackwell

Beck, U (1992) *Risk Society: Towards a New Modernity* London: Sage

Beck, U (1997) 'Democratization of the Family' 4(2) *Childhood* 151

Beck, U, and Beck-Gernsheim, E (1995) *The Normal Chaos of Love* Cambridge: Polity Press

Beck, U, and Beck-Gernsheim, E (2002) *Individualization* London: Sage

Beck, C J A, Sales, B D, and Emery, R E E (2003, In Press) 'Research on the impact of family mediation' in Folberg, J, Milne, A, and Salem, P (eds) *Mediating Family and Divorce Disputes: Current Practices and Applications* New York: Guilford Press

Berger, P L, and Kellner, H (1980) 'Marriage and the Construction of Reality' in Anderson, M (ed) *Sociology of the Family* London: Penguin

Bird, R (District Judge) (2000) 'Breaking bad family habits' 98/45 22 Nov 2000 *Law Society Gazette*

Bjornberg, U (1995) 'Family orientation among men: Fatherhood and partnership in a process of change', in Brannen, J, and O'Brien, M (eds) *Childhood and Parenthood* Institute of Education, University of London

Blackstone, W (1778) *Commentary on the Laws of England* (8th edn) Oxford: Clarendon Press

Boden, R, and Childs, M (1996) 'Paying for Procreation: Child Support Arrangements in the UK' IV *Feminist Legal Studies* 131

Bottomley, A (1985) 'What is Happening to Family Law? A Feminist Critique of Conciliation' in Brophy, J, and Smart, C (eds) *Women in Law: Explorations in Law, Family and Sexuality* London: Routledge and Kegan Paul

Bowlby, J (1953) *Child Care and the Growth of Love* (2nd edn, 1965) Harmondsworth: Penguin

Boyd, S (1991) 'Some Postmodernist Challenges to Feminist Analyses of Law, Family and State: Ideology and Discourse in Child Custody Law' 10 *Canadian Journal of Law and Society* 39

Boyd, S (1994) '(Re)Placing the State: Family, Law and Oppression' 9 *Canadian Journal of Law and Society* 39

Bradshaw, J, Stimson, C, Skinner, C, and Williams, J (1999) *Absent Fathers?* London: Routledge

Brannen, J, Meszaros, G, Moss, P, and Poland, G (1994) *Employment and Family Life: A Review of Research in the UK (1980–1994)* Department of Employment Research Series No 41 London: University of London

Brannen, J, and O'Brien, M (eds) (1995) *Childhood and Parenthood* Institute of Education: University of London

Brannen, J (1999) 'Reconsidering Children and Childhood: Sociological and Policy Perspectives' in Silva, EB, and Smart, C (eds) *The New Family?* London: Sage

Bretherington, H (2002) '"Because it's me the decisions are about" – children's experiences of private law proceedings' *Family Law* 450

Bridge, C (2001) 'Respecting Cultural Diversity', ch 26 in *Information Meetings and Associated Provisions Within the Family Law Act 1996 Final Evaluation Report* Lord Chancellor's Department London: The Stationery Office

Bridge, C, and Mitchell, S, (2001) 'Domestic Violence and Information Meetings' ch 27 in *Information Meetings and Associated Provisions Within the Family Law Act 1996 Final Evaluation Report* Lord Chancellor's Department London: The Stationery Office

Bromley, P M, and Lowe, N V (1992) *Bromley's Family Law* (8th edn) London: Butterworths

Bryan, P (1992) 'Killing us Softly: Divorce Mediation and the Politics of Power' 40 *Buffalo Law Review* 441

Burgess, A (1998) *A Complete Parent: Toward a New Vision for Child Support* London: Institute of Public Policy Research

Burgoyne, C, and Millar, J (1994) 'Enforcing Child Support Obligations: The Attitudes of Separated Fathers' 22 *Policy and Politics* 95

Canada Department of Justice (2002) *A Report to Parliament on the Federal Child Support Guidelines*

Chambers, D (2001) *Representing the Family* London: Sage

Child Poverty Action Group (1994) *Putting the Treasury First* London: Child Poverty Action Group

Children and Young People's Unit (2001) *Building a Strategy for Children and Young People*

Childright (2002) 183 'Building a strategy for children and young people: a consultation from the CYPU' 3

Chodorow, N (1978) *The Reproduction of Mothering* Berkeley: University of California Press

Clarke, K, Glendinning, C, and Craig, G (1994) 'Child Support, Parental Responsibility and the Law: An Examination of the Implications of Recent British Legislation' ch 10 in Brannen, J, and O'Brien, M (eds) *Childhood and Parenthood* London: University of London Institute of Education

Clarke, K, Craig, G, and Glendinning, C (1995) 'Money Isn't Everything. Fiscal Policy and Family Policy in the Child Support Act' 29 *Social Policy and Administration* 26

Clarke, K, Craig, G, and Glendinning, C (1996a) *Small Change: The Impact of the Child Support Act on Lone Mothers and Children* London: Family Policy Studies Centre

Clarke, K, Craig, G, and Glendinning, C (1996b) *Children's Views on Child Support* London: The Children's Society

Clarke, L, and Berrington, A (1999) 'Socio-Demographic Predictors of Divorce' Lord Chancellor's Department Research Series No 2/99 Vol 1

Cockett, M, and Tripp, J (1994, 1996) *The Exeter Family Study: Family breakdown and its impact on children* Exeter: University of Exeter Press

Cohen, J L (2002) *Regulating Intimacy* Princeton and Oxford: Princeton University Press

Collier, R (1994) 'The Campaign Against the Child Support Act "Errant Fathers" and "Family Men"' *Family Law* 384

Collier, R (1995a) *Masculinity, Law and the Family* London: Routledge

Collier, R (1995b) '"Waiting Till Father Gets Home": The Reconstruction of Fatherhood in Family Law' 4 *Social and Legal Studies* 5

Collier, R (1999) 'The dashing of a "liberal dream"? – the information meeting, the "new family" and the limits of law' 11(3) *Child and Family Law Quarterly* 257

Collier, R (2001a) 'Gender, Divorce and Information Meetings' ch 30 in *Information Meetings and Associated Provisions Within the Family Law Act 1996 Final Evaluation Report* Lord Chancellor's Department London: The Stationery Office

Collier, R (2001b) 'A Hard Time to be a Father?: Reassessing the Relationship Between Law, Policy and Family (Practices)' 28 *Journal of Law and Society* 520

Conaghan, J (2000) 'Reassessing the Feminist Theoretical Project in Law' 27 *Journal of Law and Society* 351

Cornish, W, and Clark, G (1989) *Law and Society in England 1750–1950* London: Sweet and Maxwell

Cotterrell, R (1988) 'Feasible Regulation for Democracy and Social Justice' 15 *Journal of Law and Society* 5

Cotterrell, R (1993) 'Socio-Legal Studies: Between Policy and Community' Paper presented at Socio-legal Studies Conference, on file with the author

Cotterrell, R (2002) 'Subverting Orthodoxy, Making Law Central: A View of Sociolegal Studies' 29 *Journal of Law and Society* 632

Cretney, S, Masson, J, Bailey-Harris, R (2002) *Principles of Family Law* (7th edn) London: Sweet and Maxwell

Crow, G (2002) 'Families, moralities, rationalities and social change' ch 15 in Carling, C, Duncan, S, and Edwards, R, (eds) *Analysing Families: Morality and Rationality in Policy and Practice* London: Routledge

Cunningham, H (1995) *Children and Childhood in Western Society since 1500* London: Longman

Davis, G (1988) *Partisans and Mediators* Oxford: Clarendon Press

Davis, G, Cretney, S, and Collins, J (1994) *Simple Quarrels: Negotiating Money and Property Disputes on Divorce* Oxford: Clarendon Press

Davis, G, Bevan, G, Clisby, S, Cumming, Z, Dingwall, R, Fenn, P, Finch, S, Fitzgerald, R, Goldie, S, Greatbatch, D, James, A, and Pearce, J (2000) *Monitoring Publicly Funded Family Mediation: Report to the Legal Services Commission* London: Legal Services Commission

Davis, G, and Wikeley, N (2002) 'National Survey of Child Support Agency Clients – The Relationship Dimension' *Family Law* 522

Davidoff, L, Doolittle, M, Fink, J, and Holden, K (1999) *The Family Story: Blood, Contract and Intimacy, 1830–1960* London and New York: Longman

Day Sclater, S, and Piper, C (eds) (1999) *Undercurrents of Divorce* Aldershot: Dartmouth Ashgate

Day Sclater, S (1999a) *Divorce: A Psychosocial Study* Aldershot: Dartmouth Ashgate

Day Sclater, S (1999b) 'Experiences of Divorce' in Day Sclater, S, and Piper, C, *Undercurrents of Divorce* Aldershot: Dartmouth Ashgate

Day Sclater, S, and Piper, C (2001) 'Social Exclusion and the Welfare of the Child' 28 *Journal of Law and Society* 409

Department of Social Security (1990) *Children Come First* London: HMSO

Department of Social Security (1999) *A New Contract for Welfare, Children's Rights and Parents' Responsibilities* London: The Stationery Office

Dewar, J (1992) *Law and the Family* (2nd edn) London: Butterworths

Dewar, J (1998) 'The Normal Chaos of Family Law' 61 *Modern Law Review* 467

Diduck, A (1995) 'The Unmodified Family: the Child Support Act and the construction of legal subjects' 22 *Journal of Law and Society* 527

Diduck, A (1998) 'In Search of the Feminist Good Mother' 7 *Social and Legal Studies* 129

Diduck, A (1999a) 'Justice and childhood: reflections on refashioned boundaries' in King, M (ed) *Moral Agendas for Children's Welfare* London and New York: Routledge

Diduck, A (1999b) 'Dividing the Family Assets' in Piper, C, and Day Sclater, S (eds) *Undercurrents of Divorce* Aldershot: Dartmouth Ashgate

Diduck, A (2000) 'Solicitors and Legal Subjects' ch 13 in Bridgman, J, and Monk, D *Feminist Perspectives on Child Law* London: Cavendish

Diduck, A (2001a) 'A Family by any other name ... or Starbucks comes to England' 28(2) *Journal of Law and Society* 290

Diduck, A (2001b) 'Fairness and Justice for All? The House of Lords in *White v White* 9 *Feminist Legal Studies* 173

Diduck, A, and Kaganas, F (1999) *Family Law, Gender and the State. Text, Cases and Materials* Oxford: Hart Publishing Ltd

Diduck, A, and Kaganas, F (2002) 'Law's Children' Paper presented to Sociolegal Conference, Aberystwyth

Diduck, A, and Orton, H (1994) 'Equality and Support for Spouses' 57 *Modern Law Review* 681

Dingwall, R, and Eekelaar, J (1988) 'Families and the State: An Historical Perspective on the Public Regulation of Private Conduct' 10 *Law and Policy* 341

Donzelot, J (1980) *The Policing of Families* Hurley, R (trans.) London: Hutchinson

Douglas, G (1994) 'The Intention to be a Parent and the Making of Mothers' 57 *Modern Law Review* 636

Douglas, G (2001) *An Introduction to Family Law* Oxford: OUP

Douglas, G, Murch, M, Robinson, M, and Scanlan, L (2001) 'Children's Perspectives and Experience of the Divorce Process' *Family Law* 373

Douglas, G, and Murch, M (2002) 'Taking account of children's needs in divorce – a study of family solicitors' responses to new policy and practice initiatives' 14(1) *Child and Family Law Quarterly* 57

Douglas, G, and Perry, A (2001) 'How parents cope financially on separation and divorce – implications for the future of ancillary relief' 13 *Child and Family Law Quarterly* 67

Duncombe, J, and Marsden, D (1999) 'Love and Intimacy: The Gender Division of Emotion and "Emotion Work"' 27(2) *Sociology* 221

Dunne, G A (1999) 'A Passion for "Sameness"?: Sexuality and Gender Accountability' in Silva, E B, and Smart, C (eds) *The New Family?* London: Sage

Durkheim, E (1973) *Education and Sociology: Moral Education. A Study in the Theory and Application of the Sociology of Education*, Everett K Wilson and Herman Schnurer (trans.) London: Collier Macmillan Publishers

Eekelaar, J (1991) *Regulating Divorce* Oxford: Clarendon Press

Eekelaar, J (1998) 'Should Section 25 be Reformed?' *Family Law* 469

Eekelaar, J (1999) 'Family Law: Keeping Us "On Message"' 11(4) *Child and Family Law Quarterly* 387

Eekelaar, J (2001) 'Back to Basics and Forward into the Unknown' *Family Law* 30

Eekelaar, J (2002) 'Contact – Over the Limit' *Family Law* 271

Eekelaar, J, and Dingwall, R (1988) 'The Development of Conciliation in England' in Dingwall, R, and Eekelaar, J, *Divorce Mediation and the Legal Process* Oxford: Clarendon Press

Eekelaar, J, and Maclean, M (1994) A Reader on Family Law *Oxford Readings in Socio-Legal Studies* Oxford and New York: Oxford University Press

Eekelaar, J, Maclean, M, and Beinart, S (2000) *Family Lawyers: The Divorce Work of Solicitors* Oxford: Hart Publishing

Erikson, E H (1980) *Identity and the Life Cycle* London: Norton and Co

Family Law Committee of the Law Society, (1998) 'Maintenance and Capital Provision on Divorce, The Family Law Committee's Submission to the Ancillary Relief Advisory Group' The Law Society, Appendix 10 to *Report to the Lord Chancellor by the Ancillary Relief Advisory Group* London

Family Policy Studies Centre (1995) *Families in Britain, Family Report 3*

Finch, J (1989) *Family Obligations and Social Change* Cambridge: Polity Press

Finch, J, and Mason, J (1993) *Negotiating Family Responsibilities* London: Routledge

Fineman, M (1991) *The Illusion of Equality: The Rhetoric and Reality of Divorce Reform* Chicago, London: University of Chicago Press

Fineman, M (1995) *The Neutered Mother, the Sexual Family and Other Twentieth Century Tragedies* London, New York: Routledge

Fineman, M, and Karpin, I (eds) (1995) *Mothers in Law: Feminist Theory and the Legal Regulation of Motherhood* New York: Columbia University Press

Finer, M (1974) *Report on the Committee on One Parent Families* London: HMSO, Cmnd 5629

Finer, M, and McGregor, O R (1974) *History of the Obligation to Maintain*, Appendix 5 in Finer, M (1974) *Report on the Committee on One Parent Families* London: HMSO, Cmnd 5629

Fionda, J (2001) 'Youth and Justice' in Fionda, J (ed) *Legal Concepts of Childhood* Oxford: Hart Publishing

Fisher, H E (1992) *Anatomy of Love* New York and London: W W Norton and Company

Fisher, T and Hodson, D (2001) 'Family Mediation – Did it Make Things Better?' *Family Law* 270

Fox Harding, L (1996) *Family State and Social Policy* Basingstoke: Macmillan

Freeman, M (ed) (1996) *Divorce: Where Next?* Aldershot: Dartmouth Ashgate

Freeman, M (2001) 'The Child in Family Law', in Fionda, J (ed) *Legal Concepts of Childhood* Oxford: Hart Publishing

Frenkel, J, District Judge (1997) 'Ancillary Relief Pilot Scheme in Operation' *Family Law* 726

Garrison, M (2001) 'Child Support Guideline Review: Problems and Prospects' p 437 in *International Survey of Family Law* Bristol: Jordan Publishing

Genn, H (1999) *Paths to Justice* Oxford: Hart Publishing

George, P (1997) 'In all the circumstances – s. 25' *Family Law* 729

Giddens, A (1992) *The Transformation of Intimacy* Cambridge: Polity Press

Giddens, A, and Pierson, C (1998) *Conversations with Anthony Giddens: Making Sense of Modernity* Cambridge: Polity Press

Gillespie, G (2002) 'Child Support – When the Bough Breaks' *Family Law* 528

Gilligan, C (1982) *In a Different Voice* London and Cambridge: Harvard University Press

Gillis, J (1985) *For Better or for Worse: British Marriages 1600 to the Present* Oxford and New York: Oxford University Press

Gillis, J (1997) *A World of Their Own Making: A History of Myth and Ritual in Family Life* Oxford and New York: Oxford University Press

Ginn, J, and Price, D (2002) 'Do divorced women catch up in pension building?' 14(2) *Child and Family Law Quarterly* 157

Gittins, D (1993) *The Family in Question: Changing Households and Familiar Ideologies* (2nd edn) Basingstoke: Macmillan

Gittins, D (1998) *The Child in Question* Basingstoke and London: Macmillan

Grassby, R (2001) *Kinship and Capitalism: Marriage, Family, and Business in the English Speaking World, 1580–1740* Cambridge: Cambridge University Press

Gray, C, and Merrick, S B (1996) 'Voice Alterations. Why Women Have More Difficulty Than Men With the Legal Process of Divorce' 34(2) *Family and Conciliation Courts Review* 240

Grillo, T (1991) 'The Mediation Alternative: Process Dangers for Women' *Yale Law Journal* 1545

Goldstein, J, Freud, A, and Solnit, A (1980) *Before the Best Interests of the Child* London: Burnett Books

Hart, Sir G (1999) 'The Funding of Marriage Support' A Review for the Lord Chancellor's Department London: The Stationery Office

Hatten, W, Vinter, L, and Williams, R (2002) *Dads on Dads: Needs and Expectations at Home and at Work* London: Equal Opportunities Commission

Hegel, G W F (1991) *Elements of The Philosophy of Right,* (Wood, A, ed., and Nisbet, H B, trans.) Cambridge: Cambridge University Press

Held, V (1993) *Feminist Morality: Transforming Culture, Society, and Politics* Chicago: University of Chicago Press

Hendrick, H (1990) 'Constructions and reconstructions of childhood: an interpretive survey, 1800 to the present' in James, A, Prout, A (eds) *Constructing and Reconstructing Childhood: Contemporary Issues in the Socio-logical Study of Childhood* London: Falmer Press

Hibbs, M, Barton, C, and Beswick, J (2001) 'Why Marry? – Perceptions of the Affianced' *Family Law* 197

Hillyard, P (2002) 'Invoking Indignation: Reflections on Future Directions of Socio-Legal Studies' 29 *Journal of Law and Society* 645

Himmelweit, S (2002) 'Economic theory, norms and the care gap, or: why do economists become parents?' ch 12 in Carling, A, Duncan, S, and Edwards, R (eds) *Analysing Families: Morality and Rationality in Policy and Practice* London: Routledge

Hirschmann, N (1992) *Rethinking Obligation: A Feminist Method for Political Theory* Ithaca: Cornell University Press

Holcombe, L (1983) *Wives and Property: Reform of the Married Womens' Property Acts* Toronto: University of Toronto Press

Hoggett, B, and Pearl, D (1991) *The Family, Law and Society: Cases and Materials* (3rd edn) London: Butterworths

Hoggett, B, Pearl, D, Cooke, E, and Bates, P (1996) *The Family, Law and Society: Cases and Materials* (4th edn) London: Butterworths

Hoggett, B, Pearl, D, Cooke, E, and Bates, P (2002) *The Family, Law and Society: Cases and Materials* (5th edn) London: Butterworths

Home Office (1998) *Supporting Families: A Consultation Document* London: The Stationery Office

Home Office (1999) *Supporting Families: Responses to the Consultation Document* London: The Stationery Office

House of Lords, House of Commons Joint Committee on Human Rights (2002) Adoption and Children Bill Twenty-fourth Report of the Session 2001–02 (HL Paper 177, HC 979) London: The Stationery Office

Ingleby, R (1992) *Solicitors and Divorce* Oxford and New York: Oxford University Press

Irwin, S (1999) 'Resourcing the Family: Gendered Claims and Obligations and Issues of Explanation' ch 3 in Silva, E B, and Smart, C (eds) *The New Family?* London: Sage

Jackson, R, and Pabon, E (2000) 'Race and treating other people's children as adults' 28 *Journal of Criminal Justice* 507

James, A, and James, A (1999) 'Pump up the volume: listening to children in separation and divorce' 6(2) *Childhood* p 189

James, A (1999) 'Parents: A Children's Perspective' in Bainham, A, Day Sclater, S, and Richards, M (eds) *What is a Parent?* Oxford: Hart Publishing

James, A, Jenks, C, and Prout, A (1998) *Theorizing Childhood* Cambridge: Polity Press

Jameison, L (1999) 'Intimacy Transformed? A Critical Look at the "Pure Relationship"' 33 *Sociology* 477

Jenks, C (1996) *Childhood* London: Routledge

Jolly, S (1997) 'Family Law' in Thomas, P (ed) *Socio-Legal Studies* Aldershot: Dartmouth Ashgate

KPMG (1998) 'Ancillary Relief Pilot Scheme Study' Executive Summary http://www.lcd.gov.uk/research/1998/898es.htm

Kaganas, F (1999) 'Contact, Conflict and Risk' in Day Sclater, S, and Piper, C (eds) *Undercurrents of Divorce* Aldershot: Dartmouth Ashgate

Kaganas, F (2000) '*Re L (Contact: Domestic Violence); re V (Contact: Domestic Violence); re M (Contact: Domestic Violence); re H (Contact: Domestic Violence)*' 12 *Child and Family Law Quarterly* 311

Kaganas, F, and Piper, C (1999) 'Divorce and Domestic Violence' in *Undercurrents of Divorce* Aldershot: Dartmouth Ashgate

Keating, H (1995) 'Children Come First?' 1 *Contemporary Issues in Law* 29

King, M (1999) '"Being Sensible": Images and Practices of the New Family Lawyers' 28(2) *Journal of Social Policy* 249

King, M, and Piper, C (1995) *How the Law Thinks About Children* (2nd edn) Aldershot: Arena

Kohlberg, L (1984) 'The Psychology of Moral Development. The Nature and Validity of Moral Stages' Vol 2 in *Essays on moral development* London: Harper and Row

Lacey, N (1998) *Unspeakable Subjects* Oxford: Hart Publishing

Landes, J B (1982) 'Hegel's Conception of the Family' in Elshtain, J B (ed) *The Family in Political Thought* Brighton: The Harvester Press Ltd

Lange, B (2002) 'The Emotional Dimension in Legal Regulation' 29 *Journal of Law and Society* 197

Law Commission (1966) No 6, 'Reform of the Grounds of Divorce – The Field of Choice' London: HMSO, Cmnd 3123

Law Commission (1981) No 112, *The Financial Consequences of Divorce: the Response to the Discussion Paper* London: HMSO

Law Commission (1990) No 192, *Family Law. The Ground for Divorce* London: HMSO, Cmnd 636

Law and Society Association, http://www.lawandsociety.org

Law Society (2002a) *Family Law Protocol* London: The Law Society

Law Society (2002b) *Cohabitation: The Case for Clear Law* London: The Law
   Society
Lee, N (2001) *Childhood and Society* Buckingham: Open University Press
Legal Services Commission (2002) Developing Family Advice and Infor-
   mation Services http://www.legalservices.gov.uk/fains
Levine, F J (1990) 'Goose Bumps and "The Search for Signs of Intelligent
   Life" in Sociolegal Studies: After Twenty-Five Years' 24 *Law and
   Society Review* 7
Lewis, J (1999) 'Marriage, Cohabitation and the Law: Individualism and
   Obligation' in Lord Chancellor's Department Research Series No
   1/99 London: The Stationery Office
Lewis, J (2001) 'Debates and Issues Regarding Marriage and Cohabitation
   in the British and American Literature' 15 *International Journal of Law,
   Policy and Family* 159
Lewis, J (2002) 'Individualisation, assumptions about the existence of
   an adult worker model and the shift towards contractualism' ch 3.1
   in Carling, A, Duncan, S, and Edwards, R (eds) *Analysing Families:
   Morality and Rationality in Policy and Practice* London: Routledge
Lewis, J, Datta, J, and Sarre, S (1999) 'Individualism and Commitment
   in Marriage and Cohabitation' in Lord Chancellor's Department
   Research Series No 8/99 London: The Stationery Office
Lister, R, Goode, J, and Callender, C (1999) 'Income distribution within
   families and the reform of social security' 21(3) *Journal of Social Welfare
   and Family Law* 203
Lord Chancellor's Department (1993) *Looking to the Future: Mediation and the
   Ground for Divorce* Cm 2424 London: HMSO
Lord Chancellor's Department (1995) *Looking to the Future: Mediation and the
   Ground for Divorce* Cm 2799 London: HMSO
Lord Chancellor's Department (2002) *Making Contact Work* London: The
   Stationery Office
Lord Chancellor's Department (2002) 'Sorting things out together – how
   family mediation can help you' http://www.lcd.gov.uk/family/
   fammed.htm
Lowe, N, and Douglas, G Lewis (1998) *Bromley's Family Law* (9th edn)
   London: Butterworths
Luhmann, N (1986) *Love As Passion* Cambridge: Polity Press

Maclean, M, and Eekelaar, J (1993) 'Child Support: The British Solution' 7
   International Journal of Law and the Family 205

Maclean, M, and Eekelaar, J (1997) *The Parental Obligation. A Study of Parenthood Across Households* Oxford: Hart Publishing

Mansfield, P, Reynolds, J, and Arai, L (1999) 'What Policy Developments Would be Most Likely to Secure an Improvement in Marital Stability' Lord Chancellor's Department Research Series No 2/99 Vol 2

McAllister, F (1999) 'Effects of Changing Material Circumstances on the Incidence of Marital Breakdown' Lord Chancellor's Department Research Series No 2/99 Vol 1

McCarthy, P (2001) 'The Provision of Information and the Prevention of Marriage Breakdown' ch 17 in *Information Meetings and Associated Provisions Within the Family Law Act 1996 Final Evaluation Report* Lord Chancellor's Department London: The Stationery Office

McCarthy, P, and Mitchell, S (2001) 'Meeting with a Marriage Counsellor' ch 13 in *Information Meetings and Associated Provisions Within the Family Law Act 1996 Final Evaluation Report* Lord Chancellor's Department London: The Stationery Office

McCarthy, P, Stark, C, and Walker, J (2001) 'Addressing Specific Needs and Circumstances' (including the circumstances of senior citizens, those coping with ill health and disability and members of the forces) ch 29 in *Information Meetings and Associated Provisions Within the Family Law Act 1996 Final Evaluation Report* Lord Chancellor's Department London: The Stationery Office

McMullen, R, and Kain, J (2001) 'Providing Information to People in Prison' ch 28 in *Information Meetings and Associated Provisions Within the Family Law Act 1996 Final Evaluation Report* Lord Chancellor's Department London: The Stationery Office

Morgan, D H J (1996) *Family Connections* Cambridge: Polity Press

Morgan, D H J (1999) 'Risk and Family Practices: Accounting for Change and Fluidity in Family Life' in Silva, E B, and Smart, C (eds) *The New Family* London: Sage

Morris, A, and Nott, S (1995) *All My Worldly Goods: A Feminist Perspective on the Legal Regulation of Wealth* Aldershot: Dartmouth: Ashgate

Morrow, V (1998) *Understanding Families: Children's Perspectives* London: National Children's Bureau

Mossman, M J (1994) 'Gender Equality, Family Law and Access to Justice' 8 *International Journal of Law and The Family* 357

National Family and Parenting Institute (1999) 'Is Britain family-friendly? The parents' eye view' London: National Family and Parenting Institute

Neale, B, and Smart, C (1997a) '"Good" and "bad" lawyers? Struggling in the shadow of the new law' 19 *Journal of Social Welfare and Family Law* 377

Neale, B and Smart, C (1997b) 'Experiments with Parenthood?' 31 *Sociology* 201

Neale, B, and Smart, C (1999) 'In Whose Best Interests? Theorising Family Life Following Parental Separation or Divorce', in Day Sclater, S, and Piper, C (eds) *Undercurrents of Divorce* Aldershot: Dartmouth Ashgate

Neale, B, and Smart, C (2002) 'Caring, earning and changing: parenthood and employment after divorce' ch 9 in Carling, A, Duncan, S, and Edwards, R (eds) *Analysing Families: Morality and Rationality in Policy and Practice* London: Routledge

Newcastle Conciliation Project Unit Report (1989) *Report to the Lord Chancellor on the Costs and Effectiveness of Conciliation in England and Wales* London: Lord Chancellor's Department

Nicholson, L (1997) 'The Myth of the Traditional Family' in Hilde Lindemann Nelson (ed) *Feminism and Families* New York and London: Routledge

O'Brien, M, and Shemilt, I (2003) *Working Fathers: Earning and Caring* London: Equal Opportunities Commission

O'Donovan, K (1984) 'Wife Sale and Desertion as Alternatives to Judicial Marriage Dissolution' in Eekelaar, J, and Katz, S (eds) *The Resolution of Family Conflict* Toronto: Butterworths

O'Donovan, K (1985) *Sexual Divisions in Law* London: Weidenfeld and Nicolson

O'Donovan, K (1986) 'Family Law and Legal Theory' ch 10 in W Twining (ed) *Legal Theory and Common Law* Oxford: Blackwell

O'Donovan, K (1993) *Family Law Matters* London: Pluto Press

O'Donovan, K (1997) 'Fem-Legal and Socio-Legal: An Incompatible Relationship?' in Thomas, P (ed) (1997) *Socio-Legal Studies* Aldershot: Dartmouth Ashgate

Olsen, F (1983) 'The Family and the Market: A Study of Ideology and Legal Reform' 96(7) *Harvard Law Review* 1497

Pahl, J (1989) *Money and Marriage* Basingstoke and London: Macmillan

Parker, S (1990) *Informal Marriage, Cohabitation and the Law 1750–1989* Basingstoke: Macmillan

Parkinson, L (1985) 'Conciliation in Separation and Divorce' in Dryden, W (ed) *Marital Therapy in Britain* Vol 2 London: Harper and Row

Parsons, T (1951) *The Social System* London: Routledge and Kegan Paul

Piaget, J (1952) *The Origins of Intelligence in Children,* Cook, M (trans.) New York: International Universities Press

Picciotto S, and Campbell, D (eds) (2002) 'New Directions in Regulatory Theory' 29 *Journal of Law and Society*

Piper, C (1993) *The Responsible Parent: A Study in Divorce Mediation* Hemel Hempstead: Harvester Wheatsheaf

Piper, C (1996a) 'Divorce Reform and the Image of the Child' 23 *Journal of Law and Society* 364

Piper, C (1996b) 'Norms and Negotiation in Mediation and Divorce' in Freeman, M (ed) *Divorce: Where Next?* Aldershot: Dartmouth Ashgate

Piper, C (1999) 'How do you Define a Family Lawyer?' 19 *Legal Studies* 93

Pirrie, J (2002a) 'Child Support Update, Part I' *Family Law* 195

Pirrie, J (2002b) 'The CSA Process' *Family Law* 290

Pirrie, J (2002c) 'Time for the Courts to Stand up to the Child Support Act? – An Address to District Judges' *Family Law* 114

Postman, N (1994) *The Disappearance of Childhood* New York: Vintage Books

Priest, J (1997) 'Capital Settlements and the CSA – Part I' *Family Law* 115

Putting Asunder (1966) *Putting Asunder – A Divorce Law for Contemporary Society* London: Society for Promoting Christian Knowledge, Cambridge University Press

Reece, H (1996) 'The Paramountcy Principle: Consensus or Construct?' 49 *Current Legal Problems* 267

Reece, H (2000a) 'Divorcing Responsibly' 8 *Feminist Legal Studies* 65–91

Reece, H (2000b) 'Divorcing the Children' in Bridgman, J, and Monk, D (eds) *Feminist Perspectives on Child Law* London: Cavendish

Reece, H (2003) *Divorcing Responsibly* Oxford: Hart Publishing

Regan, M C (1993) *Family Law and The Pursuit of Intimacy* New York and London: New York University Press

Regan, M C (1999) *Alone Together: Law and the Meanings of Marriage* Oxford and New York: Oxford University Press

Reynolds, J, and Mansfield, P (1999) 'The Effect of Changing Attitudes to Marriage on its Stability' Lord Chancellor's Department Research Series No 2/99 Vol 1 London: The Stationery Office

Ribbens, J (1995) 'Mothers' images of children and their implication for material response' in Brannen, J, and O'Brien, M, *Childhood and Parenthood* Institute of Education: University of London

Ribbens McCarthy, J, and Edwards, R (2002) 'The Individual in public and private. The significance of mothers and children', in Carling, A, Duncan, S, and Edwards, R (eds) *Analysing Families: Morality and Rationality in Policy and Practice* London and New York: Routledge

Ribbens McCarthy, J, Edwards, R, and Gillies V (2000) 'Moral Tales of the Child and the Adult: Narratives of Contemporary Family Lives under Changing Circumstances' 34 *Sociology* 785

Richardson, J, and Sandland, R (2000) 'Feminism, Law and Theory' in Richardson, J, and Sandland, R, *Feminist Perspectives on Law and Theory* London: Cavendish Publishing

Richards, M (1982) 'Post-Divorce Arrangements for Children: A Psychological Perspective' in *Journal of Social Welfare and Family Law* 133

Ringen, S, and Halpin, B (1997) 'Children, Standard of Living and Distributions in the Family' 26 *Journal of Social Policy* 21

Roberts, M (1997) *Mediation in Family Disputes: Principles of Practice* (2nd edn) Aldershot: Arena

Roberts, S (1983) 'Mediation in Family Disputes' 46 *Modern Law Review* 537

Roberts, S (2001) 'Family Mediation After the Act' 13(3) *Child and Family Law Quarterly* 265

Roche, J (1999) 'Children and Divorce: A Private Affair?' in Day Sclater, S, and Piper, C (eds) *Undercurrents of Divorce* Aldershot Dartmouth: Ashgate

Rodger, J (1996) *Family Life & Social Control: A Sociological Perspective* London: Macmillan Press Ltd

Rose, N (1987) 'Beyond the Public/Private Division: Law, Power and the Family' 14 *Journal of Law and Society* 61

Rose, N, and Valverde, M (1998) 'Governed by Law?' 7 *Social and Legal Studies* 541

Royal Commission on Marriage and Divorce 1951–1955 Report (1956) London: HMSO, Cmd 9678

Ruddick, S (1997) 'The Idea of Fatherhood' in Nelson, H L (ed) *Feminism and Families* London and New York: Routledge

Sarat, A, and Felstiner, W L F (1995) *Divorce Lawyers and their Clients* Oxford and New York: Oxford University Press

Sawyer, C (1999) 'Conflicting Rights for Children: Implementing Welfare, Autonomy and Justice within Family Proceedings' 21(2) *Journal of Social Welfare and Family Law* 99

Sevenhuijsen, S (1998) *Citizenship and the Ethics of Care* London: Routledge

Sevenhuijsen, S (2002) 'A Third Way? Moralities, Ethics and Families: An approach through the ethic of care', in Carling, A, Duncan, S, and Edwards, R (eds) *Analysing Families: Morality and Rationality in Policy and Practice* London: Routledge

Shanley, M L (1989) *Feminism, Marriage, and the Law in Victorian England, 1850–1895* London: Princeton University Press

Shorter, E (1975) *The Making of the Modern Family* New York: Basic Books Inc

Silva, E B (ed) (1996) *Good Enough Mothering? Feminist Perspectives on Lone Motherhood* London: Routledge

Silva, E B, and Smart, C (1999) 'The "New" Practices and Politics of Family Life' in Silva, E B, and Smart, C (eds) *The New Family?* London: Sage

Silva, E B (1999) 'Transforming Housewifery: Dispositions, Practices and Technologies' ch 4 in Silva, E B, and Smart, C (eds) (1999) *The New Family?* London: Sage

Simons, J (1999a) 'How Useful is Relationship Therapy?' Lord Chancellor's Department Research Series No 2/99 Vol 2

Simons, J (1999b) 'Can Marriage Preparation Courses Influence the Quality and Stability of Marriage?' Lord Chancellor's Department Research Series No 2/99 Vol 2

Smart, C (1984) *The Ties That Bind* London: Routledge and Kegan Paul

Smart, C (1987) '"There is of course, the distinction dictated by nature": law and the problem of paternity' in Stanworth, M (ed) *Reproductive Technologies: Gender, Motherhood and Medicine* Cambridge: Polity Press

Smart, C (1989) *Feminism and the Power of Law* London: Routledge

Smart, C (1991) 'The Legal and Moral Ordering of Child Custody' 18 *Journal of Law and Society* 485

Smart, C (ed) (1992) *Regulating Motherhood: Historical Essays on Marriage, Motherhood and Sex* London: Routledge

Smart C (1997) 'Wishful Thinking and Harmful Tinkering? Sociological Reflection on Family Policy' 53 *Journal of Social Policy* 3

Smart, C (1999) 'The "New" Parenthood: Fathers and Mothers after Divorce' in Silva, E B, and Smart, C, *The New Family?* London: Sage.

Smart, C (2000) 'Stories of a Family Life: Cohabitation, Marriage and Social Change' 17 *Canadian Journal of Family Law* 20

Smart and Neale (1999) *Family Fragments?* Cambridge: Polity Press

Smart, C, and Sevenhuijsen, S (eds) (1989) *Child Custody and the Politics of Gender* London and New York: Routledge

Smart, C, Neale, B, and Wade, A (2001) *The Changing Experience of Childhood Families and Divorce* Cambridge: Polity Press

Social Trends 28 (1998) Office for National Statistics, The Stationery Office, London

Solicitors' Family Law Association (1998) 'Proposals for Reform of Ancillary Relief Law' Orpington: SFLA, Appendix 11 to *Report to the Lord Chancellor by the Ancillary Relief Advisory Group* London

Stark, C (2001) 'Choosing a Route through the Divorce Process' ch 21 in *Information Meetings and Associated Provisions Within the Family Law Act 1996: Summary of the Final Evaluation Report* Lord Chancellor's Department, London: The Stationery Office

Stark, C, and Birmingham, C (2001) 'Mediation and Divorce' ch 19 in *Information Meetings and Associated Provisions Within the Family Law Act 1996: Summary of the Final Evaluation Report* Lord Chancellor's Department, London: The Stationery Office

Stone, L (1979) *The Family, Sex and Marriage in England 1500–1800* (abridged edition) London: Harper and Rowe

Stone, L (1990) *Road to Divorce* Oxford and New York: Oxford University Press

Strachey, J (ed) (1959) *The Standard Edition of the Complete Psychological Works of S Freud* London: Hogarth Press

Thomas, P (1997) 'Socio-Legal Studies: The Case of Disappearing Fleas and Bustards' in Thomas, P (ed) *Socio-Legal Studies* Aldershot: Dartmouth Ashgate

Thompson, E P (1978) *The Poverty of Theory, & other Essays* London: Merlin Press

Thorpe, L J (1998) 'The English System of Ancillary Relief' Paper presented at SPTL seminar, 21 March 1998, King's College, London

Trinder, L (1997) 'Competing Constructions of Childhood: Children's Rights and Children's Wishes in Divorce' 19 *Journal of Social Welfare and Family Law* 291

Tronto, J C (1993) *Moral Boundaries. A Political Argument for an Ethic of Care* New York and London: Routledge.

UK College of Family Mediators, Code of Practice (2000) London

United Kingdom Men's Movement (1997) 'The United Kingdom Divorce Racket' http://www.zynet.co.uk/gold/lymtel/ukmm/racket.htm

Van Krieken, R (2001) 'Legal Informalism, Power and Liberal Governance' 10 *Social and Legal Studies* 5

Vaughan, B (2000) 'The Government of Youth: Disorder and Dependence.' 9(3) *Social and Legal Studies* 347

Walker, J, McCarthy, P, and Timms, N (1994) *Mediation: the Making and Remaking of Co-operation Relationships – an Evaluation of the Effectiveness of Comprehensive Mediation* London: Relate Centre for Family Studies

Walker, J, Timms, N, and Collier, R (2001) 'The Challenge of Social, Legal and Policy Change' in Lord Chancellor's Department *Final Evaluation Report*, Vol 1 London: The Stationery Office

Walker, J (Research Director) (2001) *Information Meetings and Associated Provisions Within the Family Law Act 1996: Summary of the Final Evaluation Report* Lord Chancellor's Department London: The Stationery Office

Walker, J, (2001) 'Supporting the Principles of the Family Law Act', Lord Chancellor's Department *Final Evaluation Report*, Vol 3 London: The Stationery Office

Wallbank, J (1997) 'The Campaign for Change of the Child Support Act 1991: Reconstituting the "Absent" Father' 6 *Social and Legal Studies* 191

Wallbank, J (2002) 'Clause 106 of the Adoption and Children Bill: legislation for the "good" father?' 22 *Legal Studies* 276

Wallerstein, J S, and Kelly, J B (1980) *Surviving the Breakup: How children and parents cope with divorce* London: Grant McIntyre; New York: Basic Books

Warin, J, Solomon, Y, Lewis, C, and Langford, W (1999) *Fathers, Work and Family Life* London: Family Policy Studies Centre, Joseph Rowntree Foundation

Weitzman, L (1992) 'Gender Differences in Custody Bargaining in the United States' in Weitzman, L, and Maclean, M, *Economic Consequences of Divorce* Oxford: Clarendon Press

Weeks, J (2002) 'Elective families: lesbian and gay life experiments', in Carling, A., Duncan, S, and Edwards, R (eds) *Analysing Families: Morality and Rationality in Policy and Practice* London and New York: Routledge

Weeks, J, Donovan, C, and Heaphy, B (1999) 'Everyday Experiments: Narratives of Non-heterosexual Relationships' in Silva, E B, and Smart, C (eds) *The New Family?* London: Sage

Wheeler, S, and Thomas, P (2000) in Hayton, D, 'Laws Future(s) British Legal Developments in the 21st Century' ch 14 *Socio-Legal Studies* Oxford: Hart Publishing

Wikeley, N (2000a) 'Child Support – The New Formula, Part I' *Family Law* 820

Wikeley, N (2000b) 'Compliance, Enforcement and Child Support' *Family Law* 888

Wikeley, N, Barnett, S, Brown, J, Davis, G, Diamond, I, Draper, T, and Smith, P (2001) National Survey of Child Support Clients, Research Report No 152, London: Department for Work and Pensions (Summary of Report: http://www.dwp.gov.uk/asd/asd5/152summ.html)

Williamson, H, and Butler, I (1995) 'Children Speak: Perspectives on their Social Worlds', in Brannen, J, and O'Brien, M (eds) *Childhood and Parenthood* Institute of Education: University of London

Young, I M (1990) *Justice and the Politics of Difference* New Jersey: Princeton University Press

Zander, M (1997) 'The Woolf Report: Forwards or Backwards for the New Lord Chancellor?' 16 *Civil Justice Quarterly* 208

Zeldin, T (1994) *An Intimate History of Humanity* New York: HarperCollins

Index

This index covers Chapters 1 to 8. Index entries are to page numbers.